Translated Texts for Historians

This series is designed to meet the needs of students of ancient and medieval history and others who wish to broaden their study by reading source material, but whose knowledge of Latin or Greek is not sufficient to allow them to do so in the original language. Many important Late Imperial and Dark Age texts are currently unavailable in translation and it is hoped that TTH will help to fill this gap and to complement the secondary literature in English which already exists. The series relates principally to the period 300-800 AD and includes Late Imperial, Greek, Byzantine and Syriac texts as well as source books illustrating a particular period or theme. Each volume is a self-contained scholarly translation with an introductory essay on the text and its author and notes on the text indicating major problems of interpretation, including textual difficulties.

Editorial Committee
Sebastian Brock, Oriental Institute, University of Oxford
Averil Cameron, Keble College, Oxford
Henry Chadwick, Oxford
John Davies, University of Liverpool
Carlotta Dionisotti, King's College, London
Peter Heather, University College London
Michael Lapidge, Clare College, Cambridge
Robert Markus, University of Nottingham
John Matthews, Yale University
Raymond Van Dam, University of Michigan
Michael Whitby, University of Warwick
Ian Wood, University of Leeds

General Editors
Gillian Clark, University of Liverpool
Mary Whitby, Royal Holloway, London

Front cover drawing: A sea fight (after a manuscript illumination, *Vegetius De Re Militari*, f86, Fitzwilliam Museum, Cambridge)

A full list of published titles in the Translated Texts for Historians series is printed at the end of this book.

Translated Texts for Historians
Volume 16

Vegetius: Epitome of Military Science

Translated with notes and introduction by
N. P. MILNER

Liverpool
University
Press

First published 1993
2nd edition 1996 by
Liverpool University Press
Senate House, Abercromby Square
Liverpool, L69 3BX

British Library Cataloguing-in-Publication Data
A British Library CIP Record is available
ISBN 0-85323-910-X

Acknowledgements
The publishers gratefully acknowledge
the following for generous grants in
aid of publication of this book:

Christ Church, Oxford
The Jowett Copyright Trustees
The Seven Pillars of Wisdom Trust

Printed in the European Union by
Redwood Books, Trowbridge, England

Contents

Preface

This work had its genesis, appropriately enough, at an excavation of the Roman fort at Strageath, Perthshire, in September, 1983, where I was shown a copy of Vegetius' *Epitome* by Mr. N. Fuentes. It was due to his encouragement in the early stages that I embarked on the project of translation. Difficulties of interpretation along the way led to my returning to Oxford to research the topic for a D.Phil. Some of the main results of this research are incorporated here.

The technical nature of the original implies that many terms ought not to be interchangeable, and had a precise meaning for Romans which is not always easily grasped in English today. However, the translator's task is not helped by the fact that Vegetius himself was using them as a layman and did frequently interchange them or use them imprecisely. Furthermore, his interests were markedly philological; etymologies play a large part in the author's interpretation of terms. That being so, I have thought it best to adopt a fairly literal style of translation, sticking close to Latin terminology and word order, and retaining a number of Latin technical terms. Quotations by Vegetius of other authors are given in my own translations.

The rationale behind the footnotes has been first to explain my decisions at textual *cruces,* to incorporate the most relevant philological comments of previous scholars, to explain references to historical persons and events, to provide cross-references to repeated ideas or passages, to quote or cite relevant examples of language or ideas from other ancient authors, and to highlight the nature of Vegetius' method of writing as an epitomator intent on shaping and imposing a decided slant on his material. References to scholarly articles and works are provided with the aim of directing interested readers to further research if they so wish. When an ancient text has been commented upon so rarely as this has, much of what is said here must be taken as only provisional. It is intended here merely to provide an instrument for further study by others.

Most of the first edition was read in draft by Dr. R.S.O. Tomlin and Dr. Michael Whitby, to whom I remain greatly indebted for numerous improvements. For this second edition I have refined and revised the translation, augmented the notes, and expanded the introduction and bibliography. I am grateful to Dr. Gillian Clark for much help with the conversion of the disk and other editorial matters.

Introduction

§1. The work

The *Epitoma Rei Militaris* or *Epitome of Military Science* by Publius Flavius Vegetius Renatus was in the Middle Ages one of the most popular Latin technical works from Antiquity, rivalling the elder Pliny's *Natural History* in the number of surviving copies dating from before AD 1300. A number of early translations into vernacular languages were made, and frequently additions and adjustments were introduced to adapt the work to the age of Chivalry. Sections of it were often reproduced to augment more contemporary material on warfare, and in particular the "General Rules of Warfare" (III.26) were found suitable for repetition as inculcating the basic principles in an unspecific form which could be adapted to serve a great variety of military situations.[1]

In the Renaissance high esteem continued to be shown, so that it appeared along with Frontinus' *Stratagems*, Aelian's *Tactics* and "Modestus' *On terms of military science*" in several printed collections of Roman militaria already in the century from 1487. "Modestus" is itself a testament to the hunger for such material, being a pseudepigraphical abridgement of Vegetius' *Epitome* which was published in Venice in 1471 and was long regarded as one of Vegetius' sources.[2] Even now it is sometimes taken as genuine.[3]

However, it seems that one can also have too much of a good thing. Learned commentators such as G. Stewechius (Leiden 1585) expressed disappointment that it was due to the preservation of Vegetius that works by his named sources, Cato, Celsus, Frontinus and Paternus, had not survived[4] whereas Vegetius' *Epitome,* a late Christian source not from the best period of Roman culture, gave no indication which parts were owed to which classical author. This complaint is almost certainly misguided; there are a number of indications in the *Epitome* that even Vegetius worked from late epitomes of the named sources, so that it

---

[1]Cf. M. Springer, "Vegetius im Mittelalter", *Philologus* cxxiii (1979) 85–90; F.H. Sherwood, "Studies in medieval uses of Vegetius' *Epitoma Rei Militaris*", Diss. Univ. of California (Los Angeles 1980), résumé in *DA* xli (1980) 1712A; C.R. Schrader, "A handlist of extant mss. containing the De re militari of Fl. Renatus Vegetius", *Scriptorium* xxxiii (1979) 280–305; id., "The influence of Vegetius' *De re militari*", *Military Affairs* xlv (1981) 167–172.

[2]Cf. M. Jähns, *Geschichte der Kriegswissenschaften* (Munich 1889–91) I.122, A.R. Neumann, *RE Suppl.* X (1965), s.v. "Vegetius", col. 992–1020 at 997.

[3]e.g. by B. Rémy, "Notes de Lecture: Soldats de Cilicie sous l'Empire romain", *EA* x (1987) 107–109, cf. *SEG* xxxvii (1987) 1760.

[4]Reprinted in N. Schwebel, *Flavii Vegetii Renati comitis de Re Militari libri quinque* (Nuremberg 1767), augmented edn. Strasbourg, 1806, p. vi (Stewechius's *dedicatio*, Leiden 1584).

may be doubted that the latter would have had an independent chance of survival.[1] Secondly, in spite of the demand for Roman military treatises from the Carolingian period onwards, no manuscript of the lost authors can be demonstrated to have been discovered.

Vegetius' reputation further suffered by comparison with ancient historians such as Polybius in the attempt to piece together Roman military history. N. Machiavelli's *L'arte della Guerra* (Florence 1521), a thoroughgoing attempt to augment, modernize, illustrate and supplement Vegetius in the light of all the evidence of classical warfare available to him, made notable use of Polybius, Frontinus and Livy. P. Scriverius certainly regarded Vegetius as a poor substitute for the Polybius,[2] after J. Lipsius' *De militia Romana: Commentarius ad Polybium* (Antwerp 1596) had accused Vegetius of confusing the institutions of diverse periods of the Roman Empire,[3] an accusation which stuck. A long period of deepening neglect followed. Fewer printed editions of Vegetius appeared in the seventeenth century, and no new English translation was published after Lt. John Clarke's *Military Institutions of Vegetius* (London 1767), although T.R. Phillips reprinted parts of Clarke's in 1940 and 1944,[4] until L.F. Stelten's edition of 1990.[5]

Few commentaries have appeared. N. Schwebel's (Nuremberg 1767, Strasbourg 1806) was the last complete one of importance to ancient historians; D. Nisard's largely transmits the work of his predecessors.[6] Count Turpin de Crissé's *Commentaires* (Montargis 1775) are more about eighteenth-century France and its relations to antique warfare in general than an attempt to analyse the *Epitome* on its own terms. In the

[1]N.P. Milner, *Vegetius and the Anonymus De Rebus Bellicis*, D.Phil. thesis (Oxford 1991) ch. 7. Most of the arguments in this introduction are set forth more fully in the thesis.

[2]*Sic proci Penelopes, cum ad ipsam dominam accessus non pateret, cum ancillis illius miscebantur*, reprinted in Schwebel (1806) p. xii (from Scriverius' *praefatio*, Leiden 1632).

[3]R. Sablayrolles, "Bibliographie sur l'*epitoma rei militaris* de Végèce", *CGRAR* iii (1984) 142.

[4]T.R. Phillips (ed.), *Flavius Vegetius Renatus, the Military Institutions of the Romans* (Harrisburg, Pa. 1944), reprinted Westport 1985; T.R. Phillips (ed.), *The Roots of Strategy: a collection of military classics* (Harrisburg, Pa. 1940).

[5]L.F. Stelten, *Flavius Vegetius Renatus: Epitoma Rei Militaris*, edited with an English translation (New York, Bern, Frankfurt, Paris 1990).

[6]D. Nisard (ed.), *Ammien Marcellin, Jornandès, Frontin, Végèce, Modestus, avec la traduction en français*, Coll. des Auteurs Latins II.15 (Paris 1878). The translation was reprinted by F. Reyniers, *Végèce* (Paris 1948).

twentieth century, however, D.K. Silhanek produced a small unpublished commentary on books I and II,[1] and D. Schenk published a monograph of Quellenforschung.[2]

Work on the critical edition of the text of the *Epitome* has been less neglected. Since Schwebel, C. Lang edited the Teubner editions of 1869 and 1885, A. Andersson published a philological thesis on the text,[3] and L.F. Stelten produced his edition mentioned earlier, after unpublished work on books I and II.[4] New discoveries of manuscripts have for some time made new critical editions desirable, even if initial indications are that the new MSS belong to the family π whose authority Lang normally preferred to follow,[5] and another new edition was reported in progress for the Budé series in 1977.[6] There is also a new Teubner edition by A. Önnerfors which appeared in 1995.[7] The present translation is from the text of Lang's second edition, except a few cases where I have adopted a variant reading from Lang's apparatus, as indicated in the notes. I have normally not transmitted Lang's square brackets, indicating text which he considered to be interpolated by scribes, because the work of classical philologists such as M. Schanz,[8] A. Andersson and P. De Jonge[9] has all tended in the direction of vindicating the suspected text, except in a very few cases indicated in the notes.

Scholarly interest in Vegetius has slowly been rising since the nineteenth century when a number of German dissertations were devoted to the *Epitome.* If interwar activity in this area by E. Sander, F.

---

[1]D.K. Silhanek, *A translation and commentary on Vegetius' Epitoma Books I and II*, Diss. (New York Univ. 1972).

[2]D. Schenk, *Flavius Vegetius Renatus: Die Quellen der Epitoma rei militaris, Klio*, Beiträge zur alten Geschichte xxii (N.F. ix) (Leipzig 1930), repr. Nuremberg 1963.

[3]A. Andersson, *Studia Vegetiana*, Diss. (Uppsala 1938).

[4]L.F. Stelten, *Epitoma Rei Militaris of Flavius Vegetius Renatus. A critical edition of books I and II*, Diss. (St. Louis Univ. 1970), résumé in *DA* xxxi (1970) 2363A.

[5]Cf. C.E. Finch, "Codices Pal. Lat. 1571–1573 as sources for Vegetius", *TAPhA* xciii (1962) 22–29, id., "Source of codex E of Vegetius", *Classical Bulletin* xli (1965) 45–46, L. Rubio, "El ms. Scorialensis L.III.33: Nuevos datos para una futura edición del *Epitoma Rei Militaris* de Vegetius", *Emerita* xli (1973) 209–223.

[6]W. Goffart, "The Date and Purpose of Vegetius' *De Re Militari*", *Traditio* xxxiii (1977) 65 = id., *Rome's Fall and After* (London 1989) 45 n.1, cf. addendum p. 355.

[7]But see the review by M.D. Reeve, *RFIC* (forthcoming); and R.S.O. Tomlin, *Gnomon* (forthcoming).

[8]M. Schanz, "Zu den Quellen des Vegetius", *Hermes* xvi (1881) 137–146.

[9]P. de Jonge, "Ammianus and Vegetius", in *Ut pictura poesis: studia Latina Petro Johanni Enk septuagenario oblata* (Leiden 1955) 99–106.

Lammert and A.R. Neumann was not sustained post-1945, at least the results of a century of German Vegetian scholarship could be collected in Neumann's *RE* article of 1965.[1] Since then seminal articles by F. Paschoud,[2] W. Goffart[3] and G. Sabbah[4] have made considerable advances by considering Vegetius in the context of his own times, themselves greatly illuminated by the rapid growth of the study of late Antiquity.

This translation is made on the principle that since Vegetius addressed his work to a late-Roman Emperor, it is only by trying to understand what it could have meant to him that we can begin to evaluate it. To feel disappointment that Vegetius was not writing history is a symptom of having set out with the wrong preconceptions as to the nature of the work. Close examination reveals that it is highly topical, by way of offering a systematized remedy for alleged military failures in recruitment and training, army organization and strategy, and arms and equipment. It is also very selective; cavalry warfare and river patrol-boats are expressly omitted on the grounds that late-Roman progress in these areas rendered them above criticism; attacking hostile cities is largely left out presumably because the main contemporary barbarian enemies, the Goths, Huns and Alans, did not live in cities. The use of barbarian auxiliaries of various kinds is generally ignored for reasons probably determined by Vegetius' programme to apply the legionary model in the main. The late-Roman two-tier military organization of *comitatenses* and *palatini* in the field armies, and *limitanei* and *ripenses, cohortes* and *alae,* in the frontier armies is hardly visible, because Vegetius was mainly interested in the field armies.

The work also falls self-evidently into the genre of epitomes of technical treatises. As there were different types of epitome, it is important to establish which type our *Epitome* is, namely whether it is a faithful summary of other works, preserving their general order and arrangement, or whether it is a "scissors-and-paste" mosaic of other works excerpted and rearranged according to the epitomator's own system, and if the latter, whether it incorporates much additional

---

[1] A.R. Neumann, *RE Suppl.* X (1965), s.v. "Vegetius", col. 992–1020.
[2] F. Paschoud, *Roma Aeterna,* Bibliotheca Helvetica Romana VII (Neuchâtel 1967) 110–117.
[3] See above.
[4] G. Sabbah, "Pour la datation théodosienne du *De Re Militari* de Végèce", Centre Jean Palerne, *Mémoires* II (Univ. de Saint-Étienne 1980) 131–155.

material of the epitomator's own composition. Close inspection has produced opposite conclusions. Whereas Schenk thought that each of the four books was largely based on a single source—book I on Celsus, II on Paternus, and III–IV on Frontinus—it may be argued that although some signs of Frontinus' arrangement may be discerned in III and IV the work is on the whole drafted after the "scissors-and-paste" model and is extensively augmented and interpreted by the epitomator.

So much so, indeed, that in book I and II there seem grounds for thinking that Vegetius greatly expanded jejune source-material on the training and organization of the "ancient legion", using methods of subdivision of subjects, repetition of material, antiquarian etymologizing, modern glossing, embellishment with literary allusions and historical *exempla,* provision of medical explanations of phenomena and Christian pieties, reconstruction of ancient institutions from intelligent guesswork sometimes based apparently on contemporary civil service practice, and choice of material and emphasis determined by the wish to further a specific programme. The same methods may also be demonstrated for parts of book III designed to promote strategies of seizure and preservation of supplies and foodstuffs and the harrying of the enemy invader by means of guerilla actions rather than pitched battles, and in book IV in the accent placed on the defence of cities and supplies, and on themes of heavy armour and ambush pursued perhaps rather incongrously in the account of naval warfare.

In spite of all this, there are some convincing parallels between parts of book III and fragments of Cato *de Re Militari* preserved in other works, and the battle-order of the "ancient legion" retains the obsolete technical terms for the categories of combatants—*principes, hastati, triarii, velites, ferentarii, accensi*—normal in the third and second centuries BC. The background to the accounts of recruitment and training in books I, II and III also seems to link up with Cato, both in literary parallel passages and in the historical situation after the Second Punic War mentioned in significant chapters of books I and III. Furthermore the strikingly anomalous use of the verbal 2nd. pers. singular and *tuus-a-um* in book III is convincingly ascribed to the influence of Cato's original words,[1] and some of the tactics there described can be identified with battles of the Second Punic War.[2]

If the basic substrate of the "ancient legion" is Cato, many of the details of organization and administration in book II are hardly so ancient. Some seem recognizably parallel to late-Roman military and civil service grades, such as *supernumerarii, decani,* administrative *centuriones* = *centenarii,* and a *princeps* in overall charge of administration, and there is an unparalleled concatenation of imperial *praefectus legionis, praefectus castrorum* and *tribuni vel praepositi* all in command of the same unit with duties ambiguously differentiated. Some of the other details may be explained as reconstructions from obsolete terminology, such as the century of 100 men and the *praefectus fabrorum/fabrum* arbitrarily put in charge of legionary technicians and engineers.[3] The Vegetian cohort of five centuries may have been influenced by decimal subdivisions of late-Roman units.

Vegetius provides two source-notices, a fuller one in I.8 citing Cato the Censor, Cornelius Celsus, Frontinus, Paternus and the "constitutions of Augustus, Trajan and Hadrian", and a summary one in II.3 which emphasizes "Cato the Elder" and Frontinus among *alii conplures*—"many others". There is no reason to think that a different set of sources is meant for books II–IV, which came out after book I and so have a separate source-notice.

Book I, about the recruitment and training of legionaries, promises because of the subject and the frequent mention of his name to rely largely on Cato's *de Re Militari.* But in the laborious circumstances of ancient book production, it was normal for writers to cite authorities at second- or third-hand or even further removes. Caesar, for instance, named the antique Eratosthenes rather than Poseidonios whom he actually followed.[4] As there was a common ancient tendency to suppress

---

[1] D. Schenk, 60–61. Cf. V. *Epit.* III.11 note.

[2] The battle of Ilipa in 206 BC: V. *Epit.* III.20 Lang pp.108.20–109.17, cf. Livy 28.14, Polyb. 11.20–24, Sen. *de Vit. Beat.* 4.1; see M. Jähns, 54–55. The counter-tactic to elephants at the battle of Zama, 202 BC: V. *Epit.* III.24 Lang p.118.4–8, cf. Livy 30.33.1–3. The battle of Cannae, 216 BC: V. *Epit.* III.14, Florus 1.22.16, cf. 1.38.15, C. Marius later used Hannibal's "art of Cannae" to defeat the Cimbri.

[3] Cf. D. Baatz, *Bauten und Katapulte des römischen Heeres, Mavors* XI (Stuttgart 1994) 78, 133.

[4] A. Klotz, *Cäsarstudien* (1910) 27, cited by F. Lammert, *Gnomon* x (1934) 271–274.

the names of the more immediate sources,[1] or to copy authors unnamed,[2] we have to reckon with the possibility that Vegetius may have actually used epitomes of even Frontinus and Paternus. This would seem to be indicated for instance if there were signs that he had a persistent problem of too little information to go on

For most of those who cited Cato's *de Re Militari*, Verrius Flaccus is the likely source.[3] Festus', Nonius Marcellus', and Priscian's citations of linguistic peculiarities certainly or probably derive from the Augustan scholar's grammatical compilations *de Obscuris Catonis* or *de Significatu Verborum*.[4] Because of the archaic word *vitiligunt*, the elder Pliny's quotation in the preface to his *Natural History* looks suspiciously like a fragment preserved in such a source too.[5] Apart from Gellius, Vegetius is the only other citator, but if he had really had access to the original work he would surely have made more of the fact. He never explicitly quotes Cato verbatim, and in the one case where we can compare the original words, it is not clear that he knew he was quoting Cato, and his version shows linguistic modernization of the original.[6] It is obvious that if he had had the original text, he would have had to interpret dozens of archaisms, but of this, not a word is said. A work which was probably a rarity even four hundred years earlier, and which no one can be demonstrated to have seen after Gellius in the second century, was surely not in Vegetius' hands.

Moreover, Schenk's analysis of *Epitome* III suggests that "Frontinus" subsumed "Cato", at least (see below), and the fact that Celsus and Frontinus are presented in a zeugma in the source-notice at I.8, coupled with the fact that Celsus was writing under Tiberius between Cato and Frontinus, probably means that we should assume that "Frontinus" subsumed "Celsus" too. Whether or not the plan of A. Cornelius Celsus'

---

[1] Cf. Jerome's habitual citation and even quotation of Greek authors ostensibly from the originals but actually from Latin secondary literature, translations, handbooks, commentaries, etc., P. Courcelle, *Late Latin Writers and their Greek Sources* (Cambridge, Mass. 1969) 78 ff.

[2] Pliny *Hist. Nat.* praef. 21 ff.

[3] Aulus Gellius 6.4.5 is the most probable exception; this second century scholar had a strong liking for Cato's works, and took the trouble to hunt them out. Even so, he cites *de Re Militari* only once.

[4] Cf. Festus 306 M.; D. Schenk, 36–37.

[5] Pliny *Hist. Nat.* praef. 30, cf. 32, remarking Cato's compound *vitilitigatores*. For all the citations, cf. Jordan pp.80–82.

[6] *Epit.* III.20 note.

largely lost *Encyclopaedia* containing four *artes*—agriculture, medicine, rhetoric and military science—was inspired by Cato's works, which included his *de Agricultura* and *de Re Militari*, it is likely that Celsus transmitted the Catonian material on the army to Frontinus.[1] Schenk argued that Celsus was the main source for book I on stylistic grounds that have fallen victim to Andersson's demonstration that the style of the whole *Epitome* is in general (apart from the use of the 2nd. pers. sing. in book III) homogeneous.[2]

If Frontinus borrowed from Celsus, we have to ask also from what source Josephus, writing his *Jewish War* in Rome in the AD 70s[3] between Celsus and Frontinus, took his famous excursus on the Roman army and its discipline, training, philosophy, equipment and camp-construction, which has much in common with *Epitome* I–II.[4] Josephus' information on castrametation and camp discipline also shows some parallels to Vegetius' material on castrametation.[5] In two respects the latter is less detailed than Josephus; he does not discuss the system of the *tessera* that controlled the watches and sentries, and omits the traditional method of striking camp.[6] There is no good reason for these omissions. Obsoleteness does not in general deter him, and the evidence suggests anyway that the *tessera* still existed in the late fourth century AD.[7] Therefore Vegetius' source was even more concise. If Josephus' source was Celsus, then Vegetius did not make direct use of Celsus; still less did he consult Cato. But the material may well have derived from

[1] F. Marx (ed.), *A. Cornelii Celsi quae supersunt* (Leipzig–Berlin 1915) vii–viii.

[2] D. Schenk, 28 ff., A. Andersson, 21 ff.

[3] T. Rajak, *Josephus, the Historian and his Society* (London 1983) 195. N.b. Josephus could and did translate from Latin writers, cf. ibid. 235.

[4] Jos. *Bell. Iud.* 3.71, V. *Epit.* I.1, cf. Jos. *Bell. Iud.* 2.577 (Roman Empire won by valour not by fortune). Jos. *Bell. Iud.* 3.72–75, V. *Epit.* I.1, I.4, I.27–28, II.23–24, III praef., III.4, III.9 p.88.15 ff. (Lang), III.10, cf. IV.31–32 (Romans always training). Jos. *Bell. Iud.* 3.102, V. *Epit.* I.1, I.2, I.7, I.8, II.19 (training of minds as well as bodies). Jos. *Bell. Iud.* 3.88, 104–105, V. *Epit.* II.2, II.21 (Roman army behaves as one body). Jos. *Bell. Iud.* 3.106, V. *Epit.* I.8, II.2 fin. (Roman invincibility in the stationary battle primarily responsible for the size of their Empire).

[5] Jos. *Bell. Iud.* 3.76, V. *Epit.* I.21, III.8, III.10 p.92.10ff (Romans always build a camp, so are never vulnerable to surprise attack). Jos. *Bell. Iud.* 3.78, V. *Epit.* II.11 (Roman army takes with it a multitude of artificers and builders for this purpose). Jos. *Bell. Iud.* 3.79–84, V. *Epit.* II.18, cf. II.25 fin. (camp "resembles a city"). Jos. *Bell. Iud.* 3.85, V. *Epit.* II.19, III.8 (*lignatio, pabulatio, aquatio*).

[6] Jos. *Bell. Iud.* 3.87–92, Polyb. 6.34.7–12, 6.40.1–3.

[7] Amm. 21.5.13; 23.2.2; O. Douch, an archive from a limitanean unit in Egypt *c*. AD 375: *tesserarius*, nos. 12, 15, 30, 33, 41, 53; Ioh. Lyd. *de Mag.* I.46.

Celsus summarized in Frontinus or Paternus, or rather we should say from an epitome of either or both.

Despite suggestive parallels, Josephus' excursus probably did not derive from Polybius' excursus on the Roman military system preserved in his *Histories*.[1] For although, whilst omitting much archaic matter,[2] he also transmitted common details,[3] where Polybius was brief, such as for the method of striking camp, Josephus is much fuller, and where Polybius dwelt at length, for instance on the savage punishments of decimation and *fustuarium*, and on rewards for bravery, Josephus is brief. Given the Roman subject, and the prescriptive nature of Polybius' text, it seems likely that his account went back to a Latin model which was more detailed still, and that Josephus' account ultimately derived from the same more detailed Latin model. We may infer from the evidence of Vegetius-Josephus parallels that Josephus' immediate source was a presumably first-century AD military handbook such as that by Celsus that derived ultimately from Cato's *de Re Militari* and also that the latter was Polybius' main source, written by his elder contemporary.[4]

As for Sex. Julius Frontinus, who was *consul ter ordinarius* with the Emperor Trajan in AD 100, and is named both in I.8, and more particularly in II.3 as Vegetius' main source after Cato, we are unfortunate in the loss of his *de Re Militari*. However his surviving *Strategemata*, which is generally agreed to have furnished *exempla* to the lost theoretical work,[5] was analysed for parallels to the structure of

---

[1]Polyb. 6.19–6.42.

[2]e.g., Polyb. 6.19–26 (raising of consular legionary armies).

[3]Jos. *Bell. Iud.* 3.77, cf. Polyb. 6.31.10 (square-shaped camp). Jos. *Bell. Iud.* 3.83, Polyb. 6.31.10 (simile of a city). Jos. *Bell. Iud.* 3.89–92, Polyb. 6.40.1–3 (three-signal method of striking camp). Jos. *Bell. Iud.* 3.102–104, Polyb. 6.37–38 (savage discipline). Jos. *Bell. Iud.* 3.87–88, Polyb. 6.34.7–12 (*tessera*). Jos. *Bell. Iud.* 3.93–97, Polyb. 6.22–23 (infantry arms), 25 (cavalry arms).

[4]E. Rawson, *PBSR* xxxix (1971) 13 ff., argued that Polybius' excursus derived from *commentarii* of military tribunes, since it lays down the basics from their point of view. But the same would not be surprising of Cato as they were the most senior officers of the legion after the consul, who would naturally not be concerned with such details. The fact that Cato-Vegetius diverges on the order *principes–hastati–triarii* from Polybius' *hastati–principes–triarii* is without weight, given V.'s editorial method and remoteness from the original. Since Polybius' source dated from before his own day, but as Rawson observes must postdate the introduction of the military oath in 216 BC (Livy 22.38, cf. Front. *Strat.* 4.1.4), Cato as a generation older than Polybius would fit the profile. Finally, Cato *de Re Mil.* fr. 8 (Festus 298 L., 253 M. = Jordan p.81) on *procubitores* probably lies behind Polybius 6.35.5 on προκοιτία.

[5]C. Wachsmuth, *RhM* xv (1860) 575, endorsed by R. Grosse, *DLZ* lv (1934) 61–65.

Epitome III and IV by Schenk.[1] Although the structure of Frontinus' lost work remains uncertain, the *Strategemata* allows some deductions to be made about it from the order of subjects and rubrics. They imply that the Catonian tactical chapters of *Epitome* III.9–22 are embedded in the part most likely to derive from Frontinus. But there are possible exceptions to the Frontinian scheme in III.1–3, 5, 8, 26 at least, not to mention the naval chapters in book IV.

Because Frontinus may have been influenced by the *Strategikos* of Onasander, a Greek philosopher writing in Rome during the mid-first century AD, parallels between Onasander and Vegetius also support the partial reconstruction of the structure and content of Frontinus' work.[2] Not only is the general pattern of pre-battle, battle and post-battle, followed by the treatment of siege warfare, observable in Onasander as in *Epitome* III–IV and Frontinus *Strat.* I–III, but there are also numerous resemblances of detail between Onasander and Vegetius.[3] The order of subjects and the sheer number of connexions, many in addition to those collected by Schenk, make it likely that Frontinus' work included from Onasander a number of the same points which have

---

[1] D. Schenk, 44–81.

[2] E. Sander, *Philologische Wochenschrift* xlix (1929) 1230–1231, D. Schenk, 81–83, F. Lammert, *Philologische Wochenschrift* lix (1939) 236–237.

[3] Onas. 6.8, V. *Epit.* III.5 (dust-cloud and fire-signals). Onas. 6.9, V. *Epit.* III.11 (short march to battle). Onas. 7.1–2, V. *Epit.* III.6 (occupying mountain passes). Onas. 7.2, V. *Epit.* III.2 (avoiding marshes). Onas. 9.1, V. *Epit.* III.2 (continual changes of camp). Onas. 9.2, V. *Epit.* II.23 cf. I.18, III.2 (continual drill in winter). Onas. 10.1–3, V. *Epit.* I.26, cf. II.2, III.9 (infantry manoeuvres). Onas. 10.4 (armed with staves), V. *Epit.* I.11–12 (training with staves), I.13, II.23 (*armatura*), III.9, III.4 (mock-battles). Onas. 10.6, V. *Epit.* I.26, III.2 (cavalry manoeuvres). Onas. 10.10–12, V. *Epit.* III.8 (guard by night in relays). Onas. 10.13, V. *Epit.* III.22 (night retreats). Onas. 10.15, V. *Epit.* III.6 (guides). Onas. 10.20, V. *Epit.* III.11 (remaining in fortification and launching surprise attack). Onas. 10.22–24, V. *Epit.* III.6, cf. III.26 (secrecy). Onas. 11.1–5, V. *Epit.* III.6, III.22, III.25 (pursuit in broken country). Onas. 12.1–2, V. *Epit.* III.11, cf. Front. *Strat.* 2.1.1 (meal before battle). Onas. 13.1–3, V. *Epit.* III.9, III.12 (exhortation in adversity). Onas. 19.1, V. *Epit.* I.20, II.17, III.14 (intervals in the line for the light-armed). Onas. 21.1, V. *Epit.* III.15 (depth better than breadth). Onas. 21.3, V. *Epit.* III.20 (protecting the flank using natural features: 7th. *depugnatio*). Onas. 21.5–7, V. *Epit.* III.20 (crescent formation: 4th. and 5th. *depugnationes*). Onas. 21.8, V. *Epit.* III.20 (oblique formation: 2nd., 3rd. and 6th. *depugnationes*). Onas. 22.1–4, V. *Epit.* III.17–20 (tactical reserve). Onas. 26, V. *Epit.* III.5 (gestures). Onas. 28–29.2, V. *Epit.* I.20, II.12, II.14 (shining armour). Onas. 31, V. *Epit.* III.13 (choosing broken ground if enemy stronger in cavalry). Onas. 36.3–6, V. *Epit.* III.25 (exhortation in defeat). Onas. 38.7–8, V. *Epit.* III.6, III.26 (reception of defectors). Onas. 39.4–7, V. *Epit.* IV.12 (terrorizing cities). Onas. 40–41, V. *Epit.* IV.28 (night-sallies). Onas. 42.17, V. *Epit.* IV.12 (trumpets in sieges). Onas. 42.18–21, V. *Epit.* IV.25 (advice to citizens to surrender arms). Onas. 42.23, cf. V. *Epit.* IV.7 (sending non-combatants into besieged city).

finally got into *Epitome* III–IV. But at no point is there a really close verbal correspondence between Onasander, what survives of Frontinus, and Vegetius. Even where the latter has *exempla* in common with Frontinus the differences are problematic for any theory of direct use of the *Strategemata*.[1] It should be noted too that Vegetius, being on the whole ignorant of Greek (see below), would not have used Onasander directly.

The Greek origins of much of the form and substance of *Epitome* III–IV ought not to be doubted, including matter on land tactics mediated through Cato and Frontinus and the inclusion of a section on naval warfare.[2] What is far from clear is whether Frontinus included sections on shipbuilding and navigation, for *Epitome* IV.34–42 seems to carry material derived from the *libri navales* of the first century BC polymath M. Terentius Varro, cited at IV.41. A change of source is indicated both by an observable difference in treatment of the material, and the fact that what can be deduced from surviving fragments of Varro's "naval books" in Pliny, Isidorus, and Servius "Fuldensis" (a Vergilian commentator of the late fourth century AD) seems to lie directly behind the chapters on navigation IV.38–42.[3] That Varro was

---

[1] On V. *Epit.* III.10 p.93.2–11 (Lang), Val. Max. 2.7.1–2, Front. *Strat.* 4.1–2, see Schenk, 48, 59, citing A. Klotz, "Exempla und Epitoma Livii", *Hermes* xliv (1909) 211 ff. The most parallel exemplum is Front. *Strat.* 4.7.16: *Scipio Africanus dicere solitus est hosti non solum dandam esse viam ad fugiendam, sed etiam muniendam*, "Scipio Africanus used to say that a way for the enemy to flee by should not only be given to them, but even built for them," and V. *Epit.* III.21: *Ideoque Scipionis laudata sententia est, qui dixit viam hostibus, qua fugerent, muniendam*, "For this reason Scipio's axiom has won praise, when he said that a way should be built for the enemy to flee by." The differences are as striking as the similarities between Front. *Strat.* 4.7.27: *Scipio Aemilianus ad Numantiam omnibus non cohortibus tantum, sed centuriis sagittarios et funditores interposuit*, "Scipio Aemilianus at Numantia interspersed archers and slingers not just in all cohorts but in (all) centuries", and V. *Epit.* I.15: *Africanus quidem Scipio, cum adversum Numantinos, qui exercitus populi Romani sub iugum miserant, esset acie certaturus, aliter se superiorem futurum esse non credidit, nisi in omnibus centuriis lectos sagittarios miscuisset*, "Scipio Africanus, about to do battle with the Numantines who had sent armies of the Roman People under the yoke, supposed that he would only get the upper hand if he incorporated picked archers in all centuries."

[2] V. *Epit.* III praef., cf. IV.31 note; Aelian *Tact.* praef. 3 on Frontinus; Frontinus' surviving *Strategemata* covers Greek military history as well as Roman, and naval in addition to land warfare, but *not* separately.

[3] See IV.38, note.

also behind those on shipbuilding IV.34–37 is no more than a possibility.[1]

In his fuller source-notice at I.8 Vegetius also cites "Paternus, a most zealous champion of military law", and the "constitutions of Augustus, Trajan and Hadrian". Contrary to the view of Alfred Neumann and others that he used directly or indirectly the rule-book of Hadrian, which subsumed that of Augustus, itself a compilation based on Republican rule-books conjecturally going back to P. Rutilius Rufus, Scipio Africanus Minor and Cato *de Re Militari*,[2] Vegetius seems aware only of *ad hoc* military regulations.[3] Like Schanz and Grosse, Schenk felt that the *constitutiones* were available to him only in so far as they were cited by the Antonine writer and praetorian prefect P. Taruttienus Paternus, and this seems preferable.[4]

Surviving fragments of Paternus' probably juristic work in Justinian's *Digest* and John the Lydian's *de Magistratibus* show that he covered in some detail in four books[5] both antiquities of the Roman army in the age of, for example, Romulus and current regulations of the second century AD, supported by quotations from the *disciplina Augusti*.[6] Schenk, drawing attention to an alleged similarity between the *Digest* and *Epitome* II.19, and to Vegetius' announcement that he would proceed to explain the organization of the ancient legion "following the guidance of military law" (II.4), thought that book II was based mainly

---

[1]The astronomical observations for felling and hewing timber occur also in Pliny *Hist. Nat.* 16.74.190–191 and Servius ad Verg. *Georg.* 1.256, cf. V. *Epit.* IV.35 note; Pliny 16.18.42 says that the fir—*abies*—was in great demand for building ships. The further use of material deriving from Varro's works by V. may also be suggested for I.2 (*de Architectura?*) and I.6 (*Rer. Rust.*).

[2]A. Neumann, *CPh* xxxi (1936) 6–7, 9; id. *CPh* xli (1946) 223. A.A. Schiller, "Sententiae Hadrianae de re militari", in *Sein und Werden im Recht: Festgabe für Ulrich von Lübtow zum 70. Geburtstag am 21. August 1970* (Berlin 1970) 295–306, argues that there may well have been no rule-book as such.

[3]V. *Epit.* I.27 on marching drill, where he omits the name of Trajan. There is further scope in book I for use of such regulations in I.9 on marching drill and in I.5 on the height of recruits, and perhaps in II.22 on military executions; elsewhere their use seems improbable.

[4]D. Schenk, 12 ff. See V. *Epit.* I.8 note.

[5]*Dig.* index Florentinus.

[6]Cf. Ioh. Lydus *de Mag.* I.9 (Romulus), *Dig.* 50.6.7 (long list of second century AD *immunes*), *Dig.* 49.16.7 (precept on capital punishment of *proditores* and *transfugae*), *Dig.* 49.16.12 §1 (precept forbidding use of soldiers for private services, quoting from the *disciplina Augusti*, cited at V. *Epit.* II.19 note).

on Paternus.[1] But it was in I.8, the source-notice for book I which was originally published separately, that Vegetius named Paternus at all; if he lies behind the "ancient legion" in book II, he does so as part of the common background of epitomized sources. The evidence of Vegetius' late-antique reconstruction of the "ancient legion" weighs against direct use of so detailed and professional an authority as Paternus.[2]

John the Lydian cited Paternus as a Roman military rhetorician along with Celsus, a mysterious Catilina, Cato and Frontinus, and Vegetius himself.[3] There is no reason to think that John the Lydian in the sixth century, any more than John of Salisbury in the twelfth century,[4] saw all of these works, though the Lydian clearly had access to Paternus. Catilina is a shadowy figure, but most likely he was a later, third- or fourth-century, epitomator of the authors in the same tradition as that followed by Vegetius, and so a possible unnamed source used by him.

The study of Vegetius' repetitions reveals his method best, as a compiler of material epitomized from a very few secondary sources which he then wrote up with literary embellishments in a classicizing style according to a pre-arranged plan.[5] He exercised reasonable care, but not academic exactitude, throwing the material together quickly,

---

[1] Schenk, 23 ff.

[2] *Epit.* II.7 itself seems to be a post-Constantinian list of officers and under-officers inserted for supplementary purposes; V. had some but not enough ancient material for his ambitious scheme to reconstruct the "ancient legion". Ioh. Lydus *de Mag.* I.46 is a much longer list derived from a related source.

[3] Ioh. Lydus *de Mag.* I.47: μάρτυρες Κέλσος τε καὶ Πάτερνος καὶ Κατιλίνας, οὐχ ὁ συνωμότης ἀλλ᾽ ἕτερος, Κάτων <τε> πρὸ αὐτῶν ὁ πρῶτος καὶ Φροντῖνος, μεθ᾽ οὓς καὶ ῾Ρενᾶτος, ῾Ρωμαῖοι πάντες. "as witnessed by Celsus, Paternus and Catilina, not the conspirator but another, Cato before them, the first (writer), Frontinus, and after them Renatus, all Romans."

[4] Ioh. Saresb., *Policrat.* (AD 1159) 6.19. (618a): *adeat Catonem Censorium, legat et illa quae Cornelius Celsus, quae Iulius Iginus, quae Vegetius Renatus, cuius, eo quod elegantissime et diligentissime rei militaris artem tradidit licet exempla perstrinxerit, plura inserui.* "Let him consult Cato the Censor, let him read also Cornelius Celsus, Julius Hyginus, and Vegetius Renatus, of whom I have included much for the reason that he treated the art of war most elegantly and thoroughly although he made limited use of examples." Cf. M. Manitius, *Geschichte der lateinischen Literatur des Mittelalters* III (1931) 258: John excerpted Vegetius and Frontinus' *Strategemata.*

[5] F. Lammert, *Klio* xxxiii (1940) 286, observed a number of repetitions in the chapters on siege warfare, viz., *Epit.* IV.6 and 21, 5 and 24, 19 and 30, 22 and 29. These are due in part to coverage of the same tactic from the point of view of the defenders and the attackers of the city. There is a certain shift in treatment, as IV.1–11 cover fortifications and provisioning for a siege, whereas IV.12–30 are on tactics of siege-warfare, in which the presentation of attack and defence tactics is partly integrated, partly separate, but in the main weighted towards defence. Lammert, *Klio* xxxi (1938) 399, was wrong to schematize IV.8–11/12 as defence, IV.12–30 as attack.

executing an intelligent general scheme. His work stands favourable comparison with that of other contemporary semi-official authors at Court such as Eutropius and Victor, who like himself combined the writing of literature with the public life of busy hommes d'affaires.

General principles are obviously repeated because of their importance.[1] Vegetius' chapter on "General Rules of War" (III.26) is an extended list of such principles, the majority of them repeated from all parts of book III, but also including one or two from the first two books.[2] These rules were intended to provide an aide-mémoire of the main principles of field strategy and tactics; such recapitulation was a valued technique of late antique didactic writers.[3]

The repetition of wider subjects[4] is also attributable to the editorship of Vegetius, as in the course of writing he came to use the same material under different rubrics.[5] His programme of reform necessarily

---

[1]e.g., *Epit.* III.3: *saepius enim penuria quam pugna consumit exercitum, et ferro saevior fames est*, "for armies are more often destroyed by starvation than battle, and hunger is more savage than the sword"; *Epit.* III.9: *nam fames, ut dicitur, intrinsecus pugnat et vincit saepius sine ferro*, "for hunger, they say, fights from within, and often conquers without a blow"; *Epit.* III.26: *qui frumentum necessariaque non praeparat, vincitur sine ferro*, "he who does not prepare grain-supplies and provisions is conquered without a blow." Cf. Front. *Strat.* 4.7.1: *C. Caesar dicebat idem sibi esse consilium adversus hostem, quod plerisque medicis contra vitia corporum, fame potius quam ferro superandi*, "C. Caesar used to say he had the same idea for the enemy, as many doctors have against diseases of the body, that of overcoming them by starvation rather than the use of steel."

[2]*Epit.* III.26 p.122.3 (Lang): *Amplius iuvat virtus quam multitudo*, "Bravery is of more value than numbers." Cf. I.8: *In omni enim conflictu non tam prodest multitudo quam virtus*, "For in any conflict it is not so much numbers as bravery that pays off" (the clearest example). A few are not repeated from any part of the text as we have it. The most significant part of the list appears to be a summary of the seven "general actions"—*depugnationes*— of III.20.

[3]Cf. the list of *necessariae sententiae* in the probably contemporary work Palladius *de Agric.* I.6. The Byzantine military writer Maurice, at the end of the sixth century AD, included in a similar list some Greek translations of V.'s rules; e.g., *Epit.* III.26 p.121.1–2 (Lang): *In bello qui plus in agrariis vigilaverit, plus in exercendo milite laboraverit, minus periculum sustinebit*, "In war, he who spends more time watching in outposts and puts more effort into training soldiers, will be less subject to danger." = Maur. *Strat.* 8.2.2: 'Ο πλέον συναγρυπνῶ ν τῷ στρατεύματι καὶ πλέον τῷ γυμνάζειν τοὺς στρατιώτας πονῶ ν ἐλάχιστα κινδυνεύει κατὰ τὸν πόλεμον.

[4]*Epit.* I.9–20, I.26–27, II.23, III.4, III.9, III.10 (training); I.21–25, III.8, III.10 (castrametation); I.20, II.15–17, III.14 (battle-array); I.4, I.15–16, I.17(?), I.18(?), I.20, II.2, II.15, II.17, II.23, III.14, III.16–18, III.20, III.22, III.24 (legionary light-armed); II.22, III.5 (signals); III.3, IV.7 (food supplies and civilian population); II.10, III.2, IV.7 (care of sick); I.3, I.10, II.24, III.4, III.7 (swimming).

[5]*Epit.* I praef.: *per quosdam gradus et titulos antiquam consuetudinem conamur ostendere*, "we attempt to show, by a number of stages and headings, the ancient system…" A. Andersson, *Studia Vegetiana*, ch. 3, argues convincingly on grounds of style that the rubrics are by V. F. Lammert, rev. in *Philologische Wochenschrift* lx (1940) 79, reminds

required him somehow to adapt revered ancient example to contemporary conditions. This was a difficult task, and it led him to treat of a subject from both the more theoretical and practical points of view. Thus at III.14–18 the legionary array is presented in a more detailed formulation of that recommended already in II.15–17, in line with Vegetius' perception of its practical application to field campaigning, the topic of book III. Because of his chosen interest in matters of internal legionary organization and structure in book II, on the other hand, his earlier treatment serves a more theoretical aim.

Many repetitions are there to simply inform the author's abundant style. This seems the natural interpretation of repetitions of material in close succession, e.g. in IV.26–28.[1] Such *abundantia* may also explain repetitions placed farther apart, such as IV.22 and IV.29, and II.23, summarizing (with slight variations due to Vegetius' inaccuracy) the chapters on training I.9–19, 26–27. Likewise cases of the same *exempla* occurring twice.[2]

The only section of the entire *Epitome* which does not exhibit repetitions is that on shipbuilding and navigation (IV.33–42). Here he will have had sufficient rather than too little material, as he implies at one point.[3] None the less, he did not hesitate to embellish it with contemporary references in his usual style. Thus, Christian allusions in IV.34 and IV.35, a barbarian word for British spy-boats, with probably the whole *exemplum* concerning the spy-boats,[4] a circumspect reference to the festival of the *navigium Isidis* and an official decision about the date of Easter,[5] and an allusion to Vergil's *Georgics* IV.41. The other naval chapters IV.31–32, 43–46 exhibit all the familiar hallmarks of Vegetius' own editorship intended to advance his reforms, adorn his

---

us that such a framework is typical of tactical treatises such as Frontinus' *Strategemata*. Cf. also Aelian *Tact*. praef. 7. How far the plan is V.'s own, we cannot tell for sure; but much of it subserves his reformist and polemical intentions, and is thus far likely to be original.

[1]Cf. also within the same chapter, IV.25 p.146.1–8 (Lang), ibid. p.146.8–13, III.21 p.111.8–11, ibid. p.111.20–22. See P. de Jonge, "Ammianus and Vegetius", in id. (ed.), *Ut Pictura Poesis: Studia latina Petro Iohanni Enk septuagenario oblata* (Leiden 1955) 104–105.

[2]*Epit.* I.3 and I.10, II.11 and IV.24, IV praef. and IV.26, cf. IV.9.

[3]*Epit.* IV.40.

[4]*Epit.* IV.37, to be set beside the fact that V. is one of the earliest authors to use the probably Celtic word *drungus*.

[5]See *Epit.* IV.39 note.

style and amplify his source-material, including the use of repetition.[1] This pattern points to use of the same predigested sources as for the bulk of the *Epitome,* sources which he revised, redesigned and rewrote with a message for a contemporary audience, above all those in government.

The accusation that Vegetius confused the institutions of diverse periods of the Roman Empire is, therefore, beside the point. He was not interested in telling the history of the Roman army; he was not an historian, but something more akin to a politician, seeking to reform contemporary institutions and strategic thinking. He was well aware that the basic model was from Cato, albeit mediated through later authors such as Celsus, Frontinus and Paternus, and to himself probably by later epitomes of them. He largely supplemented gaps in the records available to him by intelligent conjecture based on etymologies of old military titles and knowledge of contemporary military institutions. He was not trying to avoid confusion of historical institutions but to flesh out the legion of Cato in a manner that would have relevance to the modern field army. As a strategist, he presents the "ancient legion" throughout as a model for the present. Ancient institutions and titles are set side-by-side with modern. Lessons for contemporary practice are sought and suggested. A truly historical approach was strictly irrelevant to his aims, and lack of it should not be held against him.

The *Epitome* is, then, not a true Art of War, but a political and strategic tract, an originally antiquarian account of Cato's army tricked out and rearranged as a commentary on present-day inadequacies. The circumstances of composition reflect this result. Book I, we learn from the preface to book II, was written first separately, off the writer's own bat as a paper for the Emperor's instruction and benefit on the

---

[1] Thus, the list of provinces originally served by the two fleets at Misenum and Ravenna, composed after the withdrawal of Aegyptus from Oriens in the late AD 360s (*Epit.* IV.31, cf. I.28, an editorial chapter; both lists will be of V.'s own composition), the deterrence-theory of military preparedness restated at IV.31 in a naval context in terms derived from III praef., the structure of the two naval legions under *praefecti,* and ten tribunes commanding a cohort each, resembling V.'s reconstruction of the *legio antiqua* (IV.32, cf. II.12), the heavy arms of marines (IV.44, cf. I.20 and II.15), the advantage of height presented by turrets on the ships and the use of fire-darts described in terms which derive from earlier comments on siege-warfare (IV.44, cf. IV.8, 17, 18, 19; IV.44, cf. IV.18), opportunities for ambush apparently deriving from those already listed for land warfare (IV.45), finally, three dictionary definitions given for the *asser, falx* and *bipennis* (IV.46), which could well have come from a reference book in V.'s library, cf. definitions of *alae, exercitus* and *legio* (II.1).

recruitment and training of Roman citizens, not barbarian mercenaries. This was well-received and further examples from Antiquity were commissioned by the Emperor—hence books II to IV. One Emperor who we do know admired the *duces* of the Latin age (early and middle Republic, 509–*c.*100 BC) was Theodosius I (reigned AD 379–395),[1] and it is to him that the work is most likely directed. The work covers only such areas of strategic and administrative practice as the author considered in need of reform. The impression that it is an Art of War derives from the fact that it covers much of the same ground and uses basic material from such sources. But at best it gives only an incomplete idea of the various departments of warfare.

What the Emperor really thought about it, as opposed to what he apparently said, is anyone's guess. But whereas all Emperors in the possible period of writing from AD 383 to 450 made sweeping use of barbarian mercenaries, it is evident that the driving-force behind Vegetius' reforms was the desire to reduce and down-grade the rôle of all non-Roman ethnic forces. This is most demonstrable for book I which is explicitly about the recruitment and training of legions of Roman citizens, but it is also behind the "ancient legion" of book II and the strategies for the combined infantry-and-cavalry field-armies of book III with their heavy and light divisions all patterned after the legion of Cato. Doubts are cast at the same time on the reliability and training of barbarian *auxilia (palatina)* and, although the élite barbarian cavalry are praised in I.20, the discerning will have noticed that the "ancient legion" in book II contained large numbers of "fully integrated" legionary cavalry[2] able to carry out the tactical functions outlined in III.16 ff. Vegetius' insistence that the army could no longer build camps may also be linked to the enrolment of large numbers of barbarians under their own officers, who lacked technical knowledge of Roman military traditions.[3]

Finally the whole work is informed by the need to carry on the fight with the barbarians, both within and without the system, by land and by

---

[1]Claud. *pan. de Hon. cons. IV* 399 ff., cf. Ps.-Victor *Epit. de Caess.* 48.11–12.

[2]inflated to 726 by Vegetius, more than double the 300 normal in the age of Cato.

[3]So R. Grosse, "Das römisch-byzantinische Marschlager vom 4.–10. Jahrhundert", *Byz.Z.* xxii (1913) 95–96. Cf. Amm. 18.2.6: *auxiliarii milites semper munia spernentes huiusmodi ad obsequendi sedulitatem Iuliani blanditiis deflexi...* "the auxiliary soldiers, who always refuse labours of this kind, were persuaded to complete obedience by the blandishments of Julian..." But contrast Amm. 31.8.9. For Ammianus' disapproval of barbarians under their own officers, cf. Amm. 31.16.8.

sea. For although Vegetius was aware that the barbarians had not yet posed a naval threat, he was wise enough to foresee that eventuality which was realized in the second decade of the fifth century AD.[1] Against a background of defensive operations, holding forts and cities against invasion, controlling access to foodstuffs, resisting the enemy by guerilla tactics and starvation, Vegetius proposed to purge the barbarian preponderance within the army. Nor was he alone. Synesius called for the purging of barbarians from the eastern field armies in Constantinople, AD 399,[2] and this was carried out by the party of the praetorian prefect Aurelianus for whom he spoke, for we find Alaric moves out of Dacia and Macedonia where he had been *magister militum per Illyricum* from 397 and takes to invading Italy in 401.[3] Earlier there had been a general massacre of Gothic soldiers serving in the eastern army after the disaster at Adrianople, AD 378, which was widely regarded with satisfaction as a timely safeguard.[4]

In the west the downfall of Honorius' *magister utriusque militiae* Stilicho in AD 408 was followed by a massacre of the families of Gothic Roman soldiers, 30,000 of whom responded by deserting to join forces with Alaric and precipitated the sieges of Rome in 408–409, and the sack of AD 410.[5] In AD 471 the Emperor Leo carried out another purge of selected groups of Gothic and Alan soldiers in the east.[6] The history of the period shows the Roman governments reacting violently against Gothic and other barbarian mercenaries after long periods of depending on them, whenever the balance of power swung in their favour or they could play off a new group of barbarians against those who had outstayed their welcome or abused their paymasters. If Vegetius' wish

---

[1] J.R. Moss, "The effects of the policies of Aëtius on the history of western Europe", *Historia* xxii (1973) 711–731, esp. 723–728.

[2] Synes. *De Regno* (19) 23B = 1092C–1093A: ἤδη ἀνακτητέον ἡμῖν τὰ ʻΡωμαίων φρονήματα, καὶ συνεθιστέον αὐτουργεῖν τὰς νίκας, μηδὲ κοινωνίας ἀνεχομένους, ἀλλʼ ἀπαξιοῦντας ἐν ἁπάσῃ τάξει τὸ βάρβαρον. "We must immediately recover the courage of the Romans, and get used to winning our own victories, not putting up with partners but dismissing the barbarian from every rank and post."

[3] Cf. P.J. Heather, "The anti-Scythian tirade of Synesius' *De Regno*", *Phoenix* xlii (1988) 152–172, id., *Goths and Romans* (Oxford 1991); T.D. Barnes, "Synesius in Constantinople", *GRBS* xxvii (1986) 93–112.

[4] Amm. 31.16.8, Zos. 4.26.

[5] Zos. 5.35.5–6.

[6] W. Goffart, "Zosimus, the first historian of Rome's Fall", *American Historical Review* lxxvi (1971) 429 = id. *Rome's Fall and After* (London 1989) 98 n.76 with refs., and P.J. Heather, *Goths and Romans* (Oxford 1991).

to change the demography of the army was widely held, history suggests that the late-Empire was in the grip of political and economic destinies which made it a task of the utmost difficulty; such measures seem to have succeeded, albeit partially and temporarily, only in the realm controlled by the Byzantine government. The chances are that Vegetius' Emperor, even if he agreed with his adviser in principle, was powerless to carry out such a programme, at least in the western Empire.

Writing at the threshold of the Byzantine age, Vegetius was an author for whom Cato and Frontinus were already "ancient" writers, as they are for us. The past glories he set out to re-create played an inspirational rôle for him, as they did for later potentates such as Justinian and Charlemagne, and as we have seen for his own Emperor too. The spur to his writing was provided by contemporary humiliations such as the battle of Adrianople and its after-effects. The work offered a solution based not on historical analysis, but the science and technique of warfare as it had been practised by the Romans. Whatever the shortcomings of the bald epitomes available to him, the author's judgement of his times was shrewd, and in some respects prescient, and though a civilian his strategic thinking can frequently be confirmed by parallels to contemporary professional soldiers.[1] Vegetius was thus a significant late Roman writer who not only was well-informed about the world of late Antiquity, but is in some ways a bridge beween the mediaeval and classical Roman eras.

§2. The author

Nothing is known of Vegetius except what may be deduced from his writings. Fortunately, we have two works to go on, the *Epitome* and the *Digesta Artis Mulomedicinae*,[2] a veterinary work on horse and cattle ailments, which tells us different things about the author which we could scarcely have guessed. That it was the same Vegetius who wrote both works was proved through close verbal and stylistic parallels by

---

[1] He was right in his assessment of the gravity of the threat to the survival of the Roman Empire posed by the barbarian invasions, and correctly focused on the lack of available professional field armies (after Adrianople) to meet it. He seems to have included naval warfare in unstated anticipation of barbarians acquiring a naval capability, as later happened. His belief that fortifications offered high security, both to soldiers and civilians, was grounded in the military reality of the time, cf. Amm. 31.6.4, 31.15–16. His emphatic proposals to use food as a weapon and to harry the invaders by guerilla actions are supported by strategies recorded and approved by Ammianus (noted in the commentary).

[2] E. Lommatsch (ed.), *Vegetii Digesta Artis Mulomedicinae* (Teubner edn., 1903).

C. Schoener, and is generally accepted.[1] The MS *subscriptiones* of the *Mulomedicina* give Vegetius the *praenomen* "Publius", as does the oldest MS of the *Epitome*, the seventh-century "Excerptum Vaticanum", Vat. Reg. 2077.[2] All other MSS of the *Epitome* call him Flavius Vegetius Renatus. Since it was usual in the west to call imperial servants "Flavius" plus their last name only,[3] we should have expected Flavius Renatus but this never occurs. It may be preferable to combine the two strands of evidence and make him a true Flavius: thus Publius Flavius Vegetius Renatus.[4] However, true Flavii were rare. More likely we have a reflexion of the practice (commoner in Constantinople) whereby "Flavius" was treated unproblematically as an additional name, adopted by imperial servants. Vegetius may have migrated to Constantinople, like many Spanish hangers-on of Theodosius I, or else the edition of his book prepared there by Eutropius may have affected the form of his name. At any rate, he was probably named at birth Publius Vegetius Renatus. It is also possible that he consciously chose to use the dynastic title "Flavius", to which he was entitled as an imperial servant, in order for the proposals in the *Epitome* to have more impact in Court circles, whereas he wrote the *Mulomedicina* for the private amusement of himself and his aristocratic friends (see below) who were too grand to be impressed by such a badge of service to the régime.[5]

At a time when the old *tria nomina* system of Roman nomenclature was all but dead,[6] he was unusual in having a *praenomen*, a pattern which recurs among only some fourth-century western senators and some fourth- and even fifth-century *curiales*, town-councillors and their families, from Italy and Africa.[7] Although "Vegetius" is once attested

---

[1]C. Schoener, *Studien zu Vegetius:* Programm der kgl. bayer. Studienanstalt zu Erlangen 1887–1888 (Erlangen 1888) 18ff., W.S. Teuffel et al. (edd.), *Geschichte der römischen Literatur* III (Leipzig 1913⁶) 317, M. Schanz, *Geschichte der römischen Literatur IV* (Munich 1914²) 198 f., *RE Suppl.* X (1965) s.v. Vegetius, col. 1018 (A.R. Neumann).

[2]Lang, xi.

[3]R.S. Bagnall, A. Cameron, S.R. Schwartz, K.A. Worp, *Consuls of the Later Roman Empire* (Atlanta, Georgia 1987) 38.

[4]So *PLRE* I.763, s.v. "Vegetius".

[5]Cf. B. Salway, "A survey of Roman Onomastic Practice", *JRS* lxxxiv (1994) 124–145, at 140.

[6]A. Cameron, "Polyonomy in the Late Roman Aristocracy: the Case of Petronius Probus", *JRS* lxxxv (1985) 164–182, at 173, B. Salway, art. cit., 140–141.

[7]O. Salomies, *Die römischen Vornamen. Studien zur römischen Namengebung.* Soc. Sc. Fennica, Comm. hum. litt. LXXXII (Helsinki 1987) 411–412.

as a *signum*, a name for domestic and familiar use only,[1] there are several second- and third-century examples of it as a *gentilicium*.[2] It is hazardous to draw firm conclusions from so small a number of cases, but a Celtic or Celtiberian milieu for several holders of the name emerges from the evidence, such as it is, and these Vegetii belonged to the municipal gentry in Germania superior and a remote corner of Spain. The process whereby a Latin name "Vegetus" borne by a *peregrinus* in the western provinces was transformed into a *gentilicium* "Vegetius" on the gaining of Roman citizenship was observed by Schulze.[3] There is a gap of several generations between these earlier examples and our Vegetius, but it is plausible that he came of a long line of municipal gentry owning estates in provincial Gaul or Spain, who had risen to senatorial status.[4] The personal name or *cognomen* "Renatus" is one of those which commonly denoted Christian beliefs.[5]

The *Mulomedicina* tells us further that he was a prominent breeder of horses, had travelled the Empire extensively and was familiar with and

---

[1]*CIL* 8.16561, *Fortunatus Aug(usti) n(ostri) adiutor a comm(entariis)* ... *Vegethi*, cf. 1608, 15626, 15630, Tebessa, Africa Proconsularis, *c.* third century AD; I. Kajanto, *Supernomina*, Soc. Sc. Fennica, Comm. hum. litt. XL.1 (Helsinki 1966) 89.

[2]Rome: *CIL* 6.28400, *A. Veg(etius) Diotrofes, Vegetia Victorina*, second/third century. *CIL* 6.1056 L2(42), *Vegetius Firmus* (1st coh. vigilum), AD 205. Picenum, at Septempeda: *CIL* 9.5573, *Vegetius Ingen(u)us* (Roman army), second/third century. Tarraconensis, at Conventus Bracaraugustanus: *CIL* 2.2381, *Imp. Caes. T. Aelio Hadriano Antonino Aug. Pio per T. Furnium Gal(eria) Proculum et A. Vegetium Gal(eria) Titianum*, AD 138–161. Narbonensis, at Nemausus: *CIL* 12.3826, *L. Vegetius Ingenuus*, prob. second/third century. Germania superior, from nr. Borbitomagus: *BRGK* xxvii (1937) 73 no. 77, *Mercurio Aug(usti) Vege[ti]us Gattus ob honorem aedilitatis posuit* (aedile in Borbitomagus(?), Celtic *cognomen*), late second/early third century. From nr. Eutingen-Niefern, Pforzheim: *BRGK* xl (1959) 168 no. 124, *Vegetius Pate[rnus], Ve(getius) Severus*, the former married to Sulpicia Pattua (Celtic *cognomen*), second/third century. From Vitrey, Montigny-les-Cherlieux, nr. Dijon: *CIL* 13.5910: *Mercurio Saturninus Vegetii fi(lius) v. s. l. m.*, prob. second/third century. Raetia, nr. Castra Regina: *CIL* 3.5944: *Veg(etius) Marcellin(us)* (Roman army), AD 222–235. The refs. are usefully collected by H. Solin, O. Salomies, *Repertorium nominum gentilium et cognominum Latinorum* (1994).

[3]W. Schulze, *Zur Geschichte lateinischer Eigennamen* (Berlin 1933) 53: formed after a cognate *cognomen* and conceived as a patronymic, cf. *CIL* 12.517, *Sex. Acutius Volt. Aquila Acuto patri*, beginning of first century AD.

[4]Consciousness of nobility was advertised by the use of the *tria nomina* in the late fourth century, cf. Ausonius, *Opuscula* 16. *Griphus ternarii numeri* 80: *tria nomina nobiliorum*.

[5]I. Kajanto, *The Latin Cognomina*, Soc. Sc. Fennica, Comm. hum. litt. XXXVI.2 (Helsinki 1965) 135, 355.

bred on his own studs many different breeds of horses.[1] Significantly, the breed for which he offers most information is the Hunnic warhorse.[2] Goffart has drawn attention to the considerable knowledge of the western barbarian world in Vegetius,[3] which also includes incidentally a number of Celtic and Germanic words. We may take it that Vegetius was a man who knew his barbarians when he implicitly recommended displacing them from the army.

We find from Symmachus' attempts to hire race-horses for the games staged in Rome for members of his family that Spain and Gaul were the main centres of horse-breeding, carried on in estates presided over by immensely wealthy senatorial grandees. Some of these senators may have had literary interests. Symmachus calls one major supplier by the *signum* or nickname "Euphrasius" which may allude to literary or rhetorical skills.[4] Vegetius also tells us that the demands of his friends persuaded him to add book IV devoted to cattle—they were therefore great landowners or *possessores* like himself.[5] It is justified to place Vegetius among their company, because the name though rare derives from the *cognomen* "Vegetus" which is commonest in Spain, and next commonest in Gallia Narbonensis.[6]

Also he evinces an eccentric and otherwise inexplicable interest in Sertorius, the Roman nobleman who led an armed revolt from Roman rule in Spain in the 70s BC.[7] In the chaotic conditions of the late-Empire, the central authorities in Italy were often unable to safeguard the interests of territories on the fringes, so that provinces such as Britain were repeatedly forced into taking measures for their own

---

[1]*Mul.* III.6.1: *qui propter tam diversas et longinquas peregrinationes equorum genera universa cognovimus et in nostris stabulis saepe nutrivimus.* "I who am familiar with all breeds of horses as a result of my travels which have been so various and far-flung, and have frequently bred them on my own studs." Mul. I prol. 6: *cum ab initio aetatis alendorum equorum studio flagrarem,* "since from my earliest years I was fired with zeal for breeding horses."

[2]*Mul.* III.6.5.

[3]W. Goffart, *Rome's Fall and After* (1989) 69–70.

[4]Symm. *Ep.* 4.58–63.

[5]*Mul.* IV prol. 1–2.

[6]41 out of 77 examples in A. Mócsy et al., *Nomenclator*, Diss. Pannonicae 3.1 (Budapest 1983). When his figures are adjusted to take account of the different sizes of the samples in each western province, Spain still comes first with 34%, Gallia Narbonensis second with 16%, Noricum, Gallia Belgica and the two Germanies, and Britannia roughly joint third with around 10–12%. Thus a "Vegetus" was twice as likely to come from Spain as from Narbonensis.

[7]*Epit.* I.7, I.9.

security at the price of revolting from the Emperor and putting up rivals. The revolt of the Spaniard Maximus staged from Britain in AD 383 was made easier precisely by the excessive favour shown towards Alan mercenaries by the Emperor Gratian in Milan at the expense of the regular Roman troops.[1] Gratian is strongly criticized in I.20 for military decline in his reign and after.

From *subscriptiones* to the *Epitome* we learn that Vegetius was a *vir inlustris* and Count (First class), a rank reserved for the highest échelons of the imperial bureaucracy or the army chiefs of staff. Since Vegetius disclaims all personal military knowledge and only claims to compile information from books for the Emperor or his generals to apply (I praef., I.8, I.28, II praef., II.3, II.4, II.18, III.6 init., III.10 fin., III.20 init.), we may take it for granted that he was a bureaucrat. There is no particular internal evidence weighing in favour of Praetorian Prefect, Count of the Sacred Largesses,[2] or Count of the Privy Purse, although his demonstrable interest in taxation and money-matters would suit all three. But he might equally well have been Master of the Offices, Prefect of the City or Quaestor of the Sacred Palace. Perhaps the most satisfying suggestion is by Goffart that he was Count of the Sacred Stable, frequently a *vir inlustris* from the early fifth century, at least.[3] Vegetius' extensive travels in connexion with horse-breeding, knowledge of both warhorses and luxury civilian saddle-horses, and concern with Hunnic and German breeds and the avoidance of fraud "practised upon the country" could then be explained as arising from his official duties in the procurement of military and civil mounts.[4] But one wonders that Vegetius did not advertise the fact.

MS "Π" has a *subscriptio* that he was *comes sacrum* (sic). It was suggested by Schoener that *sacrum* is an abbreviation of *sacrarum* (*largitionum*), but Vegetius' references to money suit other high offices as well as that of imperial finance minister. Rather, it may perhaps be a corruption of *comes stabuli*. A mediaeval scribe would have been

---

[1]Ps.-Victor *Epit. de Caess.* 47.6, Zos. 4.35.2–6 = Eunapius fr. 51 (Blockley).

[2]"Sacred" in the later Roman Empire was a defining epithet of the imperial court and institutions. For the various positions, see A.H.M. Jones, *The Later Roman Empire* (Oxford 1964).

[3]W. Goffart, *Traditio* xxxiii (1977) 89–90 = id., *Rome's Fall and After* (1989) 69–70. R. Scharf, "Der *comes sacri stabuli* in der Spätantike", *Tyche* v (1990) 135–147, esp. 145 and 137, assumes that V. was *comes sacri stabuli* under Valentinian III, c.440, without argument.

[4]*Mul.* III.6.

unlikely to understand *comes stabuli* as the title is rather rare, and the corruption of an uncial *stabuli* to *sacrum* is not impossible, particularly if the "ta" were transposed. The transition from "b" to "r" is easy, and the "li" could be confused with the final upright of "u" so as to suggest three uprights and hence "m". All that would remain is for uncial "t" to be confused with "c", which is also easy, since the downstroke of "t" curled to the right. The result, though a false title, might seem more satisfying to monks used to allusions to sacred things; *sacrum* was presumably misinterpreted as an abbreviated neuter plural. Another possibility is that the title was originally given in the form *comes sacri stabuli*, and the last element somehow dropped out; the corruption then of *sacri* to *sacrum* is not unduly difficult.

Vegetius makes his Christian allegiances very clear in the prefaces to both works, and the theocratic nature of the late-Roman state is affirmed by the frequent collocation of God and Emperor in almost-equal partnership. In *Epit.* II.5 he urges that soldiers should swear the oath of allegiance by the Holy Trinity and the Emperor's Majesty on the jesuitical grounds that they serve God by serving the Emperor, who is God's Representative. For the rest his analysis of Rome's military success is couched in wholly secular, pragmatic terms, and unlike many contemporary bishops he shows no signs of belief in divine intervention, or the orthodox thinking that Christian piety was a significant aid in fighting or even itself a weapon against the barbarians.[1]

Alongside his Christianity he was a traditional admirer of Vergil's poetry and the superior wisdom which was attributed rather superstitiously to him in the Latin-speaking half of the Empire, and an enthusiast for Sallust's histories and historical monographs; it is not proven that he read Livy, in spite of much parallel material. His grasp of Greek appears not to have been profound, since he abjures Greek tactical authors in *Epit.* I.8 and obtains Greek material in Latin versions according to III praef. and the prologue to *Mul.* I, where he criticizes the Latin style of Chiron and Apsyrtus, authors whose work ought to have been in Greek.[2] He seems in this typical of the late-fourth-century

---

[1] Contrast Ambr. *de Obitu Theod.* 7, *de Fide* 2.136–140, *Epp.* 17.1; Maximus of Turin (*CCSL* XXIII), *Sermo* 69.1–2, 83.1, 85.2.

[2] E. Lommatsch, op. cit., xxxvi–xxxvii.

orthodox senatorial aristocracy in the west, steeped in the Latin classics such as Vergil and Sallust, but on the whole ignorant of Greek.[1]

Finally he is consistently interested in offering explanations of military customs which presuppose a medical point of view, is fond of using medical metaphors—*remedium, medicina, vulnus*—and touches on medical concerns such as whether doctors or exercise are more conducive to health, how cholera is spread, how to protect soldiers from some of the dangers to health incidental to their profession, and the need for pure water and keeping chickens for food for the sick. Such interests are not too surprising in the author of the *Mulomedicina*, but one wonders if Vegetius ever had any medical training or was purely self-taught.

§3. The date

The upper limit is the death of Gratian, AD 383, for he is called *divus Gratianus* at I.20, and the lower AD 450, when an editor of the text called Flavius Eutropius helpfully signed a *subscriptio* with details of the place (Constantinople) and consular date, which has been copied in the MSS of class ε. Within these parameters debate continues. There is a consensus, at least, that the work was produced in the western Empire because of the mention of Gratian. Views on the identity of the dedicatee mainly divide between Theodosius I (379–395) and Valentinian III (425–455), though Honorius (393–423) has recently been proposed as a possibility. The old view that it was dedicated to Valentinian II (375–392), an adolescent cypher who never ruled in his own name, rested on *subscriptiones* added by a late copyist.[2] In what follows I shall exclude personal arguments based on the use of imperial titles, of which the evidence is too patchy to support firm arguments in favour of this or that Emperor, and Vegetius' rhetorical *topoi* offering compliments to the Emperor, of which we have no fail-safe way of judging the truth.[3]

---

[1]A.H.M. Jones, *The Later Roman Empire* (Oxford 1964) II.987, P. Courcelle, *Late Latin Writers and their Greek Sources* (Cambridge, Mass. 1969) esp. 15 ff. (Symmachus), 20 ff. (Macrobius), 78 ff. (Jerome), and 165 ff. (Augustine).

[2]Lang p.vii reports that the subscriptions to MSS D, Π, and V, three of the chief representatives of his class π, are inscribed *ad Theodosium imperatorem*, and name him elsewhere in the text too. These will be interpolations if Lang's stemma is correct, but T.D. Barnes, "The date of Vegetius", *Phoenix* xxxiii (1979) 254–257 raises the suggestion that class π diverged from ε even before Eutropius' recension of AD 450.

[3]For a fuller treatment of the date see Milner, *Vegetius*, ch. 3.

Goffart and Birley have most recently joined the ranks of Seeck and Gibbon in preferring Valentinian III.[1] Proponents of this reign object that Gratian could not have been criticized to Valentinian II, his half-brother, or Theodosius I, his half-sister Galla's husband from AD 388, five years after his death. This of course is debatable, but Theodosius, at least, was considerably less closely related. Goffart argues that Vegetius' example of the Second Punic War (I.28) presupposes a minimum time-scale of about two decades—the length of time from the First to the Second Punic War—between the end of the "long peace" and the series of disasters suffered at the hands of the Goths described in I.20. If the "long peace" were understood to be the reign of Gratian, twenty years from his death would stretch to the early 400s when a second Hannibal in the shape of Alaric was causing havoc in Italy, which culminated in the sack of Rome in AD 410. But a reaction could not set in until Honorius was dead and Valentinian III, untainted by the disasters, could preside over a recovery engineered by his *patricius* Aëtius; so it was this revival that Vegetius was in effect publicizing.[2] Birley cites a number of "Novels" or decrees of Valentinian III which allegedly attest such a military revival.[3]

However, Goffart pushes his timescale argument too hard. There is no reason to separate the analogy of the twenty or so years of peace between the First and Second Punic Wars from the "long peace" itself identified with Gratian's reign; moreover the figure "twenty" is not relevant. The period of disasters is more naturally seen as including the large-scale wars that must have terminated the "long peace" if the phrase was to have any meaning at all—thus the disastrous campaigns of AD 377–378 ending in defeat at Adrianople and the destruction of two-thirds of the eastern field army along with the eastern Emperor Valens, while Gratian was still on his way to join forces with him. The sacking of cities can be explained by the Gothic incursion into

---

[1] E. Birley, "The dating of Vegetius and the *Historia Augusta*", *Bonner Historia Augusta Colloqium* 1982–83 (1985) 57–67 = id., *The Roman Army, Papers* 1929–1986, Mavors IV (Amsterdam 1988) 58–68; W. Goffart, art.cit.; O. Seeck, "Die Zeit des Vegetius", *Hermes* xi (1876) 61–83; E. Gibbon, *Decline and Fall of the Roman Empire*, ed. J.B. Bury, III (1897) 187 n.128.

[2] Goffart, 61 ff.

[3] Note that the chief witness, which Birley quotes at second hand from L. Várady, "New evidences on some problems of the late Roman military organization", *A.Ant.Hung.* ix (1961), 333–396, is actually a Novel of Theodosius II, no. 24, from Constantinople, AD 443.

Pannonia, Dacia, Thrace and Macedonia from 378 to the peace settlements with Gratian and Theodosius I in the early 380s.[1] The mention of Gratian was only worthwhile if he was still remembered, which would not have been the case a generation later.

Secondly there was no military revival under Valentinian III. The Novels merely show the State having increasing difficulties raising recruits and money from the traditional sources of supply, so that it had to resort to new-fangled taxes and the removal of ancient privileges—a litany of decline, in fact. And whereas Vegetius aimed to restore a fully-trained national Roman standing army, Valentinian III's temporary military successes were entire due to Aëtius' ability to hire Hun mercenaries, a policy which would have been anathema to Vegetius.

C. Giuffrida argues for Honorius on different grounds extrapolated from the allegedly pacific, philo-barbarian policy followed by Theodosius I while he was alive and by Stilicho under Honorius until his fall in AD 408, contrasted with the violently anti-barbarian senatorial policy followed by the government of Honorius between 408 and the sack of Rome in 410.[2] She makes Vegetius propagandist for the nationalist senatorial interest headed by the *magister officiorum* Olympius. Her Vegetius would have been one of those directly responsible for that untimely intransigence which hastened the demise of Rome.

The argument for Honorius has the merit of explaining the mention of Gratian since the blame could scarcely be pinned on Theodosius I, the Emperor's own father. It is also probable that the desertion of 30,000 Gothic soldiers upon the massacre of their families by the Romans in Italy in 408 left them with the rump of a national army, deprived of much of its barbarian stiffening. However the policy of Theodosius I and Stilicho was hardly "philo-barbarian", but involved playing off one group of barbarians (e.g., the Tervingi) against another (e.g., the Greuthungi, heavily defeated in AD 386),[3] taking in some and resisting others. Their opposition in principle to Vegetius' plans should not be assumed. Also we must not forget the protracted circumstances of composition of the *Epitome*, book I of which appeared first and in a

---

[1]Pac. *Pan. Lat.* 2 (12) 32.3–4, cf. Them. *Or.* 34.24.62–64 (AD 382), Hieron. *Epp.* 60.16.2 (*CSEL* LIV.I.1), c. AD 397, looking back over 20 years of violence.

[2]C. Giuffrida, "Per una datazione dell'*Epitoma rei militaris* di Vegezio: politica e propaganda nell'età di Onorio", *Sic.Gymn.* xxxiv (1981) 25–56.

[3]Hydatius *Chron.* ed. A. Tranoy (1974) a. 386. 13a.viii.

separate edition from books II–IV, and in which the background of military disasters rather tails off in the latter books instead of getting worse, as we should expect.

In fact, the arguments for Theodosius I being the dedicatee are stronger than for the other candidates.[1] First, the period is right. Vegetius alludes to the battle of Adrianople (III.11)[2] but not to the sack of Rome. Rome is cited three times, no less, as the example of the inviolate city (IV praef., IV.9, IV.26), whereas this would be in poor taste, surely, after AD 410. Also one of the most dangerous groups of barbarians starting from their invasion of Gaul on 31st Dec. AD 406, to wit the Vandals, are not named by Vegetius, whereas the Goths, Huns and Alans, the victors of Adrianople, are (I.20, III.26). Moreover, he calls the Huns and Alans one nation (III.26), alluding to an event noticed also by Ammianus Marcellinus;[3] but they split up when the Alans joined the Vandals in 406,[4] and the Huns remained settled in Pannonia until AD 427.[5] Further, there was no naval war with the barbarians at the time of writing (IV.31), but the Vandals acquired a naval capability by AD 419,[6] and it was well-known that Alaric had tried to take to the sea at Rhegium in 410, and Wallia in southern Spain in 416.[7]

Further, it was still normal for *coloni* to be recruited (I.7), whereas this was banned after pressure from senatorial landowners in the early fifth century.[8] Gladiatorial games called forth no sanctimonious denunciation from Vegetius, who was normally careful in matters of piety (I.11), but Honorius temporarily closed the gladiators' schools in AD 399, and this type of entertainment was dying out after 410 even in Rome.[9] Ravenna was the site of the old Augustan eastern fleet (IV.31), but Vegetius did not mention that it was made the new capital of the

---

[1]Cf. T.D. Barnes, "The date of Vegetius", *Phoenix* xxxiii (1979) 254–257.
[2]W. Goffart, 63 n.85, G. Sabbah, 142.
[3]Amm. 31.3.1.
[4]E. Stein, *Histoire du Bas-Empire*, tr. J.-R. Palanque (Paris 1949–59) 551 n.161
[5]Marcellinus Comes, *Chron. Min.* II.76.
[6]J.R. Moss, "The effects of the policies of Aëtius on the history of western Europe", *Historia* xxii (1973) 723–728.
[7]Oros. 7.43.12.
[8]Jones, 619.
[9]*Reallexicon für Antike und Christentum* XI (1981) 27–28 s.v. Gladiator IV.

western Empire from AD 401–402, equipped with major new installations.[1]

There are more personal arguments, too. The anti-Gratian polemic (I.20) is not strong enough to be addressed to Maximus, his murderer, but too offensive to be addressed to Valentinian II, his half-brother. Theodosius I occupied a position conveniently in between these emotional poles, not being too closely related or politically involved in Gratian's realm. Secondly, a reference to a decision concerning the calculation of the date of Easter (IV.35) can be identified with one of Theodosius I's theological reforms of AD 387–388, in which Theophilus, bishop of Alexandria, worked out a paschal calendar for 100 years based on Theodosius' consulship in AD 380.[2] Thirdly, Vegetius' praise of his Emperor's city-founding programme suits an eastern Emperor, since this activity was markedly more vigorous in the east than the west, and in fact an impressive number of foundations can be attributed to Theodosius I.[3] Moreover, Theodosius is the one Emperor whose amateur interest in Republican Roman history is recorded,[4] and who we can be sure would have liked to read Vegetius' work from an antiquarian point of view.

How then to reconcile a western author with an eastern Emperor? First, Theodosius was the senior Augustus from AD 383 to his death in 395.[5] Secondly, he stayed at Milan for three years following his victory over Maximus in AD 388; without having to travel to Constantinople or Thessalonica, Vegetius would have had ample opportunity to address such a work to him, even on the subject of the reform of the field armies, not just those of the west, and to meet and perhaps serve the Emperor in person. It is consistent with the hypothesis that the work seems to widen in scope after the polemic against Gratian's army in book I.

---

[1] M. Reddé, *Mare Nostrum* (Rome 1986) 659–660.
[2] Sabbah, 145.
[3] Milner, *Vegetius*, ch. 3 (d).
[4] Claud. *pan. de Hon. cons. IV* 399 ff., Ps.-Victor *Epit. de Caess.* 48.11–12, cf. SHA *Alex. Sev.* 16.3, possibly inspired by a contemporary ideal.
[5] Oros. 7.35.

§4. The late-Roman army

The classic, comprehensive survey of the late-Roman army is ch. XVII of A.H.M. Jones' *Later Roman Empire.* D. Hoffmann's *Das spätrömische Bewegungsheer und die Notitia Dignitatum* is the major work of scholarship since. The late-Roman army is very different from the army of the Principate, but grew out of it under the reforms of Constantine, who built on a duality set up by Diocletian's field army and frontier defences, but relied largely on élite barbarian mercenaries to bolster his own position in the State. But Vegetius criticized it against the standard of the army of the middle Republic as transmitted by sources from the Principate. Hence the non-specialist reader requires an up-to-date synopsis of all three armies, middle Republican, Principate and late-Roman. He is respectfully referred to *The Roman World*, ed. J. Wacher, with articles on "The army of the Republic", by G.R. Watson, "The imperial army", by Alistair Scott Anderson, and "The army of the late Empire", by R.S.O. Tomlin.[1]

For an understanding of Vegetius, the last of these armies is perhaps least familiar and most important. Briefly, the late-Roman army in the late-fourth century AD was of two main kinds, (I.) regular and (II.) mercenary. (I.) Regular units comprised three categories, (1.) infantry and cavalry and river patrols distributed around the frontier provinces as *limitanei* under the command of *duces* who controlled sectors called "duchies", (2.) élite units of infantry and cavalry called *comitatenses*, concentrated in important cities and imperial capitals to provide field armies which could be quickly mobilized to deal with any large-scale invasion beyond the resources of the *limitanei,* and (3.) élite units of mounted Imperial Guard called *scholae palatinae,* who protected the Emperor's person and fought with the *comitatenses.* Of the mobile or "field" troops, the *scholae palatinae* were very heavily barbarized, as were also the cavalry *vexillationes* and the infantry *auxilia palatina* among the *comitatenses,* leaving only the *legiones* as less barbarized and having more Romans in them. It is these field troops that Vegetius was writing to reform, by creating units which combined the specializations of the various *comitatenses* under the umbrella of reformed and greatly enlarged legions, with their more Roman military traditions and manpower.

---

[1]*The Roman World,* ed. J. Wacher (London–New York 1987), Vol. I, Pt. 3, pp.75–135, with further bibliography.

(II.) The cause was lost, however. The use of mercenaries at precisely the time of writing was sharply on the increase, at the expense of keeping fewer units of regulars and failure to maintain paper-strengths of existing units, a process particularly evident in the West. The reign of Theodosius I was a watershed for the increased reliance on mercenaries, many or most of whom were (1.) *foederati,* treaty-troops raised from barbarians settled both within and without the Empire, while others will have been (2.) *buccellarii,* private armies raised by individual barbarian leaders and even Roman generals from motley sources, although the distinction between these terms became increasingly blurred. (3.) A third source of such irregulars was prisoners-of-war or *dediticii.*[1] The horde-type armies with which Theodosius engaged the usurpers Maximus (388) and Eugenius (394) marks the start of a new era in which Roman governments were chiefly dependent on barbarian condottieri for temporarily hired military forces which they no longer maintained themselves. The mobile legions which Vegetius tried to save and revivify disappear from the historical record in the western Empire in the next century, although many of their counterparts survived unreconstructed in the East into the sixth century at least.

---

[1] See J.H.W.G. Liebeschuetz, *Barbarians and Bishops: Army, Church, and State in the Age of Arcadius and Chrysostom* (Oxford 1990) 32 ff., A.H.M. Jones, 663 ff.

Ancient Synopsis[1]

The First book discusses the selection of recruits,[2] from what localities what sort of men should be approved as soldiers, and in what military exercises they should be trained. The Second book comprises the organization of the ancient army, in accordance with which an infantry army may be instituted.[3] The Third book illustrates all kinds of strategic skills which seem necessary to land warfare. The Fourth book lists all the machines used to attack and defend cities; precepts of naval warfare also are appended.

Book I

Preface.

In ancient times it was the custom to commit to writing one's studies in the liberal arts and offer them summarized in books to Emperors.[4] For nothing is begun rightly unless after God the Emperor favours it, nor is it appropriate that anyone should have superior or wider knowledge than the Emperor, whose learning can benefit all his subjects. That Octavian Augustus[5] and good Emperors after him readily thought so is clear from many examples. Thus with the testimonials of rulers, eloquence flourished, while boldness was not rebuked.[6] Spurred on to emulate this, when I reflected that Your Clemency was better able than others to excuse temerity in literature, I hardly felt my great inferiority to ancient authors. Yet in this opuscule neither linguistic elegance nor intellectual acumen was needed, but painstaking and faithful labour, to put into the public domain for the benefit of Rome

---

[1]There is no reason to think that the Synopsis was not written by V.

[2]Like the Theodosian Code, V. uses *iunior* and *tiro* synonymously for "recruit".

[3]V. is mainly concerned to reverse a supposed decline in the Roman infantry armies (legions) at the expense of mainly barbarian élite cavalry (*vexillationes* or *equites*) and light infantry (*auxilia palatina*)—cf. I.20, II.1, II.3, III.9—but in fact large numbers of legionary cavalry too are included in the "ancient legion" described in Book II.

[4]Aelian *Tact.* 1.7 cites Plato's *Leges* 625e–626b on the nomothete of the Cretans for the view that art of war is the most useful of all, since mankind is on a constant war-footing, there being by nature undeclared war between all cities. Cf. III praef, III.10. Celsus' encyclopaedia contained four "arts"—agriculture, medicine, rhetoric and military science. Polyb. 9.20.9 called war "the most honourable and serious of all arts".

[5]The first Emperor of Rome, reigned 27 BC–AD 14, never called "Octavian Augustus" until by historians of late antiquity, cf. Amm. 26.1.13, Vict. *Caess.* 1.1, Eutrop. *Brev.* 1.12.2, Rufius Festus *Brev.* 19.

[6]Cf. Verg. *Georg.* 1.40: *da facilem cursum atque audacibus adnue coeptis.* "Grant an easy course and support my bold undertaking."

matters which lay scattered and hidden in the pages of various historians and teachers of military science.[1]

We attempt to show then, by a number of stages and headings,[2] the ancient system of levying and training recruits. Not that those things would appear unfamiliar to you, Invincible Emperor,[3] but so that you may recognize in your spontaneous dispositions for the safety of the State the principles which the builders of the Roman Empire long ago observed,[4] and in this little book find whatever you think needful to affairs of State, which are ever pressing.

(Recruitment, ch. 1–7)

1. That the Romans conquered all peoples solely because of their military training.

In every battle it is not numbers and untaught bravery so much as skill and training that generally produce the victory.[5] For we see no other explanation of the conquest of the world by the Roman People than their drill-at-arms, camp-discipline and military expertise. How else could small Roman forces have availed against hordes of Gauls? How could small stature have ventured to confront Germanic tallness?[6] That the Spaniards surpassed our men not only in numbers but in physical strength is obvious. To Africans' treachery and money we were always

---

[1] The motif of inability to do justice to the subject was common in encomiastic literature, cf. E. Curtius, *European Literature and the Latin Middle Ages*, tr. W.R. Trask (New York 1953) 83 ff., L.B. Struthers, "The rhetorical structure of the *encomia* of Claudius Claudian", *HSCPh* xxx (1919) 57.

[2] This indicates that the rubrics are the author's; their style is homogeneous with the text, and they share in the same systems of *variatio*, cf. A. Andersson, *Studia Vegetiana* (Uppsala 1938) ch. III, pp.44–47.

[3] MS *D* reads *princeps invicte O Theodosi divorum augustorum praecellentissime*, probably an interpolation. "Invincible Prince, O Theodosius, most Excellent of the deified Augusti."

[4] i.e., during the middle Republic, third to second centuries BC, the age of Cato the Censor. V. evades the problem how to inform the "omniscient" by attributing to the Emperor full knowledge of what he is about to tell him anyway.

[5] This sentence belongs here in the "vulgate"; in the best MSS it is placed at the head of the capitulation of Book I. The vulgate is to be preferred because the sentence does not fit the capitulation and otherwise I.1 would open with an inferential conjunction *enim*, contrary to V.'s usage.

[6] Cf. Amm. 16.12.47 on Roman discipline being a match for German height and strength, cf. Caes. *Bell. Gall.* 2.30.4: *plerumque omnibus Gallis praemagnitudine corporum suorum brevitas nostra contemptui est*, ibid. 4.1.9, 1.39.1. "Because of the excessive size of their bodies our shortness has usually been a subject of contempt for all the Gauls."

unequal.[1] No one doubted that we were surpassed by the arts and intelligence of the Greeks.[2] But what succeeded against all of them was careful selection of recruits, instruction in the rules, so to speak, of war, toughening in daily exercises, prior acquaintance in field practice with all possible eventualities in war and battle, and strict punishment of cowardice.[3] Scientific knowledge of warfare nurtures courage in battle. No one is afraid to do what he is confident of having learned well. A small force which is highly trained in the conflicts of war is more apt to victory: a raw and untrained horde is always exposed to slaughter.[4]

2. From what regions recruits should be levied.

The order of our subject demands that the first part should treat of the provinces and peoples from which recruits should be levied. Now it is common knowledge that cowards and brave men are born in all places. However, nation surpasses nation in warfare, and climate exerts an enormous influence on the strength of minds and bodies. In this connexion let us not omit what has won the approval of the most learned men.[5] They tell us that all peoples that are near the sun, being parched by great heat, are more intelligent but have less blood, and therefore lack steadiness and confidence to fight at close quarters, because those who are conscious of having less blood are afraid of wounds. On the other hand the peoples of the north, remote from the sun's heat, are less intelligent, but having a superabundance of blood are readiest for wars. Recruits should therefore be raised from the more temperate climes. The plenteousness of their blood supplies a contempt for wounds and death, and intelligence cannot be lacking either which

---

[1]alluding to Jugurtha's dictum (Sall. *Jug.* 35.10): *urbem venalem et mature perituram, si emptorem invenerit.* "(Rome) ...a city for sale and soon to pass away, if it finds a buyer."

[2]alluding to the likes of Verg. *Aen.* 6.847–853 and Horace's dictum: *Graecia capta ferum victorem cepit et artes / intulit agresti Latio,* (*Epist.* 2.1.156–157). "Captive Greece captured its fierce victor and brought the arts to wild Latium." The whole argument resembles Cic. *de Harus. Resp.* 9.19.

[3]Front. *Strat.* 4.1–2, Val. Max. 2.7, Polyb. 6.37.9 ff.

[4]Small, highly-trained (legionary) armies are at the core of V.'s recommendations, cf. II.4, III.1.

[5]Arist. *Pol.* 1327b adapted by Posidonius, probably transmitted to V. through Varro, cf. W. Theiler (ed.), *Poseidonios, Die Fragmente* (Berlin 1982) II.72 fr. 71. The fullest expression of it may be found in Vitr. 6.1. V. omits the climax that the perfect mix of qualities was to be found in the Roman People and peoples of Italy, but allows the inference to be drawn that barbarians were unsuitable.

preserves discipline in camp and is of no little assistance with counsel in battle.

3. Whether recruits from the country or from the city are more useful.

The next question is to consider whether a recruit from the country or from the city is more useful. On this subject I think it could never have been doubted that the rural populace is better suited for arms.[1] They are nurtured under the open sky in a life of work, enduring the sun, careless of shade, unacquainted with bathhouses, ignorant of luxury, simple-souled, content with a little, with limbs toughened to endure every kind of toil, and for whom wielding iron, digging a fosse and carrying a burden is what they are used to from the country.

Sometimes however necessity demands that city-dwellers also be conscripted. These, when they have given in their names for military service, must first learn to work, drill, carry a burden and endure heat and dust; they must adopt a moderate, rural diet, and camp now under the sky, now under tents.[2] Only then should they be trained in the use of arms and, if a long campaign is in prospect, they should be detained for considerable periods on outpost-duty and be kept far away from the attractions of the city, so that by this means their physical and mental vigour may be increased.[3]

It is undeniable that after the City was founded[4] the Romans always set out for war from town. But in those days they were not enervated by luxury. Youth would wash off sweat collected in running and field exercises, swimming in the Tiber.[5] The same man was both warrior and farmer, merely changing the style of equipment. This was so far true that by all accounts Quinctius Cincinnatus was offered the dictatorship

---

[1]Cf. Cato *de Agric.* praef. 4: *at ex agricolis et viri fortissimi et milites strenuissimi gignuntur.* "From farmers both the bravest men and the strongest soldiers are born."

[2]Cf. Hor. *C.* 1.8.4: *cur apricum ¦ oderit Campum patiens pulveris atque solis,* "...why he shuns the open Campus (Martius), having learned to endure dust and sun." Onas. 10.5: θάλπεσιν ἀσκιάστοις καὶ κρυμοῖς ὑπαίθροις ἐγγυμναζόμενα.   "...exercising in summer heat without shade and in the icy cold in the open air."

[3]On the mental as well as physical benefits of training, cf. II.23, Onas. 9.2–3.

[4]The traditional date for the foundation of Rome is 753 BC.

[5]Porph. ad Hor. *C.* 3.7.25, 1.8.8. V. repeats the example at I.10. Cf. also Cic. *pro Cael.* 36. A grassy plain in Rome along the Tiber, consecrated to Mars, the Campus Martius was the place for army musters and exercises, and meetings of the *comitia centuriata*, the Roman People in military order, during the Republic. From the first century BC onwards it was gradually filled in with monumental buildings.

while he was ploughing.[1] From the country, then, the main strength of the army should be supplied. For, I am inclined to think, a man fears death less if he has less acquaintance with luxury in his life.[2]

4. At what age recruits should be approved.[3]
Next let us examine at what age it is appropriate to levy soldiers. Indeed if ancient custom is to be retained, everyone knows that those entering puberty should be brought to the levy.[4] For those things are taught not only more quickly but even more completely which are learned from boyhood. Secondly military alacrity, jumping and running should be attempted before the body stiffens with age. For it is speed which, with training, makes a brave warrior. Adolescents are the ones to recruit, just as Sallust says: "Directly as soon as youth was able to endure war, it learned military practice in camp through labour."[5] For it is better that a trained young man should complain that he has not yet reached fighting age, than that he should regret that it has passed.[6]

He should also have the time to learn everything. For the art of war does not seem a slight or trivial matter, whether you wish to train a cavalryman, a foot-archer or a *scutatus*,[7] or teach all the routines and all

---

[1]Traditional date, 458 DC. Cf. Livy 3.26.9, Eutrop. *Brev.* 1.17.1: *is, cum in opere et arans esset inventus...* "while he was found at work, ploughing..." Livy also reports an alternative tradition that he was digging a ditch.

[2]Alcibiades was said to have declared that the Spartans welcomed death in battle because of the tough régime by which Sparta lived; cf. Aelian *Var. Hist.* 13.38.7.

[3]The scrutiny of recruits known as *probatio* or "approval" was carried out by the civil authorities, often provincial governors in person, to check the identity, height, age and status-qualifications of candidates for military service, before despatch to a unit. Cf. R.W. Davies, "Joining the Roman Army", *Service in the Roman Army,* ch. I, 3–30.

[4]V. exaggerates; the ancient evidence was for recruitment from 16 years at the earliest, cf. Livy 22.57.9, Serv. ad Verg. *Aen.* 7.162. But from AD 364 Valentinian I allowed the enrolment of young sons or relatives of established *domestici* in the élite *scholae protectorum domesticorum*, which functioned like a staff college for military commanders; the boys were to stay *in sedibus*—at the home base—but drew pay and rations of four *annonae*. In time they would be old enough to bear arms and go on campaign; cf. *CTh* 6.24.2–3, and Jones, 638. In the fourth century AD recruitment to ordinary army units began at 19 years, cf. *CTh* 7.13.1 (AD 326 S.), 7.22.4 (=12.1.35) (AD 343 S.).

[5]Sall. *Cat.* 7.4.

[6]Elderly soldiers were not uncommon in the late Empire, perhaps because they could be enlisted at as late as 35 years, cf. Jones, 616 n.19, 635 n.60, J.R. Rea, "A Cavalryman's Career, AD 384 (?)–401", *ZPE* lvi (1984) 84, letter iii. But cf. Tac. *Ann.* 1.35.2, for men who had served 30 years and more in AD 14.

[7]infantryman armed with a shield and darts, cf. I.17, II.15, III.14. V. also includes light *scutati* (as well as heavy) at III.14, at least, who seem likely to be late-antique.

the gestures of the *armatura*,[1] not to desert one's post, not to disorder the ranks, to hurl the javelin with a true aim and great force, to know how to dig a fosse and plant stakes in scientific fashion, handle a shield and deflect oncoming missiles with oblique movements, avoid a blow intelligently and inflict one boldly. For this recruit so trained, fighting against all manner of enemies in battle will be no terror but a delight.

5. At what height recruits should be approved.

The height of recruits was, I know, always required to be up to the *incomma*,[2] so that men of 6 ft. (= 5 ft. 9½ in., 1·77 m.)[3] or at least 5 ft. 10 in. (= 5 ft. 7½ in., 1·72 m.) were approved for the *alares* cavalry[4] or the First cohorts of the legions.[5] But in those days the population was greater, and more followed a military career. For civilian careers did not then take away the better class of youth.[6] So if necessity demands, it is right to take account not so much of stature as of strength. Even Homer himself is not wanting as a witness, since he records that Tydeus was small in body but a strong warrior.[7]

6. That the potentially better recruits are recognized at selection from the face and physical posture.

He who is charged with carrying out the levy procedure should take great pains to choose those able to fill the part of soldiers from the face, from the eyes, from the whole conformation of the limbs. For quality is indicated not only in men, but even in horses and dogs, by many

---

[1]A special and perhaps ancient drill, practised as a sport by late-Roman officers and Emperors, considered by V. to be the hallmark of the ancient legionary; cf. I.13.

[2]Greek for "incised mark" = standard height.

[3]Roman measures (modern equivalents in brackets): the Roman foot measured 295·7 mm., shrinking to 294·2 mm. in the third century AD, as opposed to the modern imperial foot of 304·8 mm., cf. F. Hultsch, *Griechische und römische Metrologie* (Berlin 1882²) 94–97.

[4]i.e. service in the *alae*.

[5]*CTh* 7.13.3 (AD 367) reduced the minimum height for Italians for entry into unspecified regular units from 5 ft. 10 in. to 5 ft. 7 in. (= 5 ft. 4⅔ in., 1·64 m.); cf. also 7.1.5 showing that one could be too weak or small for military service; 7.22.8, showing that lower physical standards were applied for recruits for the *ripenses* than for the *comitatenses*.

[6]Cf. *CTh* 7.22.6–10 (AD 349–380), imperial constitutions forbidding veterans' sons entry to the civil service, apparently with less than total success.

[7]Hom. *Il.* 5.801.

points, as is understood in the teaching of the most learned men.[1] Even in bees, the Mantuan author says, it is to be observed:

"Two kinds there are, the better by its face
Distinguished and bright with ruddy scales;
The other type is shaggy and inert
And drags along its fat, cowardly paunch."[2]

So let the adolescent who is to be selected for martial activity have alert eyes, straight neck, broad chest, muscular shoulders, strong arms, long fingers, let him be small in the stomach, slender in the buttocks, and have calves and feet that are not swollen by surplus fat but firm with hard muscle. When you see these points in a recruit, you need not greatly regret the absence of tall stature. It is more useful that soldiers be strong than big.[3]

7. Of what trades recruits should be selected or rejected.

The next matter is for us to examine from what crafts soldiers should be selected or rejected utterly.[4] Fishermen, fowlers, pastrycooks,[5] weavers and all who shall seem to have dealt in anything pertaining to textile-mills[6] should in my view be banned far from camp. Masons, blacksmiths, wainwrights, butchers and stag- and boar-hunters may

---

[1]Varro *Rer. Rust.* 2.7.4–5 (points of a horse), 2.9.3–4 (dog), 2.5.7–8 (cattle), Verg. *Georg.* 3.49–59 (cattle), 72–88 (horses).

[2]Verg. *Georg.* 4.92–94.

[3]The selection of recruits according to lists of points useful in stockbreeding is not attested in the sources, which speak merely of *statura* and *robur,* and may well be V.'s own idea.

[4]Cf. *CTh* 7.13.8 (AD 380), forbidding slaves, innkeepers, brothel-workers, cooks, bakers, or practitioners of "degrading" occupations from being recruited to the field army (?) or at least the "cavalry". The Romans had persistent and deep-seated qualms about the moral qualities of various kinds of tradesmen, cf. Cic. *de Off.* 1.150. Those who pursued dishonourable professions included *infames* such as actors, gladiators, charioteers and brothel-keepers, cf. M. Kaser, "Infamia und ignominia in den römischen Rechtsquellen", *ZRG* lxxiii (1956) 220–278. The list of professions that disqualified one from military service, or at least the higher branches of it, was apparently considerably longer in the late Empire, and included e.g. weavers and linen-workers, on which see below.

[5]Purveyors of luxury foods were notoriously prized by officers for their tables; cf. Ambr. *de Elia* 46 on officers' parties, and Pac. *Pan. Lat.* 2 (12) 14.3, SHA *Claud.* 14.11 on fowlers, fishermen and huntsmen enrolled in the army for the purpose.

[6]*gynaecea* = lit. "women's quarters", but denoting in the fourth century State-owned textile factories, making among other things military uniforms. Weavers and textile workers were among the many categories banned by law from the army. Such workers were originally State-slaves, although by the mid-fourth century their condition had so far improved that they had become *de facto* free persons bound by an hereditary tie to their trade, cf. Jones, 836.

usefully be joined to the military. This is a matter on which the safety of the entire State depends, that recruits be levied who are outstanding both in physique and moral quality. The strength of the realm and the foundation of the Roman Empire depend on the initial examination of the levy.[1] Let it not be thought an unimportant duty, nor one which may be delegated to anyone, anywhere. It is well-known that among his considerable range of qualities Sertorius was praised by the ancient (writers) for this in particular.[2] For the youth in whose hands is to be placed the defence of provinces, the fortune of battles, ought to be of outstanding breeding if numbers suffice, and morals. Decent birth makes a suitable soldier, while a sense of shame prevents flight and makes him a victor.[3]

For what benefit is there in training a coward, of his spending several years' service in camp? An army never makes fast progress if the selection procedure in approving recruits has been awry. And as we know from practice and experience, it is from this cause that so many defeats have been inflicted on us everywhere by our enemies, whilst during long years of peace the levying of soldiers has been neglected, while all those of decent birth have been pursuing civilian careers, while recruits levied from landowners have through the corruption or neglect of those granting approval been joined to the army only when they were of the sort their lords disdained to keep.[4] So suitable recruits should be levied with great care by great men.

---

[1] On physical strength and good character of recruits, cf. Jos. *Bell. Iud.* 2.580–582, 5.306, cf. 6.38, *Dig.* 49.16.4.1–9 (Menander), 49.16.2.1 (Menander), 49.16.16 (Paulus) showing that convicted felons were not allowed in the army. In normal circumstances freedmen were not allowed to enlist, either.

[2] As *quaestor* in 90 BC Q. Sertorius early distinguished himself recruiting troops and procuring arms for use in the Social War, cf. Plut. *Sert.* 4.1. Later, exiled from Rome, he organized the Spanish tribes and equipped them with Roman-style arms to fight Rome on equal terms from 80 BC until his assassination in 73 or 72, cf. Plut. *Sert.* 14, Flor. 2.10.

[3] On shame, cf. Ajax's advice, Hom. *Il.* 15.561–564. On decent birth, cf. Tiberius' complaint, Tac. *Ann.* 4.4.4.

[4] Cf. Amm. 19.11.7, 31.4.4, on the detrimental effect of using barbarian manpower to fill positions in the regular army, merely because of the reluctance of Romans to serve. On the recruitment of *coloni* or tenantry, resisted by senatorial landowners even during the war with Gildo in AD 397, and subsequently banned in the early fifth century, see Jones, 184, 619; V. must have been writing before this ban. Cf. Anon. *de Reb. Bell.* 4, denouncing corrupt *exactores* from the governor's *officium* involved in raising recruits, and Symm. *Ep.* 9.10.2, denouncing the local authorities for the same.

(Training, ch. 8–28)

8. When recruits should be marked.[1]

The recruit should not be tattooed with the pin-pricks of the official mark as soon as he has been selected, but first be thoroughly tested in exercises so that it may be established whether he is truly fitted for so much effort. Both mobility and strength are thought to be required of him, and whether he is able to learn the discipline of arms, whether he has the self-confidence of a soldier. For very many, though they seem not unacceptable in appearance, are yet found unsuitable in training. Therefore the less useful ones should be rejected and in their place the most energetic should be substituted. For in any conflict it is not so much numbers as bravery that pays off.[2]

So once the recruits have been tattooed the science of arms should be shown them in daily training. But neglect due to long years of peace has destroyed the tradition of this subject. Whom can you find able to teach what he himself has not learned?[3] We must therefore recover the ancient custom from histories and (other) books. But they wrote only the incidents and dramas of wars, leaving out as familiar what we are now seeking. The Spartans, it is true, and the Athenians and other Greeks published in books much material which they call *tactica,* but we ought to be inquiring after the military science of the Roman People, who extended their Empire from the smallest bounds almost to the regions of the sun and the end of the earth itself. This requirement made me consult competent authorities and say most faithfully in this opuscule what Cato the Censor wrote on the science of war, what Cornelius Celsus, what Frontinus thought should be summarized, what Paternus, a most zealous champion of military law, published in his books, and

---

[1]C.P. Jones, "Stigma: tattooing and branding in Graeco-Roman antiquity", *JRS* lxxvii (1987) 139–155, has established that soldiers were tattooed, not branded, without noticing V.

[2]A general principle of V. is the belief in the superiority of quality to quantity. On the four or so months' preliminary testing of recruits, not attested elsewhere, cf. II.5. This may be an invention of V.'s, or it may have been used by such units as regularly filled vacancies from a large pool of soldiers' sons or *adcrescentes,* where they would have been able to pick and choose, cf. II.3, Anon. *de Reb. Bell.* 5.7–8.

[3]Partly rhetorical hyperbole, partly true statement (so far as V. was concerned). V. exaggerates his points for better effect. For the continued existence of at least some contemporary training, cf. Ambr. *de Off.* 1.32, Synes. *de Regno* 13–14 (14 A–D), 19 (21 D).

what was decreed by the constitutions of Augustus, Trajan and Hadrian.[1] For I claim no authority to myself, but merely write up the dispersed material of those whom I have listed above, summarizing it as if to form an orderly sequence.[2]

9. Recruits should be trained in the military step, in running and in jumping.[3]

So, at the very start of the training recruits should be taught the military step.[4] For nothing should be maintained more on the march or in battle, than that all soldiers should keep ranks as they move. The only way that this can be done is by learning through constant training to manoeuvre[5] quickly and evenly. For a divided and disordered army experiences danger from the enemy which is always most serious. So at the military step 20 miles should be covered in five hours, at least in summer time.[6] At the full step,[7] which is faster, 24 miles should be covered in the same

---

[1]Perhaps Trajan is introduced merely to please Theodosius I, who liked to be thought of as a second Trajan, for at I.27 only Augustus and Hadrian are mentioned. Cf. Ps.-Victor *Epit. de Caess.* 48.8–10, K.H. Waters, "Trajan's character in the literary tradition", in *Polis and Imperium; Studies in honour of Edward Togo Salmon* (Toronto 1974) 238–240, Claud. *pan de Hon. cons. IV* 19, Them. *Or.* 14.205a. Also Pac. *Pan. Lat.* in editing such a collection headed by Pliny's and his own panegyrics may have been hinting at a Trajan–Theodosius parallel.

[2]P. Taruttienus Paternus, *ab epistulis Latinis* to Marcus Aurelius in the AD 170s and then *praefectus praetorio* almost certainly under Marcus Aurelius and Commodus, then Commodus alone *c.* AD 180–82, wrote a juristic work on the Roman army of which a few fragments survive, cf. *Dig.* 49.16.12, 50.6.7, Ioh. Lydus *de Mag.* 1.8, 47. This was probably the source for the imperial constitutions, cited by V. at I.27 only. Repeated signs of late-Roman educated guesswork and reconstruction based on jejune material suggest that V. had only late epitomes of Paternus and Frontinus, which subsumed the earlier authors; thus, none of the named authorities was directly used. The second source-notice at II.3, which serves for the rest of the work, names Cato and Frontinus and "many others", i.e. the same collection of material as here. The account of the Ancient Legion "following the guidance of military law" in II.4 ff. may also derive in some measure from Paternus.

[3]Cf. in general for training R.W. Davies, "Fronto, Hadrian and the Roman army", *Service in the Roman Army*, ch. III, 71–90.

[4]*militaris gradus.*

[5]For the technical sense of the verb *ambulo = decurro,* cf. A.R. Neumann, "Römische Rekrutenausbildung im Lichte der Disziplin", *CPh* xlii (1947) 157 n.3.

[6]i.e. 18 miles, 658 yds. (29·57 km.) in 5 x $^{14·5}/_{12}$ hr., or about 3·04 m.p.h. (4·89 km./h.). The Romans counted 12 hours of daylight, which averaged about 14½ modern hours in summer and 9½ in winter at the latitude of Rome. 1 standard Roman mile measured *c.*1,617 yds. (1,478·5 m.). Cf. F. Hultsch, *Griechische und römische Metrologie* (Berlin 1882²) 98, and W. Kubitschek, *Grundriss der Antiken Zeitrechnung*, Handbuch der Altertumswissenschaft I.7 (Munich 1928) 183.

[7]*plenus gradus.*

time.[1] If you add anything to this, it now becomes running, for which a distance cannot be defined. But recruits should particularly be accustomed to running too, so as to charge the enemy with greater impetus, occupy favourable positions swiftly when need arises and seize them first when the enemy wish to do the same, to go out on scouting expeditions speedily, return more speedily, and overtake fugitives with greater ease.[2]

The soldier should also be trained at jumping, whereby ditches are vaulted and hurdles of a certain height surmounted, so that when obstacles of this kind are encountered he can cross them without effort. Furthermore, in the actual conflict and clash of arms the soldier coming on by a running jump makes the adversary's eyes flinch, frightens his mind and plants a blow before the other can properly prepare himself for evasive or offensive action.[3] Of the training undertaken by Gneus Pompeius Magnus, Sallust records: "He would compete with the speedy at jumping, with the swift at running, and with the strong at fencing."[4] For he could not otherwise have been a match for Sertorius, had he not prepared himself and his soldiers for war with frequent exercises.[5]

10. Recruits should be trained in the art of swimming.
Every recruit without exception should in the summer months learn the art of swimming, for rivers are not always crossed by bridges,[6] and armies both when advancing and retreating are frequently forced to swim. Torrents often tend to flood after sudden falls of rain or snow, and ignorance of swimming incurs risk not only from the enemy but the water also. Therefore the ancient Romans, who were trained in the

---

[1] i.e. 22 miles, 86 yds. (35·48 km.) in 5 $x^{14·5}/_{12}$ hr., or about 3.65 m.p.h. (5·87 km/h.). Cf. Livy 9.45.15 *pleno gradu*, cf. 30.5.4 *modico gradu*. Sall. *Jug.* 98.4 *pleno gradu*. The *militaris gradus* is unique to V. It will correspond to the speed of the "standard march" or *iustum iter* known from Caesar *Bell. Civ.* 3.76, defined as a normal route-march on good roads in good weather between camps, leaving time to build the camp and *curare corpora,* and leave in good time the next day; cf. G. Veith, in J. Kromayer, G. Veith (edd.), *Heerwesen und Kriegführung der Griechen und Römer* (Munich 1928) 352.

[2] Cf. Onas. 10.1–6.

[3] Cf. II.23, and Serv. ad Verg. *Aen.* 11.284, quoted ad loc.

[4] Sall. *Hist.* frag. 2.19 (Maurenbrecher).

[5] Q. Sertorius is something of a hero with V., which supports a Spanish origin for him. Cn. Pompeius Magnus held command as proconsul of Hither Spain against Q. Sertorius from 77–71 BC.

[6] A sardonic allusion to *urbani milites,* modern field army men who were used to being garrisoned in imperial capitals and, spoiled by the amenities of civilization, would allegedly be unready to wade through rivers; cf. III.8 init.

whole art of warfare through so many wars and continual crises, selected the Campus Martius next to the Tiber in which the youth might wash off sweat and dust after training in arms, and lose their fatigue from running in the exercise of swimming.[1] It is highly advantageous to train not just infantry but cavalry and their horses and grooms, whom they call *galearii*,[2] to swim as well, lest anything should happen to them on account of their inability in the hour of need.[3]

11. How the ancients trained recruits with wicker shields and with posts.[4]

The ancients, as one finds in books, trained recruits in this manner. They wove shields from withies, of hurdle-like construction, and circular, such that the hurdle had twice the weight that a government shield[5] normally has. They also gave recruits wooden foils likewise of double weight, instead of swords. So equipped, they were trained not only in the morning but even after noon[6] against posts. Indeed, the use of posts is of very great benefit to gladiators as well as soldiers. Neither the arena nor the battle-field[7] ever proved a man invincible in armed combat, unless he was judged to have been thoroughly trained at the post. Each recruit would plant a single post in the ground so that it

---

[1]Cf. I.3.

[2]See under III.6. Cf. Jos. *Bell. Iud.* 3.69 for the military training of soldiers' servants.

[3]Arguably an allusion to the calamitous crossing of the Tigris by Jovian's army in AD 363, cf. Amm. 25.8.1: *aut imperitia nandi gurgite fluminis absorbebantur...* "or were sucked under by the river's current through their inability to swim." V. uses hyperbaton to add pregnancy to his words *quid imperitis... eveniat*; cf. his allusion to the battle of Adrianople, III.11 fin.

[4]Cf. Scipio Africanus Maior at Carthago Nova, 209 BC, Polyb. 10.20, Livy 26.51.3 ff. V. omits the next stage, fencing with a live opponent, cf. Antyllus apud Oribasius *de Rem.* 6.36.2–4. Cf. Juv. 6.247 for use of posts in training gladiators. Cato *de Re Mil.* fr. 14 also mentions gladiatorial training, so that P. Rutilius Rufus, cos. 105 BC, will not have been the first to introduce gladiatorial methods of training to the army, despite Val. Max. 2.3.2. Cf. also Auct. *de Bell. Afr.* 71 and Amm. 16.12.49.

[5]*scutum publicum.* V. inserts a "modernizing" gloss having reference, probably, to the late Roman army, in which arms issued to soldiers by the *armorum custos* remained state property, subject to be handed back, cf. *refundere*, I.20 init. See M.P. Speidel, "The Weapons Keeper, the *fisci curator*, and the ownership of weapons in the Roman army", *Roman Army Studies* II (1992) 131–136.

[6]V.'s consistent emphasis on afternoon training as something remarkable suggests that Cato's army did not observe the siesta, already a Roman custom by the first century BC, when it was called the *meridiatio.*

[7]*campus.* The meaning varies according to context: I.11, II.25, III.15, 17, 20, 24, 25, IV.45 (battle-field); I.18, 26, II.7, 22, 23, III.2 (training-field); I.27, II.1, 18, III.2, 6, 9, 19, IV.1 (plain); I.22, III.8 (camping ground).

could not move and protruded six feet. Against the post as if against an adversary the recruit trained himself using the foil and hurdle like a sword and shield, so that now he aimed at as it were the head and face, now threatened the flanks, then tried to cut the hamstrings and legs, backed off, came on, sprang, and aimed at the post with every method of attack and art of combat, as though it were an actual opponent. In this training care was taken that the recruit drew himself up to inflict wounds without exposing any part of himself to a blow.

12. Recruits should be taught to strike not with the edge, but with the point.

Further, they learned to strike not with the edge, but with the point. For the Romans not only easily beat those fighting with the edge, but even made mock of them, as a cut, whatever its force, seldom kills, because the vitals are protected by both armour and bones. But a stab driven two inches in is fatal; for necessarily whatever goes in penetrates the vitals. Secondly while a cut is being delivered the right arm and flank are exposed; whereas a stab is inflicted with the body remaining covered, and the enemy is wounded before he realizes it. That is why, it is agreed, the Romans used chiefly this method for fighting.[1] The hurdle and foil of double weight they gave out so that when the recruit took up real, and lighter arms, he fought with more confidence and agility, as being liberated from the heavier weight.

13. Recruits should be taught *armatura*.

Further, the recruit should be taught the type of drill known as *armatura*,[2] handed down by drillmasters.[3] This practice even partly

---

[1] The real reason was the introduction of the Spanish *gladius*, a short stabbing sword, during the Second Punic War (probably on occasion of the reforms of Scipio Africanus at Carthago Nova in 209 BC, cf. *Suda* M.302 s.v. μαχαίρα, following a lost portion of Polyb. book 29); but V.'s medical explanation is surely part of the reason for the change, which made close-order tactics possible. An upward stab wound is far more dangerous that a slash. The terms *caesa, puncta* are morphologically late forms, cf. A. Souter, *A Glossary of Later Latin to 600 AD* (Oxford 1949) s. vv.

[2] A "special drill" attested as used only in the late-Roman sources Ammianus, cf. Firmicus Maternus *Math.* 8.6.3, and V., see *TLL* s.v. 606. But cf. Livy 44.9.2–7 for similar displays of manoeuvres and tactics by Roman youths in the Circus already commonplace by 169 BC, as under the Empire, cf. II.23. The equestrian display of the *lusus Troiae* is a related custom which lasted centuries. *Armatura pedestris* was practised by the Emperors Julian and Constantius II, and Ursicinus' sons' expertise in it could be represented as a threat to Constantius II, cf. Amm. 16.5.10, 21.16.7, 14.11.3. V.'s Emperor is praised for his *armatura (equestris)* at III.26 fin., as probably too is Constantius II at Amm. 21.16.7.

survives. For it is well-known that even now *armaturae*[1] fight better than the rest in all battles. Hence it should be appreciated how much better is a trained soldier than an untrained, when *armaturae*, whatever their proficiency, outstrip the rest of their comrades in the art of warfare.

The discipline of training was so strictly maintained by our ancestors that weapons instructors[2] were rewarded with double pay, and soldiers inadequately proficient in this mock-battle were forced to accept barley instead of corn. Wheaten rations were not restored to them until they had shown, by giving demonstrations in front of the Prefect of the legion,[3] tribunes and senior officers,[4] that they had completed all that was contained in the military art.[5] For there is nothing stabler nor more fortunate or admirable than a State which has copious supplies of soldiers who are trained. For it is not fine raiment or stores of gold, silver and gems that bend our enemies to respect or support us;[6] they are kept down solely by fear of our arms. Secondly, in other matters, as Cato says, mistakes can be corrected afterwards; errors in war do not admit of amendment, because the penalty follows immediately upon the slip. For those who fight without courage or expertise either perish

---

Claud. *pan. de Hon. cons. VI* 621–640 describes it. Also called *pyrrhicha militaris*, the drills were set to music. See Grosse, 221–222.

[3]*campidoctores*, first attested in the Praetorian Guard under Septimius Severus, were senior NCOs in late-Roman infantry units. *CIL* 2.4083 from Tarraco may attest a centurion acting as *campidoctor* of the provincial governor's *equites singulares* already under Commodus.

[1]*Armaturae* may stand here for all *scholares* though properly designating *scholae* units with this name only. *Scutarii* is similarly and more often used as a generic term, cf. Hoffmann, 292. *Scholae palatinae* were élite mounted regiments belonging to the imperial guard, cf. Jones, 613–614, Grosse, 93–96. V. has made a false etymology in all probability, as there is no known connexion between the name of the regiments and that of the drill which is likely to be much older, as stated above.

[2]*doctores armorum.*

[3]*praefectus legionis*, cf. II.9.

[4]*principia*, cf. II.7.

[5]V. modernizes the officers and may invent the occasion. In the early Empire, at least, the drill was taught by *centuriones evocati* acting as *exercitatores*, cf. Ruggiero s.v. Barley-rations as punishment may not have survived after Augustus, cf. Suet. *Aug.* 24, Front. *Strat.* 4.1.25, 37, Livy 27.13.9, Polyb. 6.38.3. They are absent from the military punishments mentioned by the jurists Ulpian, Modestinus, Paul, Aem. Macer and Arrius Menander, cf. *Dig.* 49.16. Double pay for the higher NCO grade of *armaturae* is mentioned at II.7, where V. may misidentify these with *doctores armorum.*

[6]i.e., subsidies to barbarians.

immediately, or turn to flight and dare not stand up again to their victors.[1]

14. Recruits should be trained at throwing javelins.
But I return to my subject. The recruit who is being trained with the foil at the post is also made to launch spear-shafts of heavier weight than the real javelins will be against the above-mentioned post as though against a man. In this activity the instructor in arms sees to it that he hurl the spear-shaft with great force, and drive the missile with a true aim into or next to the post.[2] For by this exercise the arms gain strength, and skill and experience in throwing javelins is acquired.

15. Recruits should be thoroughly trained in arrows.
About a third or a quarter of recruits, who prove to have more aptitude, should be trained constantly with the aforesaid posts using wooden bows and mock arrows. Instructors should be chosen for this training who are experts, and greater care should be taken that (recruits) hold the bow scientifically, string it smartly, keep the left hand firm, draw the right with calculation, let the eye and mind concentrate together on the target to be hit, and learn to shoot straight whether from horseback or on foot. This art needs to be learned thoroughly and maintained by daily use and exercise. How much utility good archers have in battle was clearly shown by Cato in his books On Military Science, and by Claudius, who overcame an enemy to whom he had previously been unequal by establishing and training numerous darters.[3] Scipio Africanus, about to do battle with the Numantines who had sent armies of the Roman

---

[1]Cf. III.10 fin.

[2]Probably V.'s guesswork. One would not be permitted to miss the mark, surely, and in any case the *doctor armorum* sounds suspiciously like the late-Roman *campidoctor*. But an early *doctor cohortis* is attested among the Praetorian Guard probably in the second century AD, who was promoted *campidoctor* of *cohors I praetoria* in *CIL* 6.533. *Doctor armorum*, at least, does not seem to occur in inscriptions, cf. Ruggiero, s.v.

[3]M. Porcius Cato the Censor's *de Re Militari*, written in the mid-second century BC, is lost apart from a few fragments, collected by H. Jordan, *M. Catonis praeter librum de re rustica Quae Extant* (Leipzig 1867). There is no reason to think V. had access to the original. Appius Claudius Pulcher is probably credited here with the invention of *velites* or light-armed sharp-shooters at the siege of Capua in 211 BC, but his proconsular colleague Q. Fulvius Flaccus is usually more prominent in the tradition, cf. Val. Max. 2.3.3, Livy 26.4.4–10. V. seems to be thinking of both archers—*sagittarii*—and darters—*iaculatores*.

People under the yoke, supposed that he would only get the upper hand if he incorporated picked archers in all centuries.[1]

16. Recruits should be trained at firing stones from slings.[2]

It is advisable that recruits be thoroughly trained at casting stones by hand or with slings. The inhabitants of the Balearic Isles are said to have been first to discover the use of slings and to have practised with such expertise that mothers did not allow their small sons to touch any food unless they had hit it with a stone shot from a sling.[3] Often, against soldiers armed with helmets, cataphracts[4] and cuirasses, smooth stones shot with a sling or "sling-staff"[5] are more dangerous than any arrows, since while leaving the limbs intact they inflict a wound that is still lethal, and the enemy dies from the blow of the stone without loss of blood.[6] That slingers served in all battles of the ancients is known to everyone. This weapon should be learned by all recruits with frequent exercise, because it is no effort to carry a sling.[7] It often happens too that warfare is carried on in stony places, that some mountain or hill has

---

[1]The sack of Numantia, Spain, 133 BC, by P. Cornelius Scipio Africanus Aemilianus, after several years of war. Cf. Front. *Strat.* 4.7.27: *Scipio Aemilianus ad Numantiam omnibus non cohortibus tantum, sed centuriis sagittarios et funditores interposuit.* "Scipio Aemilianus at Numantia interspersed archers and slingers not just in all cohorts, but in all centuries."

[2]Cf. W.G. Griffiths, "The Sling and its place in the Roman Imperial Army" in *5th Roman Military Equipment Conference,* ed. C. van Driel-Murray, BAR Int. Ser. 476 (1989) 255–280, T. Völling, "Funditores im römischen Heer", *SJ* xlv (1990) 24–58.

[3]Cf. Flor. I.43.5: *(Baleares) certos esse quis miretur ictûs, cum haec sola genti arma sint, id unum ab infantia studium? Cibum puer a matre non accipit, nisi quem ipsa monstrante percusserit.* "Who can wonder that (the Baleares) are sure of aim, when this is their only national arm, this their sole interest from infancy? A boy does not receive food from his mother, unless he shall hit it when she points to it." V. provides a colourful exemplum here, perhaps again because of his national pride as a Spaniard.

[4]*cataphractae,* coats-of-mail or scale-armour, metallic or horn on a leather foundation, cf. IV.9 fin. V. uses the term interchangeably with *lorica*—"cuirass"—, cf. I.20, or else in addition to it, as here.

[5]*fustibalus.* A kind of sling attached to a staff, also known in the Middle Ages, but introduced in the late-Roman period. Cf. T.G. Kolias, *Byzantinische Waffen* (Vienna 1988) 255.

[6]Probably a reminiscence of David and Goliath, cf. Biblia vulgata *I. Sam.* 17.23, 49, since the idea is militarily unsound. V. pads out and embellishes from his own medico-Christian perspective. Note the medical explanation.

[7]V. is sarcastic about the modern, "urban" soldier's ability to carry weights, cf. I.19. I.20.

to be defended, or barbarians kept from storming forts or cities,[1] by using stones and slings.

17. On training with lead-weighted darts.[2]

Training with lead-weighted darts, which they call *mattiobarbuli,* should also be provided to recruits. In Illyricum once there were two legions which had 6,000 men apiece and were called Mattiobarbuli after their skilful and brave handling of these weapons. By them, as is well-known, long ago all wars were concluded in a most vigorous manner; so much so, in fact, that when Diocletian and Maximian acceded to the throne they decreed that these Mattiobarbuli be called Joviani and Herculiani in recognition of their valour, and are (thereby) judged to have preferred them to all other legions.[3] They usually carried five *mattiobarbuli* each, slotted inside their shields. If soldiers throw them at the right moment, it seems almost as if shield-bearing infantry[4] are imitating the rôle of archers.[5] For they wound the enemy and his horses before they can get not merely to close quarters, but even within range of javelins.

---

[1]*Civitas* or "city" frequently means a small fort or fortified settlement in late-Latin, cf. Goffart, 65–66, but it is probably neutral here.

[2]*(Sagittae) plumbatae,* known to the elder Pliny *Hist. Nat.* 10.97, 12.85 after Arist. *Hist. An.* 9.616 simply as "arrows weighted with lead", as used in hunting for nests of the cinnamon bird when they were shot from a bow, may have originated in military use as the *cestrus,* a short wooden dart with an iron head, thrown from a sling, described by Livy 42.65.9 and Polybius 27.11 (9).1 as having been first introduced *c.*171 BC. From the Anon. *De Rebus Bellicis* 10 we find it developing into a kind of throwing-mace in late antiquity, also attested as such in Byzantine times, its weight increasing the while. But they came in a wide variety of shapes and sizes from the late-Roman period, some clearly darts for firing from engines, others for throwing by hand. There are no earlier examples so far discovered by archaeology. Cf. T. Völling, "Plumbata–mattiobarbulus– μαρτζοβά ρβουλον. Bemerkungen zu einem Waffenfund aus Olympia", *AA* (1991) 287–298, J. Bennett, "Plumbatae from Pitsunda (Pityus), Georgia, and some observations on their probable use", *JRMES* ii (1991) 59–63, R. Degen, "Plumbatae: Wurfgeschosse der Spätantike", *HA* xxiii (1992) 139–147.

[3]V. is the only source to attest the use of lead-weighted darts by the Joviani and Herculiani, the most senior pair of *legiones palatinae* of the fourth century AD, cf. Hoffmann, I.215–217. See also T. Drew-Bear, "Les voyages d'Aurélius Gaius, soldat de Dioclétien", in *La Géographie administrative et politique d'Alexandre à Mahomet,* Actes de Colloque de Strasbourg 14–16 juin 1979 (Univ. de Strasbourg 1982) 97, 101–102. Vict. *Caess.* 39.18 implies that they were originally *auxilia,* a statement which may arise from confusion with the Jovii. Diocletian acceded to the throne in AD 284 and Maximian as his colleague in 286, and they created a number of units named after their divine surnames "Jovius" and "Herculius". For late-Latin *doceantur,* "are judged", cf. III.6 fin. note.

[4]*scutati,* cf. II.15.

[5]*sagittarii.*

18. How recruits should be trained in mounting horses.

The vaulting of horses has always been rigorously demanded of both recruits and of soldiers with many years' service. It is clear that this exercise has survived to the present day, albeit now with neglect.[1] Wooden horses were set up under cover in winter, in summer on the training-field.[2] Over them recruits were made to vault at first unarmed, until they had gained experience, then in arms. Such care was taken that they learned to jump on and off both from the right-hand side and from the left, even holding drawn swords and lances.[3] This they likewise performed with constant practice naturally so as to be able to mount without delay in the stress of battle, having trained with such dedication in peace.

19. Recruits should be trained in carrying a burden.

Recruits should very frequently be made to carry a burden of up to 60 lb.[4] and route-march at the military step, since on arduous campaigns they have necessarily to carry their rations together with their arms.[5] This should not be thought hard, once the habit has been gained, for there is nothing that continual practice does not render very easy. We know that the ancient soldiers used to do this exercise from the evidence of Vergil himself, who says:

---

[1] Perhaps as part of *armatura equestris*, cf. Amm. 16.5.10, 21.3.7, Claud. *pan. de Hon. cons. VI* 621–639, Grosse, 222. Polyb. 6.25.4 suggests that the vaulting of wooden and live horses while holding arms was originally devised for *velites* in the third century BC.

[2] Cf. II.23, III.2. Cf. R.W. Davies, "Roman Military Training Grounds", in E. Birley, B. Dobson, and M.G. Jarrett (edd.), *Roman Frontier Studies 1969, Eighth international congress of Limesforschung* (Cardiff 1974) 20–26, id., "The training grounds of the Roman cavalry", *Service in the Roman Army*, ch. IV, 93–124.

[3] Cf. Arr. *Tact.* 43.3–4.

[4] = *c*.43 lb. 5 oz. avoirdupois, 19·647 kg. 1 Roman pound = 0·7219 lb. avp. or 327·45 grammes, cf. F. Hultsch, *Griechische und römische Metrologie* (Berlin 1882[2]) 161.

[5] Cf. Amm. 17.9.2: *...ex annona decem dierum et septem, quam in expeditionem pergens vehebat cervicibus miles, portionem subtractam,* "...a portion removed from the rations for 17 days, that a soldier going on expedition carried at his neck..." SHA *Alex. Sev.* 47.1: *...nec portarent cibaria decem et septem, ut solent, dierum nisi in barbarico,* "...nor would they carry rations for 17 days, as is normal practice, except in barbarian territory." Front. *Strat.* 4.1.7: *C. Marius recidendorum inpedimentorum gratia, quibus maxime exercitus agmen oneratur, vasa et cibaria militis in fasciculos aptata furcis inposuit, sub quibus et habile onus et facilis requies esset: unde et proverbium tractum est "muli Mariani".* "To cut down on baggage, which weighs an army column down more than anything else, C. Marius had the individual soldier's cups and rations tied up in bundles and put upon forked props, under which the burden might be manageable and respite easy: hence the phrase passed into proverb, 'Marius' mules'." See N. Fuentes, "The mule of a soldier", *JRMES* ii (1991) 65–100.

"Just as the bold Roman in his national arms
Cruelly laden takes the road, and before
The enemy expects it stands in formation, having pitched camp."[1]

20. What kind of arms and armour the ancients used.[2]

The place (in our narrative) demands that we attempt to state the kind of arms with which recruits should be equipped and protected. But on this subject ancient practice has been utterly destroyed. For despite progress in cavalry arms thanks to the example of the Goths, and the Alans and Huns,[3] the infantry as is well-known go unprotected. From the founding of the City down to the time of the deified Gratian,[4] the infantry army was equipped with both cataphracts[5] and helmets. But upon the intervention of neglect and idleness field exercises ceased, and arms which soldiers rarely donned began to be thought heavy. So they petitioned the Emperor that they should hand in[6] first the cataphracts, then helmets. Thus with their chests and heads unprotected our soldiers have often been destroyed in engagements against the Goths through the multitude of their archers. Even after so many defeats, which led to the

---

[1]Verg. *Georg.* 3.346–348.

[2]V.'s rhetorical allegation that infantry (legionaries) had cast off heavy armour has for long been taken at face value and generalized incautiously. In fact it plays on a commonplace used also by Tac. *Ann.* 13.35.1 and Fronto *Princ. Hist.* 11–12. For a discussion of the evidence for generally undiminished use, at least in the East, of heavy armour, cf. J.C.N. Coulston, "Later Roman armour, 3rd.–6th. centuries AD", *JRMES* i (1990) 139–160.

[3]Cf. E.A. Thompson, *A History of Attila and the Huns* (Oxford 1948) 53 on the Hun bow, and V. *Mul.* III.6 on the Hunnic horse.

[4]Reigned in the West, AD 375–383, murdered at Lugdunum (Lyons) by Andragathius on the order of Magnus Maximus, who invaded from Britain leading the regular troops against Gratian, and exploited their hatred of him on account of his favouritism towards his Alan mercenaries, cf. Zos. 4.35.2–6 = Eunapius fr. 51 (Blockley). Maximus reigned as Augustus in the prefecture of Gaul until defeated and killed by Theodosius I at the battle of Aquileia, AD 388.

[5]*cataphractae*, coats-of-mail or scale-armour, metallic or horn on a leather foundation, cf. IV.9 fin. V. uses the term interchangeably with *lorica*—"cuirass"—, cf. below, or else in addition to it, as at I.16.

[6]I follow Otto's emendation *se de<be>re refundere*. For *refundere*, cf. SHA *Claud.* 14.5: *loricam unam, quam refundat.* The circumstantial detail of a petition—cf. *Nov.* Theod. II 21 (441) for such a procedure followed by the *scholae palatinae*—may suggest an historical event, but its scope is wholly a matter of conjecture. V. probably exaggerates and generalizes a particular case, but the point was to stress the broken-backed state of Gratian's field infantry.

sacking of so many cities,[1] no one has troubled to restore either cataphracts or helmets to the infantry.

The result is that those who in battle are exposed unprotected to wounds, think not about fighting but fleeing. For what is a foot-archer to do, without a cataphract or a helmet, when he cannot hold a shield along with a bow? What are the dragon-bearers[2] themselves and the standard-bearers to do in battle, who control the poles with the left hand, and whose heads and chests are obviously unprotected? But a "cuirass"[3] or helmet seems heavy to an infantryman who perhaps rarely exercises, perhaps rarely handles arms; yet daily use makes light work even if heavy equipment is worn. But these men, not being able to endure the labour of wearing the old protective armour, because their bodies are uncovered are forced to risk wounds and deaths, and worse still, to be captured or betray the State by taking flight. So while they refuse training and hard work, they are butchered in the greatest disgrace, like cattle.[4]

Why else was the infantry army called a "wall" among the ancients,[5] if not because the serried ranks of legions shone in their shields, cataphracts and helmets? So much so, indeed, that archers were equipped on the left arm with an arm-guard, and the shield-bearing infantry were made to wear iron greaves on the right leg, as well as cataphracts and helmets. Such was the armour of those who, fighting in

---

[1]I translate *tantarum* as = *tot*, as often in late Latin, and see no reference to the sack of Rome. V. talks rhetorically of *innumerabiles urbes* at IV praef. The cities are likely to have been in the Danube-lands, including such famous fortresses as Carnuntum, abandoned between AD 375 and *c*.390, cf. Amm. 30.5.2.

[2]In the Roman army the dragon was originally an auxiliary cavalry standard, described as Scythian in a detailed account by Arr. *Tact.* 35.2–4, but it first appears on Trajan's column in use among the Dacians, cf. Cichorius Pl. XXIII, scene xxxi, Pl. XLV, scene lxiv, Pl. LIX, scene cxliv, Pl. LXIV, scene clix. Later it spread to the whole Roman army, including legionary infantry units, by the fourth century AD, cf. Grosse, 231–232, and see J. Garbsch, *Römische Paraderüstungen* (Munich 1978) 88 and Pl. 48 for an actual dragon-standard found at Niederbieber on the upper German *limes*. See also M.P. Speidel, "The Master of the Dragon Standards and the Golden Torc", *TAPhA* cxv (1985) 283–287, and J.C.N. Coulston, "The 'draco' standard", *JRMES* ii (1991) 101–114.

[3]*lorica*, = cataphract, cf. above.

[4]Cf. Sall. *Jug.* 44.1, 44.5, Tac. *Ann.* 13.35.1, Fronto *Principia Historiae* 11–12, Fronto *ad Verum Imp.* 2.1, echoed by contemporary sources such as Amm. 16.2.1, 18.6.2, 18.8.2, 22.4.6–7, 27.9.1, 27.9.6, 29.4.6, Liban. *Or.* 2.38, 47.6, SHA *Tac.* 2.4, Symm. *Epp.* 6.73, 7.38, Claud. *In Eutrop.* 2.580 ff. Cf. R. MacMullen, *Corruption and the Decline of Rome* (Yale 1988) 175–176. Cic. *Tusc. Disp.* 2.16.37 gives the ideal.

[5]V. may have in mind a Latin translation of Hom. *Il.* 4.299 ἕρκος πολέμοιο, "bulwark of war." Cf. II.17; also Amm. 16.12.49: *instar turrium*, "like towers."

the First line, were called *principes*,[1] in the Second line *hastati*,[2] and in the Third line *triarii*.[3] The *triarii* would wait in reserve behind their shields on bended knees, lest they be wounded while standing by oncoming missiles and, when circumstances required, would attack the enemy with more violence for having rested. They often gained the victory, it is said, after the *hastati* and those who stood at the front had fallen.[4]

However, there were also in ancient times men among the infantry called "light armament", slingers, and light-armed troops.[5] They were mainly located on the wings, and undertook the opening phase of the fighting. They were chosen for their great speed and fitness; they were not very numerous. If the course of battle compelled it, they would

---

[1]"frontlinesmen".

[2]"spearmen".

[3]"thirdlinesmen". These categories are from the manipular army of the third and second centuries BC, essentially that described at greater length by Polyb. 6.22–23, and Livy 8.8 (which projects a manipular army back into the age of the Latin wars), and by V. at II 15–17, III 14. V. greatly exaggerates the use of cataphract-armour, under late-antique influence, for it was worn originally only by the wealthiest soldiers, cf. Polyb. 23.14–16. He also inverts the canonical order *hastati–principes* of the First and Second lines, probably on etymological grounds; in practice, too, they could really be inverted, cf. Livy 8.8.9–10, 22.5.7, 40.27.6.

[4]Cf. Livy 8.8.9–13 (allegedly 340 BC): *Ubi his ordinibus exercitus instructus esset, hastati omnium primi pugnam inibant. Si hastati profligare hostem non possent, pede presso eos retro cedentes in intervalla ordinum principes recipiebant. Tum principum pugna erat; hastati sequebantur; triarii sub vexillis considebant, sinistro crure porrecto, scuta innixa humeris, hastas suberecta cuspide in terra fixas, haud secus quam vallo saepta inhorret acies, tenentes. Si apud principes quoque haud satis prospere esset pugnatum, a prima acie ad triarios se sensim referebant. Inde rem ad triarios redisse, cum laboratur, proverbio increbuit. Triarii consurgentes, ubi in intervalla ordinum suorum principes et hastatos recepissent, extemplo compressis ordinibus velut claudebant vias unoque continenti agmine, iam nulla spe post relicta, in hostem incidebant; id erat formidolosissimum hosti, cum velut victos insecuti novam repente aciem exsurgentem, auctam numero, cernebant.* "When the army had been drawn up in these lines, the *hastati* began the battle first of all the rest. If the *hastati* could not overcome the enemy, falling back at the double they were received between intervals in the lines of the *principes*. Then the battle belonged to the *principes*; the *hastati* were behind them; the *triarii* sat under their insignia, with the left leg forward, holding their shields rested against the shoulders, their spears fixed in the ground with points lowered, just as if the line were bristling with a fence of stakes. If the *principes* also had insufficient success in the fight, they slowly withdrew from the front line to the *triarii*. Hence it became proverbial to say that 'the thing was down to the *triarii*', when in difficulty. The *triarii* rose up and received the *principes* and *hastati* between intervals in their ranks, and then suddenly closing ranks they as it were shut off the pathways and made a single continuous line, whereupon with no other hope left to fall back on they attacked the enemy. It was a most terrible thing for the enemy when, pursuing apparently defeated men, they suddenly saw a new array rising up against them in increased numbers."

[5]*ferentarii.*

retire and be received between the front ranks of the legions, in such a way that the line remained unmoved. Almost down to the present day the custom survived whereby all soldiers wore leathern caps which they called "Pannonians". This was observed so that the helmet should not seem heavy to a man in battle, who was used always to wearing something on his head.[1]

The javelins that the infantry army used were called *pila*, having thin, triangular iron heads 9 in. or 1 ft. long, such as once lodged in a shield could not be broken off and, when thrown skilfully and with force, might easily pierce a cuirass.[2] Weapons of this type are now rare with us, but barbarian shield-bearing infantry use these particularly, calling them *bebrae,* and carrying two or three each in battle.[3] It should be noted, also, that when missiles are being exchanged, soldiers should have the left foot forward;[4] this way the throw is stronger for hurling darts.[5] But when it comes to what they call "to javelins",[6] and the fighting is hand-to-hand with swords,[7] soldiers should have the right foot forward,[8] so as to draw the flank away from the enemy lest they be wounded, and to have the right hand closer so it can land a blow.

Obviously, therefore, recruits should be equipped and protected with every ancient type of arms. For a man who does not fear wounds because he has his head and chest protected must acquire sharper courage for battle.

---

[1] V.'s medical exegesis again. The caps are thought to be those depicted in artistic representations of soldiers in non-battle dress, familiar from the famous relief of the Tetrarchs on St. Mark's, Venice, cf. H. Ubl, "Pilleus pannonicus, die Feldmütze des spätrömischen Heeres", in *Festschrift für R. Pittioni* II (Vienna 1976) 214–241. Leathern caps are mentioned because the source mentioned the headgear of *velites* here, cf. Polyb. 6.22.3, *RE* VII (1910) 572 s.v. Galea (Fiebiger), J. Kromayer, G. Veith, *Heerwesen* (1928) 327, D. Schenk, 36.

[2] Cf. under II.15.

[3] J.G. Kempf, "Romanorum sermonis castrensis reliquiae collectae et illustratae", *Jahrbücher für klassische Philologie,* Suppl. xxvi (1901) 367, identifies this with a hypothetical Celtic *berva* = spear.

[4] *in ante,* a late-Latinism, cf. E. Löfstedt, *Late Latin* (1959) 164 n.1.

[5] *spicula,* cf. II.15.

[6] *ad pila.*

[7] V. means the close-quarters phase of battle, called *ad spathas et ad pila,* "to broadswords and to javelins" at III.14.

[8] *proximior,* a late-Latinism quoted by Priscian *Inst.* 3.21.

21. On building camps.[1]

The recruit should also learn how to build camps, for nothing is found so safe or so indispensable in war, since if a camp has been properly constructed, soldiers spend days and nights so secure behind the rampart—even if the enemy is besieging it—that they seem to carry a walled city about with them everywhere.[2] But knowledge of this technique has altogether perished; for no one now for a long time has built a camp with lines of fosses and a stockade fixed above it.[3] For this reason, as we know, many armies have frequently been harmed in day or night-attacks by barbarian cavalry. But it is not only when they bivouac without building a camp that they suffer this: when in battle they begin to retreat for some reason, they lack the fortification of the camp to retire to and fall unavenged, like animals, and there is no end to the killing until the enemy's will to pursue flags.

22. In what kind of places camps should be built.

Camps—especially when the enemy is near—should be built always in a safe place, where there are sufficient supplies of firewood, fodder and water, and if a long stay is in prospect choose a salubrious site. Care must be taken lest there be a nearby mountain or high ground which could be dangerous if captured by the enemy. Thought must be given that the site is not liable to flooding from torrents and the army to

---

[1] I.21–25 on castrametation are not well-adapted to the training of recruits but appear to have been put together by V. and inserted incongruously into the training chapters. For the recruit would actually need to acquire trenching, building and stockading skills, mentioned at I.4, II.25, III.4, III.10, whereas the strategic calculations which V. summarizes here were relevant only to senior officers. The material is repeated with a few variations and additions at III.8. Cf. R.W. Davies, "Roman Wales and Roman military practice-camps", *Service in the Roman Army*, ch.V, 125–139, and R. Grosse, "Das römisch-byzantinische Marschlager vom 4.–10. Jahrhundert", *Byz.Z.* xxii (1913) 90–121, arguing that the fourth-century army still built camps until growing barbarization lost the technique.

[2] Cf. II.18, II.25 fin. The mobile city is a peculiarly late-Roman concept, inspired by the Gothic *carrago* which is cited as an example for Roman castrametation at III.10. Note that V. includes circles among possible shapes of camps at I.23, III.8. But the image of the camp as a city goes back at least as far as Polyb. 6.31.10, cf. Front. *Strat.* 4.1.14.

[3] A rhetorical exaggeration, also at III.10, but even élite barbarian units such as *auxilia palatina* do not appear usually to have had the same skills in castrametation or tolerance of hard work (cf. II.3) as the trained legions. Cf. Amm. 18.6.2: *auxiliarii milites semper munia spernentes huiusmodi*, "auxiliary soldiers who always refuse tasks of this sort", and 19.5.2, but contrast 31.8.9.

suffer harm in this event.[1] The camp should be built according to the number of soldiers and baggage-train, lest too great a multitude be crammed in a small area, or a small force in too large a space be compelled to be spread out more than is appropriate.

23. In what shape camps should be marked out.

Camps should be made sometimes square, sometimes triangular, sometimes semicircular, according as the nature and demands of the site require. But the gate which is called *praetoria*[2] should either face east, or the direction which looks towards the enemy, or if on the march it should face the direction in which the army is to proceed.[3] Within it the First centuries, that is cohorts, pitch tents and set up the dragons and standards.[4] The gate called *decumana*[5] is behind the headquarters;[6] through it delinquent soldiers are taken out to be punished.

24. The sorts of fortification of a camp.

There are three different sorts of fortification of a camp. When there is no pressing danger, turves are cut from the earth and from them a kind of wall is built, 3 ft. high above the ground, with the fosse from which the turves were lifted in front. Then there is a temporary fosse 9 ft. wide and 7 ft. deep. But when more serious forces of the enemy threaten it is advisable to fortify the perimeter of the camp with a proper fosse, 12 ft. wide and 9 ft. deep below the "line", as it is called.[7] Above it revetments are built on either side[8] and filled with earth that has been raised from the fosse, rising to a height of 4 ft. The result is that (the fosse) is 13 ft. deep and 12 ft. wide. Above are fixed stakes of very strong wood, which the soldiers are accustomed to carry with them.

---

[1]Cf. Ps.-Hyg. 57 for the same regulations. Caesar at Ilerda in 49 BC made the mistake of camping between two rivers, Caes. *Bell. Civ.* 1.48.

[2]Main gate.

[3]V. adds the probably Christian eastward orientation to the traditional regulations given also by Ps.-Hyg. 56.

[4]V. normally identifies centuries with cohorts, giving them dragon-standards, obviously under the influence of late-Roman usage.

[5]Rear gate.

[6]*praetorium.*

[7]i.e. ground-level.

[8]i.e. on either side of the intended embankment, which was on the inner side of the fosse, cf. III.8.

For this work it is advisable always to have in readiness mattocks, rakes, baskets and other kinds of tools.[1]

25. How a camp should be built when under threat from the enemy. It is easy to build a camp when the opposition are absent, but if the enemy threatens, then all the cavalry and half the infantry are drawn up in line to repel attack[2] while the remainder build the camp behind them, digging fosses. The herald announces which century is the first, which the second and third, to have completed all its work. After this the fosse is inspected and measured by the centurions, and punishment is inflicted on any who may have worked carelessly.

Therefore the recruit should be trained in this technique, so that when need arises he may be able to build a camp without difficulty, quickly and in safety.

26. How recruits are trained to keep ranks and intervals in the line. It is agreed that nothing is more advantageous in battle, than that by dint of their constant exercises soldiers should keep their appointed ranks in the line,[3] and not mass together or thin out the formation at any point inconveniently. For when densely packed they lose room to fight and impede one another, and when too thinly spread and showing the light between them they provide the enemy with an opening to breach. It is inevitable that everything should at once collapse in panic if the line is cut and the enemy reach the rear of the fighting men. Therefore recruits should be led out constantly to the exercise-field and drawn up in line following the order of the roll, in such a way that at first the line should be single and extended, having no bends or curvatures, and there should be an equal and regular space between soldier and soldier.[4] Then the command should be given that they at once double the line, so that in an actual assault that arrangement to which they are used to conform may be preserved. Thirdly the command should be given suddenly to

---

[1]Cf. II.25. See N. Fuentes, "The mule of a soldier", *JRMES* ii (1991) 65–100.

[2]Cf. III.8, indicating that the cavalry and half the infantry were exempted by rank from camp-construction.

[3]The traditional penalty for failure to do this was death, cf. Livy 2.59.11, Diod. Sic. 12.64.3. But while training his troops at Numantia in the 130s BC, Scipio Africanus Minor punished such errors with flogging only, cf. Livy Epit. 57.

[4]Cf. III.15.

adopt a square formation,[1] and after this the line itself should be changed to triangular formation, which they call a "wedge".[2] This formation is usually of great advantage in battle. Next they are commanded to form circles,[3] which is the formation commonly adopted by trained soldiers to resist a hostile force that has breached the line, to prevent the whole army being turned to flight and grave peril ensuing.[4] If recruits learn these manoeuvres by continual practice they will observe them more easily in actual battle.

27. The distance that they should advance and retire, and how often a month the exercise should take place, whereby soldiers are led out on marching manoeuvres.

Next, the ancient procedure both survived and is enacted by constitutions of the deified Augustus and Hadrian, that thrice a month both cavalry and infantry should be led out *ambulatum*.[5] That is the term by which they call this type of exercise: the infantry were commanded to advance ten miles at the military step, armed and equipped with all their weapons, and then to retire to camp, completing some part of the march at the brisker running pace.[6] The cavalry also, divided by troops[7] and armed, similarly traversed the same distance, performing equestrian manoeuvres, now pursuing, now retreating, and by some rally renewing the charge.[8] Both formations had to go not merely on the flat but to go down and up in hilly and difficult terrain, to the end that nothing, even quite by chance, could befall the fighting

---

[1] *quadrata acies,* a marching formation with a hollow centre in which the baggage-train could be escorted; cf. III.6.

[2] *cuneus,* in fact a marching formation formed from two converging lines, only metaphorically like a triangle or wedge; cf. F. Lammert, "Der Keil in der Taktik des Altertums", *Gymnasium* li (1940) 15–31. Cf.III.17–20.

[3] *orbes.*

[4] Cf. Sall. *Jug.* 97.5, Caes. *Bell. Gall.* 4.37.2, 5.33.3, Amm. 29.5.41, 28.5.6.

[5] "on manoeuvres". Every seven days, according to SHA *Avid. Cass.* 6.3; every five days, according to SHA *Maxim.* 6.2. The present tense *praecavetur* appears to refer to the constitutions of Augustus and Hadrian as an extant document, but is probably merely copied from the source derived from Paternus; this is the only instance of V. citing *constitutiones,* despite I.8. For the technical sense of the verb *ambulo = decurro,* cf. A.R. Neumann, "Römische Rekrutenausbildung im Lichte der Disziplin", *CPh* xlii (1947) 157 n.3.

[6] Cf. I.9 for the different paces.

[7] *turmae.*

[8] Cf. R.W. Davies, "The Training grounds of the Roman cavalry", *Service in the Roman Army,* ch. IV, 93–123.

men, which good soldiers had not learned to deal with beforehand by the constant practice.[1]

28. On encouraging military science and Roman valour.

This material, having regard for faithfulness and devotion to truth, I have brought together in this little book, Invincible Emperor, abridged from all the authors who have written down the technique of military science, so that should anyone wish to be diligent in raising and training recruits he may be able easily to strengthen an army in emulation of ancient military virtue. For martial energy has not declined in mankind, nor are the lands exhausted that produced the Spartans, the Athenians, the Marsians, Samnites, Paeligni, the Romans themselves.[2] Were not once the Epirotes very powerful in arms?[3] Did not the Macedonians and Thessalians overcome the Persians and penetrate as far as India on campaign?[4] Clearly the Dacians, Moesians and Thracians have always been warlike, for fables tell us that Mars himself was born among them.[5] But it is tedious if I attempt to list the strength of all the provinces, when they all belong under the sway of the Roman Empire.[6]

However, a sense of security born of long peace[7] has diverted mankind partly to the enjoyment of private leisure, partly to civilian

---

[1]Cf. Jos. Bell. Iud. 3.98 on leaving nothing to chance.

[2]The Marsians and Paeligni, Italian tribes of the central Apennines, were the core of the unsuccessful last great challenge to Roman power in Italy mounted by these and other peoples, including the Samnites, during the Social War, 91–87 BC. Earlier Rome had fought three major wars with the Samnites, a powerful Italian tribal confederation of the southern Apennines, between 343 and 290 BC for hegemony in the Italian peninsula.

[3]A mountainous state abutting the NW Greek coast, Epiros became a Hellenistic military great power based on its capital Ambracia, pushed back the empire of Macedon, and annexed most of north Greece for a time under its formidable king, Pyrrhus. He reigned 297–272 BC, and among ceaseless campaigns fought the Romans in Italy and the Carthaginians in Sicily, 280–275.

[4]Under Alexander III, the Great, king of Macedon, reigned 336–323 BC, conquered and overthrew the Persian Empire 331, went on expedition to India 327–325.

[5]The story of Mars' birth is told only by Ovid Fasti 5.251–260.

[6]The list of provinces and peoples picks up that at I.1 which began with the peoples of the west before moving to Greece. The manpower reserves of the whole Empire are meant. Hieron. Epp. 60.16.2 (AD 397) may possibly ironically echo this passage and the 20+ years of neglect mentioned below.

[7]Cf. I.5, I.7, II.3, II.18, III.10. V. is under the influence of the literary topos in Juvenal 6.292: nunc patimur longae pacis mala. "Now we are suffering the evils of long peace." He really means a lengthy period of neglect of the army. It is not clear how long the "long peace" is envisaged as being, although it was certainly running in Gratian's reign (cf. I.20).

careers.[1] Thus attention to military training obviously was at first discharged rather neglectfully, then omitted, until finally consigned long since to oblivion.[2] Neither let anyone wonder that this happened in the preceding age,[3] because after the first Punic war twenty and more years of peace so enervated those all-conquering Romans as a result of private leisure and neglect of arms, that in the second Punic war they could not stand up to Hannibal. So it was that after so many consuls, so many generals, so many armies lost, they only finally achieved victory, when they had been able to learn military science and training.[4] Therefore recruits should constantly be levied and trained. For it costs less to train one's own men in arms than to hire foreign mercenaries.[5]

---

[1]Cf. I.5, III.10.

[2]Cf. I.8, I.20, and I.21. The closing strictures on the failure to train parallel those on the failure to recruit, I.7. Cf. also II.3, II.18 fin., and III.10 fin.

[3]*Superiore aetate*, i.e. the recent past, cf. III.12: *superiore vel nostra aetate*, referring to AD 378; so perhaps translate "the preceding reign".

[4]A ref. to Scipio Africanus' training programme at Carthago Nova, 209 BC, cf. Polyb. 10.20, Livy 26.51.3 ff. The First Punic War lasted 264–241 BC, the Second 218–201 BC.

[5]Cf. refs. to expenses of the army at II.1, II.3, II.18, III.3. See also Introduction §1 fin., and I.2, II.1–3, III.1, III.10, obliquely referring to over-reliance on barbarians, as cavalry, *auxilia palatina,* and as irregulars.

Book II

Preface.

It is demonstrated by continual victories and triumphs that Your Clemency abides by our ancestors' precepts for the armed forces to the full, and with very great expertise, if indeed the outcome of events is an undoubted proof of one's ability. But Your Tranquillity, Invincible Emperor, with loftier counsel than an earthly mind could have conceived, requires ancient examples from books, whilst surpassing antiquity itself by fresh deeds. Therefore when I was commanded to collect this material in a written epitome for Your Majesty not so much to learn as to recollect, devotion to the truth often contended with embarrassment. For what could be more audacious than to address some statement about the practice and science of warfare to the Lord and Emperor of the human race, the Conqueror of all barbarian races, unless of course he had ordered to be done what he had done himself?[1] Then again, not to obey the commands of so great an Emperor seemed full of sacrilege and danger.

So, in a wonderful way, I was rendered bold in obeying, by fearing to appear still more bold by refusing. The previous indulgence of Your Eternity encouraged me to this act of temerity. For I offered earlier in all humility a booklet on the levying and training of recruits,[2] and yet escaped without blame. Nor am I afraid under orders to tackle a work which, when it was voluntary, came off with impunity.

(The armed services, ch. 1–3)

1. Into how many categories military science is divided.[3]

Military science, as the most excellent of Latin authors bears witness in the opening of his poem, consists of "arms and men".[4] These are divided into three parts, cavalry, infantry and navy. The cavalry squadrons[5] were so called because they covered the battle-line on each

---

[1] The titles were applied to several fourth- and fifth-century Emperors, cf. A. Chastagnol in A. Donati (ed.), *La Terza Età dell' Epigrafia*, Atti del Convegno, Univ. di Bologna, ottobre 1986 (Faenza 1988) 24–25.

[2] preserved as Book I.

[3] A traditional subject in the *tactici*, defining the terms in which the science is organized; cf. Arr. *Tact*. 2 ff.

[4] alluding to Verg. *Aen*. I.1: *arma virumque cano*. "Arms and a man I sing..."

[5] *alae*, "wings" = squadrons.

side like wings;[1] they are now called "vexillations"[2] after the flag,[3] for they use flags, that is flame-coloured ensigns.[4] There is also another type of cavalry, called "legionary" because they were joined to the legion; "greaved" cavalry were established on their model.[5] There are likewise two sorts of navy, one of warships,[6] the other of river patrol-boats.[7] Plains are held by the cavalry, seas and rivers by the navy, hills, cities, flat and broken country by the infantry. From this it is clear that infantry are more vital to the State, as they can be useful everywhere; also a greater number of soldiers is maintained at less cost and expense.[8]

The army[9] received its name from the actual fact and action of exercise, so that it was never permitted to forget what it was called.[10] The infantry itself was divided into two parts, namely into auxiliary units[11] and legions. The *auxilia* were supplied by the Allies[12] and "federated peoples";[13] whereas Roman manpower mainly predominated

---

[1]Cf. Cincius apud A. Gell. 16.4.6: *alae dictae exercitus equitum ordines, quod circum legiones dextra sinistraque tamquam alae in avium corporibus locabantur.* "The lines of cavalry of an army were called 'wings', because they were stationed about the legions on the right and left-hand sides just as wings on the bodies of birds."

[2]*vexillationes.*

[3]*velum,* i.e. *vexillum.*

[4]*flammulae,* see III. 5. Cf. Amm. 20.6.3: *et matutinae lucis exordio, signo per flammeum erecto vexillum, circumvaditur civitas...* "and at first light, as the signal of the flame-coloured ensign was hoisted, the city was surrounded." Cf. Leo *Tact.* 5.4, 6.2.

[5]*ocreati equites.* They may be identical to Procopius' mounted archers wearing cuirasses and greaves, cf. Procop. *Bell.* 1.1.8–16. Cf. also Arr. *Tact.* 4.8 who may allude to their ancestor. V. seems to imply that *ocreati equites* were created after the abolition of legionary cavalry, i.e., in the early fourth century AD. Cf. Grosse, 17, 36, 49.

[6]*liburnae.*

[7]*lusoriae.*

[8]V. is often accused of reacting against the late-Imperial rise of cavalry, but in fact regular cavalry units only made up one-third of the number of units listed for instance in the eastern *Notitia Dignitatum,* cf. Hoffmann I.193 ff., Liebeschuetz 33. When V. talks of the need for infantry, he means Roman legionary infantry, as opposed to barbarian *auxilia* or *vexillationes.* He may have regarded both the latter as little better than the barbarian mercenaries who also cost more (cf. I.28 fin.).

[9]*exercitus.*

[10]Cf. Varro *de ling. lat.* 5.87: *exercitus, quod exercitando fit melior.* "'Army' (*exercitus*), because it is made better by means of 'exercise'."

[11]*auxilia.*

[12]*socii* (Latin, Italic and other allies).

[13]*foederatae gentes,* i.e. *civitates foederatae.*

in the ranks of the legions.[1] The legion was named after "selecting",[2] because their appellation requires the good faith and conscientiousness of persons approving soldiers. In the *auxilia* a smaller number, in the legions a far greater number of soldiers was usually enrolled.[3]

2. The difference between legions and *auxilia*.[4]

The Macedonians, Greeks and Dardanians[5] had phalanxes, such that in one phalanx 8,000 soldiers were counted. The Gauls, Celtiberians, and many other barbarian nations used hordes[6] in battle, in which there were 6,000 soldiers. The Romans had legions, in each of which there traditionally were 6,000 servicemen, sometimes more.[7] I shall explain what the difference is between legions and *auxilia*. When auxiliaries are taken on campaign, coming as they do from diverse stations and diverse units, they have nothing in common with one another either in training, in acquaintance, or morale. Their methods differ, the use of arms is different among them. Further, those who disagree before they fight must achieve victory more slowly. For instance, although it is of great importance on campaign that all soldiers wheel at the bidding of a single command,[8] those who were not together before cannot carry out their orders evenly. But these same units are of no little assistance if they are hardened by the various customary exercises almost daily. For *auxilia* were always joined to the (old) legions in battle as light

---

[1] In the middle Republic there were legions of *socii* and Latins, as well as those of Roman citizens; cf. Livy 37.39.7.

[2] *eligendum*. Cf. Varro *de ling. lat.* 5.87: *legio, quod leguntur milites in delectu*, cf. ibid. 6.66. "'Legion', because soldiers are 'selected' in the 'selection'-process."

[3] Referring to the smaller size of auxiliary as compared to legionary units. The rubric to ch. 2 has perhaps become displaced and should rather go before *Quid autem inter... expediam*—"I shall explain...".

[4] *Auxilia* for V.'s generation meant élite barbarian light regiments of *auxilia palatina*, cf. Hoffmann, I.72. V. blames them for part of the disparateness of the modern field army. But V.'s source was referring to the old auxiliary units which assisted the old legions in a more subordinate rôle. V. surreptitiously uses criticisms of the old to attack the new *auxilia*.

[5] The Dardanians were a warlike people of the central Balkans, N. of Macedonia, in what is now the plain of Kosovo. Subdued by the Macedonians in 335 BC and by the Romans in the first century BC, they proved difficult to control in practice, but were a fruitful source of army recruits to both empires.

[6] *catervae*.

[7] Cf. Isid. *Etym.* 9.3.46: *proprie autem Macedonum phalanx, Gallorum caterva, nostra legio dicitur*. "Properly speaking, 'phalanx' is said of the Macedonian, 'horde' (*caterva*) of the Gallic, and 'legion' of our own unit."

[8] Cf. Jos. *Bell. Iud.* 3.88, 105.

armament, so that they were used more as an aid to fighting than the main reserve force.[1] But when the legion is fully complemented with its own cohorts, when it has the heavy armament, that is *principes, hastati, triarii,*[2] *antesignani,*[3] and also the light armament, that is *ferentarii,*[4] *sagittarii,*[5] *funditores,*[6] *ballistarii,*[7] when it has its own legionary cavalry incorporated in it and on the same rolls,[8] when it acts with one mind and equal commitment to fortify a camp, draw up a line, do battle, complete in every part and needing no external additions,—it usually defeats any numbers of the enemy.[9] Proof of this is the great size of the Roman State, which always fought with legions and conquered as many enemies as either it wished or the nature of the world permitted.[10]

3. What caused the legions to become depleted.

The name "legion" survives in the army even today, but its strength of former times has been broken by neglect, since corruption usurped the rewards of valour and soldiers were promoted through influence when they used to be promoted for actual work.[11] Secondly, when ordinary soldiers had completed their years of service and were duly discharged with testimonials, others were not substituted. Also, inevitably some are

---

[1]*subsidium.* The *auxilia palatina* appear to have had just such a rôle, cf. Amm. 16.12.45 (Batavi and Reges, paired *auxilia palatina*), 24.6.9 (perhaps the same pair), 25.6.2–3 (Jovii and Victores), 31.13.9: *Batavos in subsidiis locatos,* "the Batavians placed in reserves." The proper *subsidium* to which V. refers belonged to the *triarii,* cf. Varro *de ling. lat.* 5.89: *Pilani triarii quoque dicti, quod in acie tertio ordine extremi subsidio deponebantur; quod hi subsidebant ab eo subsidium dictum, a quo Plautus: "Agite nunc, subsidite omnes quasi solent triarii".* "The *pilani* were also called *triarii,* because they were placed in the third line in reserve, last in the battle-array. Because they 'sat down' (*subsidebant*), the word 'reserve' (*subsidium*) was derived from it; hence Plautus: 'Come now, sit down all as the *triarii* do'."

[2]Cf. I.20.

[3]Cf. II.7, II.16, where they are considered akin to standard-bearers, drillmasters, NCOs.

[4]"light troops", cf. I.20.

[5]"archers", cf. I.15.

[6]"slingers", cf. I.16.

[7]"catapultiers and crossbowmen", cf. II.15 fin., III.14.

[8]Cf. I.20, II.15–17, III.14. This legion with its own light-armed derives from Cato's lost *de Re Militari,* but V. is unreliable on details and habitually updates some of the weaponry.

[9]V. implies that the late-Roman field army, which was a hotch-potch of different types of forces, was weakened by its composition; he is also criticizing the separate existence of (mainly barbarian) light infantry and cavalry units.

[10]Cf. Jos. *Bell. Iud.* 3.107, Flor. 1.34, 19.1, 5.

[11]Cf. Sall. *Cat.* 52.22: *omnia virtutis praemia ambitio possidet,* "corruption takes all the rewards due to bravery." Cf. Amm. 20.5.7, Zos. 4.27.1–3.

weakened by disease and are discharged, others desert or die for various reasons;[1] an army becomes depleted, however numerous, unless every year, or rather virtually every month, a host of recruits succeeds to the places of those who have left. There is also another reason why the legions have become attenuated: the labour of serving in them is great, the arms are heavier, the duties[2] more frequent, the discipline more severe. To avoid this many flock to the *auxilia*[3] to take the oaths of service, where the sweat is less and the rewards come sooner.[4]

Cato the Elder, since he was unbeaten in war and as consul had often led armies, thought he would be of further service to the State if he wrote down the military science. For brave deeds belong to a single age; what is written for the benefit of the State is eternal.[5] Several others did the same, particularly Frontinus, who was highly esteemed by the deified Trajan for his efforts in this field.[6] These men's recommendations, their precepts, I shall summarize as strictly and faithfully as I am able.[7] For although both a carefully and a neglectfully

---

[1] Cf. Aem. Macer *de Re Mil.* II apud *Dig.* 49.16.13 §3. *Missionum generales causae sunt tres: honesta causaria ignominiosa. Honesta est, quae tempore militiae impleto datur: causaria, cum quis vitio animi vel corporis minus idoneus militiae renuntiatur; ignominiosa causa est, cum quis propter delictum sacramento solvitur* "There are three general reasons for discharge: honourable, causal and ignominious. The honourable is that which is granted on the completion of the period of military service. The causal is when one is declared unfit for military service because of some fault of mind or body. The ignominious reason is when one is released from the oath of service because of some crime." By a law of Constantine, soldiers in the field armies and the riparian legions were permitted *honesta missio* after a minimum of 20 years' service, but not the full privileges of veterans—*emerita missio*—for which 24 years was the minimum; cf. Jones, 635.

[2] *munera*, fatigues, services to officers.

[3] i.e., *auxilia palatina.*

[4] A comment on a failure to maintain the paper strength of the late-Roman legions, small as they were, rather than on reductions in paper strength from the 6,000-strong old legion. The same problem of unattractive conditions leading to vacancies is tackled by the Anon. *de rebus bellicis* 5. On the lighter service of the *auxilia palatina,* cf. Amm. 18.2.6: *auxiliarii milites semper munia spernentes huiusmodi ad obsequendi sedulitatem Iuliani blanditiis deflexi...* "the auxiliary soldiers, who always refuse labours of this kind, were persuaded to complete obedience by the blandishments of Julian..." with Hoffmann, I.72. Note V.'s unmarked transition to modern *auxilia.*

[5] Cf. Sall. *Cat.* 3.1. V. goes beyond Sallust's argument that writing is as good as doing.

[6] Sex. Julius Frontinus was *consul ter ordinarius* in AD 100 with Trajan. But his *Stratagems* were written under Domitian. Possibly V. wished to hint that his own relations with his Emperor had parallels with those between Frontinus and Trajan. See I.8 note above on Theodosius–Trajan.

[7] Cf. I.8 for the source-notice to book I. This source-notice to book II seems to do duty for II–IV, which were all published to commission to complement book I which was not. The other sources to book I are subsumed under *alii conplures* here, so that the sources in general are the same for all books.

ordered army cost the same expense, it is to the benefit of not only the present but of future generations also if, thanks to Your Majesty's provision, August Emperor, both the very strongest disposition of arms be restored and the neglect of your predecessors amended.

(The formation and structure of the Ancient Legion, ch. 4–14)

4. How many legions the ancient generals led to war.

In all the authorities it is found that individual consuls led against the most numerous hostile forces no more than two legions each, with *auxilia* of the Allies added.[1] So great was their training, such their confidence, that two legions were deemed sufficient for any war.[2] Accordingly I shall explain the organization of the ancient legion following the guidance of military law.[3] If this description seems rather obscure or incomplete, it is proper to blame not myself but the difficulty of the actual subject. Therefore the details should be read repeatedly with an attentive mind so that with memory and intelligence they may be understood. For the State must inevitably be invincible, whose Emperor, having learned the military art, may make as many armies as he wishes fit for war.

5. How the legion is formed.

So when recruits have been carefully selected who excel in mind and body, and after daily training for four or more months,[4] a legion is formed by order and auspices of the invincible Emperor. The soldiers are marked with tattoos in the skin which will last and swear an oath, when they are enlisted on the rolls. That is why (the oaths) are called

---

[1] *socii* (Latin, Italic and other allies).

[2] Cf. Polyb. 3.107.10–15, 6.19–20, Livy 22.36.2–4. The Romans first fielded more than four legions (eight) at Cannae 216 BC.

[3] *Ius militare* is defined by Isid. *Etym.* 5.7.1–2 as rules of conduct of war in the widest sense, including both international relations, army discipline in the field, and the differentiation of pay, rank and rewards. But here it may simply allude to material derived from the jurist P. Taruttienus Paternus, "a most zealous champion of military law", cf. I.8.

[4] Cf. R.W. Davies, "Joining the Roman army", *Service in the Roman Army*, ch.1, 3–30. He saw *probatio* as followed by the recruit's arrival at his unit with a letter from the provincial governor and a *viaticum,* followed in turn by four months' training and tests of proficiency before *signatio* and formal oath-taking and passing-out parade as a fully qualified and trained soldier (p.26); however he was building on V. Cf. I.8.

the "sacraments" of military service.[1] They swear by God, Christ and the Holy Spirit, and by the Majesty of the Emperor which second to God is to be loved and worshipped by the human race. For since the Emperor has received the name of the "August",[2] faithful devotion should be given, unceasing homage paid him as if to a present and corporeal deity. For it is God whom a private citizen or a soldier serves, when he faithfully loves him who reigns by God's authority. The soldiers swear that they will strenuously do all that the Emperor may command, will never desert the service, nor refuse to die for the Roman State.[3]

6. How many cohorts there are in a legion, and how many soldiers in a cohort.

Note that in a legion there ought to be ten cohorts. But the First cohort exceeds the remainder in the number of soldiers and in rank, for it seeks out the most select men as regards birth and instruction in letters. It protects the eagle, which was always the especial and distinctive sign in the Roman army of a whole legion. It undertakes the worship of the images of the Emperors, that is the divine and propitious *signa*.[4] It has 1,105 infantry, 132 cavalry cuirassiers, and is called a milliary cohort. This is the head of the legion; from it when there is to be a battle the First line begins being drawn up. The Second cohort has 555 infantry,

---

[1]*sacramenta.* Cf. F.J. Dölger, *Antike und Christentum* II (1930) 268–280. The whole process of oath-swearing, tattooing and enrollment was part of a religious dedication. V. thinks of it as something akin to Christian rites such as Ash Wednesday or Baptism, in which the candidates are marked (with the sign of the Cross). The contemporary word for this was *signo, consigno*, cf. M. Bonnet, *Le Latin de Grégoire de Tours* (Paris 1890) 240.

[2]*Augustus.*

[3]V. probably serves the Christian theocratic State enforced by Theodosius I in seeking to justify swearing by God and the Emperor, instead of traditionally by the Emperor alone, and to persuade people who were in any case loyal to the Emperor that they were really loyal to God. The original pagan oath was first administered to the expanded army of 216 BC, cf. Livy 22.38.1–5. But V.'s appears to be the late-Roman form, cf. hints in Zos. 4.26.1, 4.33.3, Amm. 21.5.10, 16.10.40, *Nov. Th.* II 7.1 (439). It does not follow the pattern of oaths sworn to uphold the *salus* of the pagan Emperors and their families, cf. T. Mommsen, *Römisches Staatsrecht* (Leipzig 1887³) I.622 ff., II.792.

[4]effigies on standards; also = standards themselves. V.'s reliable information on the First cohort ends here. Cf. Ps.-Hyginus 3. The plan of Inchtuthil shows that it had 10 normal-sized centuries and only 5 centurions, the *primus pilus* thus commanding a double century, and the other 4 *primi ordines* commanding double centuries, cf. L.F. Pitts, J.K. St. Joseph, *Inchtuthil: the Roman legionary fortress excavations, 1952–65, Britannia* monograph series VI (London 1985) 164–169. The *pilus posterior* was apparently removed from the First cohort before extant records begin.

66 cavalry, and is called a quingenary cohort. The Third cohort similarly has 555 infantry, 66 cavalry, but it is customary to approve stronger men for this Third cohort because it stands in the centre of the line. The Fourth cohort has 555 infantry, 66 cavalry. The Fifth cohort has 555 infantry, 66 cavalry, but the Fifth cohort also needs strong soldiers because like the First on the right the Fifth is placed on the left wing. These five cohorts are drawn up in the First line. The Sixth cohort has 555 infantry, 66 cavalry; to it, too, recruits of proven ability should be assigned because the Sixth cohort stands in the Second line behind the eagle and images. The Seventh cohort has 555 infantry, 66 cavalry. The Eighth cohort has 555 infantry, 66 cavalry, but it too needs brave men because it stands in the centre of the Second line. The Ninth cohort has 555 infantry, 66 cavalry. The Tenth cohort has 555 infantry, 66 cavalry; it also is accustomed to take good warriors because it holds the left wing in the Second line. With these ten cohorts the full legion is formed, having 6,100 infantry, 726 cavalry.[1] Therefore there should not be a smaller number of soldiers in a legion; but sometimes a greater number is customary if it shall have been ordered to receive more than one milliary cohort.[2]

7. The titles and grades of officers of the legion.
Having set out the ancient battle-order of the legion, I shall list the titles and ranks of *principales milites* or, to use the proper term, *principia*, according to present-day rolls.[3] The greater tribune is appointed by

---

[1]So the "vulgate", which gives the correct sum of cavalry; the best MSS offer 730 or 736. The sums are artificially conceived from the basic assumption of (100 *contubernales* x 5 *centuriae* =) 500 *contubernales* + (10 *decani* x 5 *centuriae* =) 50 *decani* + 5 *centuriones* = 555 infantry and (32 *turmales* x 2 *turmae* =) 64 *turmales* + 2 *decuriones* = 66 cavalry for cohorts II–X, doubled for cohort I.

[2]V. conceives the legion as made up of combinations of milliary and quingenary cohorts, when the terms otherwise refer exclusively to auxiliary units of the Principate. His presupposition may be determined by late-Roman unit-sizes. The standard hypothesis of the size of the "new legion" created by Diocletian (?) is 1,000 men, cf. E. Ritterling, *RE* XII (1950) 1350, Hoffmann, I.4, 215.

[3]V. confuses *principia* with *principales:* whereas the latter properly means "under-officers", the former means "officers" in general, cf. Amm. 22.3.2: *praesentibus Iovianorum Herculianorumque principiis et tribunis,* "in the presence of the *principia* and tribunes of the Jovians and the Herculiani", 25.5.1: *collecti duces exercitus advocatisque legionum principiis et turmarum super creando principe consultabant,* "the assembled generals of the army summoned the *principia* of the legions and cavalry troops and consulted about creating a new Emperor". 28.6.17: *numerorum principiis,* "the *principia* of the units", 15.5.16: *principiorum vertices*—"top brass" or senior army officers under Silvanus *magister peditum* in Gaul AD 355. V. appears to list such officers of the "ancient

sacred letter on the Emperor's judgement. The lesser tribune arrives by actual work.[1] The tribune is named after the tribe, because he is in charge of soldiers whom Romulus originally chose by tribe.[2] *Ordinarii*[3] is the title of those who, since they are first,[4] lead the *ordines*[5] in battle. *Augustales* denotes those who were added to the *ordinarii* by Augustus. *Flaviales* also, as second *Augustales,* were added to the legions by the deified Vespasian.[6] Eagle-bearers[7] carry the eagle. Image-bearers[8] carry the images of the Emperor. *Optiones*[9] are called after "adopting",[10] because when the above officers are out of action through illness, these are accustomed to take charge of everything as their adopted substitutes.[11] Standard-bearers[12] carry the standards; they are now called

---

legion" as still survived in the modern organization, before going on to describe the obsolete officers in II.8–14. The modern list seems to be related in the order of items to the much longer list of "parts of the legion" given by Ioh. Lydus *de Mag.* I.46.

[1] i.e. in the unit. The distinction probably refers to that between the late-Roman legionary commander (*tribunus*) and his *vicarius,* who might also call himself *tribunus* with reference to function if he stood in for the tribune, although he was normally the *primicerius* of the unit. Cf. Jones, 675.

[2] Cf. Varro *de ling. lat.* 5.81: *tribuni militum, quod terni tribus tribubus Ramnium, Lucerum, Titium olim ad exercitum mittebantur.* "'Tribunes' of the soldiers, (so called) because three each were sent by the three 'tribes' of the Ramnes, Luceres and Tities to the army long ago."

[3] = centurions.

[4] *primi,* perhaps like *priores* meaning "officers".

[5] = centuries. One of V.'s home-made etymologies, probably, like the two following.

[6] On *ordinarii,* cf. J.R. Rea, "Ordinatus", *ZPE* xxxviii (1980) 217–219, J.F. Gilliam, "The ordinarii and ordinati of the Roman Army", *Mavors* II (Amsterdam 1986) 1–22; the term *ordinarius* or *ordinatus* supplanted *centurio* in the late third century. Confusingly, it could also refer to ordinary soldiers in an *ordo* or century, cf. SHA *Quadr. Tyr.* 14.2. We know that the *adiutor* counted among the officer *ordinarii* of the late-Roman army. *MAMA* 1.168: Παύλου ἀπὸ καμπιδουκτόρων ὠρδεναρίου, ibid. 1.169a: Φλάβ. Εὐάνδρος αὐγουστάλιος ἀρι[θμ]οῦ τῶν γεννεοτάτ[ω]ν Λαγκιάρις (fourth or fifth century, field-army, Laodicea Combusta); P.Monac 1. no.8.46 (sixth century): ὀρδ(ινάριος) ἀγουστάλιος Σεήνης (limitanean, stationed at Syene); BGU 369 (sixth century): φλαουιαλίῳ ἀριθμοῦ (τῶν καθοσιωμ(έ νων) Τραν]στιγριτανῶ ν (*leg. pseud.* cf. Hoffmann, I.419–420), *SB* I.4779 corrected by J.G. Keenan, "An instance of the military grade Flavialis", *BASP* x (1973) 43–46, q.v. (late-fourth century onward). *Flaviales* were named after the Constantinian dynasty, not Vespasian, cf. Keenan, loc. cit.

[7] *aquiliferi.*

[8] *imaginarii.* Otherwise always *imaginiferi,* which may be the true reading here too, supported by several MSS. Cf. R.W. Davies, "Some notes on military papyri from Dura", *BASP* v (1968) 31.

[9] centurions' deputies.

[10] *adoptandum.* Cf. Varro *de ling. lat.* 5.91, Paul. Fest. 201.23 L., for the etymology. In the late Empire they were commissary officials and paymasters, cf. Jones, 626, 667.

[11] *vicarii,* "vicars", i.e. lieutenants.

dragon-bearers.[1] *Tesserarii* announce the *tessera*[2] through the soldiers' 10-man sections.[3] The *tessera* denotes the general's order, by which the army is mobilized for some task, or for battle.[4] *Campigeni*,[5] that is, *antesignani*, are so named because it is owing to their efforts and toughness that the general type (*genus*) of drill is improved on the training-field (*campus*).[6] Surveyors[7] go on ahead and choose the site for a camp. *Beneficiarii*[8] are so called because they are promoted by the *beneficium*[9] of tribunes.[10] *Librarii*[11] are so called because they enter in books[12] the accounts pertaining to the soldiers. Trumpeters,[13] hornblowers[14] and buglers[15] normally launch the battle with the trumpet, bronze horn or bugle. *Armaturae duplares* are those who get double pay;[16] *simplares* get single pay. Quartermasters[17] measure out the places

---

[12]*signiferi.*

[1]*draconarii.* Cf. II.20. V. assumes just ten standard-bearers (= dragon-bearers), one for each dragon, the late-Roman cohort standard. There were no longer such things as centuries or century *vexilla,* described as antique in II.13.

[2]password or written orders.

[3]*contubernia,* 8-man sections in Ps.-Hyginus 1.

[4]Cf. Amm. 21.5.13; 23.2.2, Ps.-Hyginus 43, *viva tessera*; O. Douch, an archive from a limitanean unit in Egypt *c.* AD 375, has several instances of a *tesserarius,* nos. 12, 15, 30, 33, 41, 53.

[5] = *campidoctores,* arms instructors, drillmasters.

[6]*campigeni* is unattested elsewhere. The rather far-fetched etymology is probably V.'s. *Antesignanus* appears to denote a standard-bearer or senior NCO in Amm. 19.6.12: *horum campidoctoribus ut fortium factorum antesignanis... armatas statuas... locari iusserat imperator.* "The Emperor ordered armed statues to be set up in honour of their *campidoctores* as leaders of their brave deeds."

[7]*Metatores,* cf. *mensores* below.

[8]adjutants.

[9]patronage.

[10]Not only of tribunes, another of V.'s confusions. They continue to occur as staff-officers in the bureaucracies of civil governors throughout the fourth century AD: *P.Oxy.* xlix (1982) 3480, *P.Lips.* 55. *CTh* 8.4.7 (361) treats *beneficiarii* as a grade of *cohortales.* On *beneficiarii consularis* of the Principate, cf. N.B. Rankov, *Beneficiarii Consularis,* D.Phil. thesis (Oxford 1986), and on *beneficiarii* generally, cf. E. Schallmayer et al. (edd.), *Der römische Weihebezirk von Osterburken I: corpus der griechischen und lateinischen Beneficiarier-Inschriften des römischen Reiches* (Stuttgart 1990).

[11]clerks.

[12]*libri.*

[13]*tubicines.*

[14]*cornicines.*

[15]*bucinatores.*

[16]Cf. I.13, where it is the instructors who are so treated.

[17]*mensores.*

in camp according to the square footage[1] for the soldiers to pitch their tents, or else assign them billets in cities.[2] Wearers of the torque on double, and on single pay:[3] the torque of solid gold was a prize of valour, winners of which sometimes gained double pay, in addition to praise.[4] *Duplares, sesquiplares*: *duplares* got double pay, *sesquiplares* got pay-and-a-half.[5] *Candidati duplares, candidati simplares.*[6] These are the under-officers,[7] who are vested with privileges. The rest are called "service-men",[8] because they have to do services.[9]

---

[1]*podismus*

[2]The Codes make no distinction between *metatores* and *mensores*, cf. *CTh* 7.8, *DE METATIS*, ib. 7.8.4 (393), *mensorum*. *Mensores* occur as government quartermasters in *CTh* 7.8.4 (393), and *metatores* as the same in Th. II *Nov.* 25, line 24 (444), cf. *CTh* 7.8.10 (413); 7.8.16 (435). Sixth-century Byzantine sources do attempt some distinction: Ioh. Lydus *de mag.* 1.46: μήνσωρες, προμέτραι — μητάτωρες, χωρομέτραι; Mauricius *Strat* · ἀντικένσορας (*antecessores*) ἤτοι πρεπαρά τορας (*praeparatores*) — μήνσορας (1.3.33, 1.9; 2.12). Cf. Ps.-Hyginus 37, 46, and M. Lenoir (ed.), § 127.

[3]*torquati duplares, torquati simplares.*

[4]The torque was a contemporary decoration: Zos. 4.40.8, cf. 2, in which a unit of Gothic *comitatenses(?)* stationed outside Tomi *c.* AD 386 and attacked by *limitanei(?)* under Gerontius appear to have worn the *torques* as the badge of rank of their unit. Cf. Ambr. *de ob. Val.* 68.9: *torques autem insignia esse victoriae dubitari non potest, cum hi, qui in bello fortiter fecerint, torquibus honorentur.* "That the torque is the insignia of victory cannot be doubted, since those who have done bravely in war are honoured with torques." Cf. also SHA *Prob.* 5.1, perhaps reflecting the age in which it was written. Cf. also M.P. Speidel, "The Master of the Dragon Standards and the Golden Torc", *TAPhA* cxv (1985) 286–287 = *Roman Army Studies* II, 390–395. Why V. regards it as obsolete is unclear, the more so as he has it from "present-day rolls", but cf. II.3 on corruption having "usurped the rewards of valour".

[5]Late-Latin forms corresponding to *duplarius, sesquiplarius*, in use in the second and third centuries AD, themselves abbreviated forms of *duplicarius, sesquiplicarius*.

[6]*TLL* s. v. *candidati militares* (238 C) wrongly takes V.'s summary of the list as the explanation of *candidati*. There were imperial bodyguards associated with the *scholae palatinae* called *candidati*, cf. Jones, 613 n.11, Grosse, 96–97, but V's are less exalted. In the third century AD there were *candidati legionis*, who were often seconded to governors' staffs like *beneficiarii*, but lowlier, cf. *Ann.Épigr.* 1917.57. They are likely to be *beneficiarii* in waiting; hence V.'s are *principales* in waiting. They fall naturally at the bottom of any list of under-officers, and may have seemed self-explanatory to V. Cf. *optio candidatus* in M.P. Speidel, "The career of a legionary", *TAPhA* cii (1982) 209–214 = *Roman Army Studies* II, 197–202.

[7]*milites principales.* V. again seems to equate modern *principia* or "officers" with *principales.*

[8]*munifices.*

[9]*munera*, cf. II.19. Cf. *munifex* appointed *catafractarius* in the same unit, J.R. Rea, "A Cavalryman's Career, A.D. 382 (?)–401", *ZPE* lxvi (1984) 82.

8. The titles of the officers who led the ancient centuries.[1]

Ancient practice stipulated that the chief centurion[2] was promoted from the First centurion of the *principes*[3] of the legion; he was in charge of the eagle and controlled four centuries, that is, 400 soldiers, in the First line. As head of the entire legion, he received benefits and perquisites.[4]

Correspondingly, the First centurion of the *hastati*[5] led two centuries, 200 men, in the Second line; he is now called a *ducenarius*.[6] But the *princeps* of the First cohort[7] controlled a century-and-a-half, 150 men. Almost all general administration within the legion fell to him. The Second centurion of the *hastati*[8] also commanded a century-and-a-half, 150 men. The *triarius prior*[9] controlled 100 men. Thus the ten centuries of the First cohort were controlled by five centurions.[10] The ancients set up great privileges and great honour for them, to encourage the rest of the soldiers from the entire legion to strive with every effort and loyal service to gain these great rewards.

---

[1] *ordines.* In contrast to the modern officers listed in II.7 we have obsolete officers from here to the end of II.14, and then the old battle-array (II.15–17), followed by an appeal to the Emperor to restore it (II.18), and the administrative arrangements of the "ancient legion" (II.19–end), with various hopeful modern equivalents (often incorrectly) supplied.

[2] *centurio primi pili,* centurion of the *primus pilus.*

[3] *primus princeps,* i.e. *primus princeps prior,* according to traditional terminology. Cf. M.P. Speidel, "The Centurions' Titles", *Epigraphische Studien* XIII (Cologne 1983) 43–61, repr. with addendum in id., *Roman Army Studies* II, 21–39, for the correct forms, which V. misconceives.

[4] *commoda,* cf. *CJ* 12.62.1 (AD 253–268): *commoda primipilatus post administrationem deberi incipiunt, et si is, qui ea percipere debuit, prius rebus humanis eximatur, heredibus petitio salva sit.* "Perquisites of the primipilate start to fall due after the period of service, and if one who was due to receive them shall be removed first from human affairs, let the claim be safe for the heirs." According to B. Dobson in D.J. Breeze, B. Dobson, *Mavors* X (Stuttgart 1993) 183, the *commoda* included a gratuity which bestowed equestrian rank. Cf. also M.P. Speidel, *Roman Army Studies* II, 368, and cf. II.21.

[5] *primus hastatus,* i.e. *primus hastatus prior.*

[6] Probably V.'s equation, by a false etymology, *ducenarius* < *ducenti.* The *ducenarius* and *centenarius* were middle-ranking late-Roman NCOs in *vexillationes, auxilia* and *scholae,* but their functions are not clearly established, cf. Grosse, 117–118, Jones, 634. V. likens centurions to them.

[7] V. means again the First centurion of the *principes.*

[8] *secundus hastatus,* i.e. *primus hastatus posterior.* V.'s terminology presupposes no more than one cohort for the unit, when in fact he is trying to describe the structure of a ten-cohort unit.

[9] Not a traditional title of a centurion under the Principate, when *triarii* were called *pili,* and we have already met the *primus pilus,* who was not balanced by a *pilus posterior* in the First cohort; in any case V. does not make the connexion. He has omitted the *primus princeps posterior.*

[10] *ordinarii.*

There were also centurions, who looked after single centuries; these are now called *centenarii*.[1] There were "deans"[2] too, in charge of ten soldiers each; they are now called *caput contubernii*.[3] The Second cohort had five centurions, and so did the Third and Fourth, and so on to the Tenth, cohorts. In the whole legion there were 55 centurions.[4]

9. The duties of the Prefect of the legion.[5]

Ex-consuls used to be sent out to the armies as legates of the Emperor.[6] All legions and *auxilia* obeyed them in the administration of peace or the exigency of war. In their place the Illustrious Men[7] the Masters of the Soldiers[8] are, it is well-known, now substituted, controlling not merely pairs of legions, but greater numbers also. But the individual commanding officer[9] was the Prefect of the legion, who had the rank of "Count of the First class".[10] In the absence of the legate, he retained as his "vicar"[11] supreme power.[12] The tribunes, centurions and the rest of the soldiers obeyed[13] his commands. The *tessera*[14] for the night-watches

---

[1]Probably V.'s equation, by a false etymology, *centenarius* < *centum*. See note above under *ducenarius*.

[2]*decani.*

[3]"captain of 10-man section". *Decani* do not appear in our records before the fourth century AD. The *caput contubernii* may be identical with the *caput z* from Concordia cemetery, cf. Hoffmann, II.28 n.206; I.76. The title seems only temporarily to have displaced *decanus*.

[4]i.e. 55 centuries, but V. forgets that the 10 centuries of the First cohort were under 5 *ordinarii*, so that his figures add up to 50 centurions only.

[5]*praefectus legionis*. The title is not known before the second century AD; cf. B. Dobson, *Die Primipilares* (Cologne 1978) 69.

[6]i.e. as consular governors. Cf. C. Lessing, *Scriptorum historiae Augustae Lexicon* (Leipzig 1901–06) 88, s.v. "consul 5)".

[7]*inlustres viri*, the highest rank of the fourth century AD.

[8]*magistri militum.*

[9]*iudex* or "judge", a general term for provincial governor or equivalent.

[10]*comitiva ordinis primi*. See III.1 for the equation of the ancient consul with the modern *magister militum*, and the ancient *praetor* with the modern *comes rei militaris*. Here V. thinks of the *praefectus legionis* as like a *comes rei militaris*. On the *praef. leg.*, identical to the *praef. castr.*, cf. B. Dobson, loc. cit., 68–74.

[11]*vicarius*, i.e. deputy.

[12]This parallels the relation between the *tribunus* and *vicarius* = *minor tribunus* in II.7. V. does not appear to know of the *tribunus laticlavius* who ranked between the legate and the *praef. leg.* before his abolition c. AD 260. Cf. M. Christol, *Essai sur l'évolution des carrières sénatoriales dans la seconde moitié du IIIe siècle ap. J.C.* (Paris 1986) 39–44.

[13]On the late-Latin vogue for *servo* = *observo*, popular in V., cf. A. Andersson, 46.

[14]written order or password.

or the march was obtained from him.[1] If a soldier committed some crime, he was sent by a tribune for punishment on the authority of the Prefect of the legion. The arms of all soldiers, likewise the horses, uniforms and pay and rations[2] were part of his responsibility. The enforcement of discipline, and the training both of infantry and legionary cavalry were looked after daily at his command. In his person he was just, conscientious and sober, and by means of constant labours he trained the legion entrusted to him in every act of loyal and attentive service, in the knowledge that the excellence of those under him redounded to the Prefect's praise.

10. The duties of the Prefect of the camp.

There was also a Prefect of the camp,[3] who while inferior in rank was still occupied with important concerns. He was responsible for the siting of the camp and the assessment of the rampart and fosse. The soldiers' tents or huts, along with all baggage, were taken care of under his command. Moreover sick soldiers, the doctors who tended them, and payments,[4] belonged to his duties. He saw to it that there were never any shortages of wagons, pack-horses, or iron tools for sawing and felling timber, opening fosses, building a rampart or an aqueduct; likewise, of firewood, straw, battering-rams, mangonels,[5] catapults[6] and other kinds of torsion-engines. He was selected after lengthy and tested service as the most experienced of the men, to teach others correctly what he had himself done with merit.[7]

---

[1]The *praef. leg.* had a *tesserarius* on his staff, cf. M.P. Speidel, *Roman Army Studies* I (1984) 287.

[2]*annona.*

[3]The *praefectus castrorum* was a creation of Augustus, cf. Dobson, loc. cit., 68. The division of duties between this and the preceding officer is probably invention; the two are not attested simultaneously in the same legion. The duties also are perhaps invented along etymological lines. What we know of the duties of the *praef. castr./leg.* implies that he was a campaigning regimental commander, not a bureaucrat tied to the camp, cf. Dobson, 71, and Tac. *Ann.* 12.38.3, 13.39.2.

[4]*expensae*, cf. III.3.

[5]*onagri*, or stone-throwing engines.

[6]*ballistae*, or arrow-shooting machines.

[7]At III.2 the *praefectus legionis* and *tribuni* and *principia* are all responsible for the care of the sick; the *annona* is taken care of by the *praefectus legionis* in II.9, but *expensae* belong to the *praefectus castrorum* in II.10; the training of the men is the duty of the *praefectus legionis* in II.9, but teaching responsibility belongs to the *praefectus castrorum* in II.10. Also the duty to see that supplies are constantly available appears to be arbitrarily divided between the *praefectus castrorum* in II.10 and *praefectus fabrum* in II.11.

11. The duties of the Prefect of engineers.[1]
Moreover the legion has engineers, carpenters, masons, wagon-makers, blacksmiths, painters and other artificers, ready-prepared to construct buildings for a winter camp, or siege-engines, wooden towers and other devices for storming enemy cities or defending our own, to fabricate new arms, wagons and the other kinds of torsion-engines, or repair them when damaged. They used to have workshops, too, for shields, cuirasses and bows, in which arrows, missiles, helmets and arms of every type were made.[2] For the main aim was to ensure that nothing which the army was thought to require should be lacking in camp, to the extent that they even had sappers[3] who, after the fashion of the Bessi,[4] sank mines underground, and dug through the foundations of walls to emerge unexpectedly and capture hostile cities.[5] The particular officer responsible for these matters was the Prefect of engineers.[6]

12. The duties of the Tribune of soldiers.[7]
We have said that a legion has ten cohorts. But the First was a milliary cohort, into which were sent soldiers favoured by their wealth, birth, literacy, physique and strength. This was under the command of the

---

[1]*praefectus fabrorum.* V. uses the unusual form of the gen. pl. here and perhaps, according to some of the best MSS, below. This officer was an aide-de-camp, often only in an honorary capacity, in the late Republic and early Empire, so the duties assigned to him were probably an etymological interpretation. It may be argued from Paternus apud *Dig.* 50.6.7 that the *optio fabricae* and *architectus* took care of the technical side of the legion's activities and services under the Principate. See B. Dobson, "The Praefectus Fabrum in the Early Principate", in D.J. Breeze, B. Dobson, *Mavors* X (Stuttgart 1993) 218–241.

[2]Under Diocletian's reforms these services were centralized in permanent munitions factories, cf. S. James, "The *fabricae*: State arms factories of the Later Roman Empire", in *Roman Military Equipment. Military Equipment and the Identity of Roman Soldiers,* Procs. of the 4th. Roman Military Equipment Conference, ed. J.C. Coulston, BAR Int. Ser. 394 (Oxford 1988) 257–332.

[3]*cunicularii.*

[4]Cf. IV.24. The Bessi were a gold-mining tribe in Thrace, cf. Claud. *de cons. Mall. Theod.* (AD 399) 38–41; Pac. *Pan. Lat.* 2 (12).28.2; cf. Amm. 31.6.6.

[5]Ordinary *legiones palatinae* and *auxilia palatina* dug mines, cf. Amm. 24.4.13, 24.4.21–22 called *cunicularii*, Zos. 3.22.2. Perhaps V.'s *cunicularii* were the technical consultants for the operations; more likely, however, V. is enlarging upon jejune source-material off the top of his head.

[6]*praefectus fabrum.* D. Baatz, "Katapultbewaffnung und -produktion des römischen Heeres in der frühen und mittleren Kaiserzeit", *Mavors* XI (Stuttgart 1994) 127–135, at 133, argues that V. has substituted *praef. fabr.* for *praef. castr.* in his source because of the etymology.

[7]*tribunus militum.*

tribune who was outstanding in military knowledge, physical strength and honourable character. The remaining cohorts were governed by tribunes or "provosts",[1] according as the *princeps* decided.[2]

The supervision of training the soldiers was taken very seriously. Tribunes or "provosts" would order the ordinary soldiers entrusted to them to train daily under their gaze, but also encouraged them to imitate their own example, since they were themselves perfect in the art of bearing arms. It is the tribune who is praised for his conscientiousness and hard work, when a soldier goes forth immaculate in his uniform, well-protected and gleaming in his arms, and versed in the practice and system of his training.[3]

13. The centuries and ensigns[4] of infantry.

The chief standard[5] of the entire legion is the eagle, carried by the eagle-bearer.[6] Dragons are also carried into battle one for each cohort by dragon-bearers.[7] But the ancients knew that in battle once fighting commenced the ranks and lines quickly became disordered and confused. To avert this possibility they divided the cohorts into centuries and established individual ensigns for each century. The ensign was inscribed with letters indicating the century's cohort and ordinal number within it. Seeing and reading this, soldiers could not stray from their

---

[1] *praepositi*, i.e. "officers commanding".

[2] *princeps*, i.e. the senior administrative officer equated with the old First centurion of the *principes* (II.8). V.'s idea of him is anachronistic. As the chief of the bureaux of all military officials, including the *magistri militum*, *comites* and *duces*, the late-Roman *princeps* wielded great power; cf. Grosse, 120 ff. V.'s conception of tribunes resembles the major and minor types of the modern army (see II.8) rather than the laticlave/angusticlave of the Principate. The minor type appear interchangeable with *praepositi* also in *CJ* 12.42.1 (323): *ne cui liceat praepositorum vel tribunorum cohortium vel vicariorum...* R.E. Smith, "Dux, praepositus", *ZPE* xxxvi (1979) 263–278, traces the history of the term *praepositus* without always separating legionary vexillations from auxiliary. Cf. M. Christol, "L'armée des provinces pannoniennes et la pacification des révoltes maures sous Antonin le Pieux", *Ant.Afr.* xvii (1981) 133–141 on auxiliary vexillations.

[3] The training-rôle of tribunes is identical to that already given to the *praefectus legionis* in II.9. Hence the details are probably reconstructed.

[4] *vexilla*.

[5] *signum*.

[6] *aquilifer*.

[7] *draçonarii*.

comrades, whatever the confusion of battle.[1] They also detailed centurions, now called *centenarii*—very much battle-ready, clad in a cuirass,[2] wearing transverse crests on their helmets to make it easier for them to be recognized—to command individual centuries. This was so that no deviation would arise, since the soldiers in groups of a hundred followed their own ensign and the centurion who had the sign on his helmet. The centuries were themselves subdivided into 10-man sections.[3] For every ten soldiers living under one tent, there was one in charge as "dean",[4] now called "section-captain".[5] The 10-man section used to be called a "maniple"[6] because they fought in groups (*manûs*) joined together.[7]

14. The troops[8] of legionary cavalry.

As the term "century" or "maniple" is used among infantry, so the corresponding expression among cavalry is the *turma*. One troop contains 32 cavalrymen. The officer-in-charge is called a "decurion". As

---

[1]V. forgets that the average soldier could not read, as we know from numerous documents on papyri written by amanuenses and as we can see from II.19. The description of the *vexilla* is probably V.'s own reconstruction, prompted by information in his source about shield-emblems and the labelling of the shield with the owner's name and century, whose purpose (to prevent mistaken ownership or theft) V. has wrongly lumped together with that of the emblems, cf. II. 18. The existence of century standards under the Principate is uncertain, cf. W. Zwikker, "Bemerkungen zu den römischen Heeresfahnen in der älteren Kaiserzeit", *BRGK* xxvii (1937) 7–22. It seems certain that they did not exist under the Republic, cf. Varro *de ling. lat.* 5.88, Livy, 27.14.8.

[2]i.e. not bureaucrats as the few remaining centurions are likely to have been in the fourth century AD. Cf. also II.8.

[3]*contubernia.*

[4]*decanus.*

[5]*caput contubernii*, cf. II.8.

[6]*manipulus.*

[7]V. seems to regard *manipulus* as a diminutive of *manus.* Cf. Ovid *Fasti* 3.118 for the conventional identification with the "handful" of straw of the primitive standard. See also R. Maltby, *A lexicon of ancient Latin etymologies* (Leeds 1991), s.v. *manipulus.* Varro *de ling. lat.* 5.88, cf. 6.85, derived it from *manûs*—groups. For the late-antique use of *manipulus = contubernium*, cf. SHA *Pesc. Nig.* 10.5–6, of a unit of 10 or 11 *commanipulones.* For the size, cf. also Maur. *Strat.* 12. B (8) 9, 12. B (8) 6: κατὰ δεκαρχίαν ἤτοι κοντουβέρνιν "by decarchy or *contubernium.*" In Ps.-Hyginus *Castr.* 1 the tent covers only an 8-man mess.

[8]*turmae.*

110 infantrymen are controlled by one centurion under one ensign, so 32 cavalrymen are governed by one decurion under one ensign.[1]

Moreover, in the same way as a centurion is chosen for great strength and tall stature, as a man who hurls spears and javelins skilfully and strongly, has expert knowledge how to fight with the sword and rotate his shield and has learned the whole art of *armatura*,[2] is alert, sober and agile, and more ready to do the things ordered of him than speak, keeps his soldiers[3] in training, makes them practise their arms, and sees that they are well clothed and shod, and that the arms of all are burnished and bright,—in the same way the man who is to be chosen as decurion to be put in charge of a troop of cavalry, should above all be physically able to mount a horse while cuirassed and girded with all his arms in highly impressive style, to ride heroically, wield the lance[4] with skill and shoot arrows expertly, instruct his *turmales,* that is, cavalrymen placed under his charge, in all things needed for cavalry warfare, and make them frequently clean and look after their cuirasses and cataphracts, lances and helmets. The glitter of arms strikes very great fear in the enemy.[5] Who can believe a soldier warlike, when his inattention has fouled his arms with mould and rust? It is advantageous to school not just the men, but the horses too through constant training. So responsibility for the fitness and training of both men and horses devolves upon the decurion.

---

[1] There were no *decuriones* in the legion of the Principate, cf. M.P. Speidel, *Roman Army Studies* I (1984) 294, id. "The captor of Decebalus: a new inscription from Philippi", *JRS* lx (1970) 145 n.34, D. Breeze, "The organization of the legion: the First cohort and the equites legionis", *JRS* lix (1969) 50–55. The source derives from Cato, in whose day there were, cf. Polyb. 6.25.1–2, describing 10 *turmae* (30-strong) each under 3 *decuriones,* one of whom was senior commander of the *turma.* Cf. Livy 4.38.2, 22.38.3–4.

[2] special drill, cf. I.13.

[3] *contubernales.*

[4] *contus.*

[5] e.g. Gratian's court troops in 378, Amm. 31.10.10, 14. Cf. Donatus ad Verg. *Aen.* 7.626: *quoniam fulgor armorum plurimum hostibus terroris importat,* "since the shine of arms conveys very great fear to the enemy", and 8.402: *plurimum enim terrorem hostibus incutit etiam splendor armorum,* "for the glitter of arms also strikes very great fear in the enemy", with Vegetius' words here: *Plurimum enim terroris hostibus armorum splendor inportat.*

(The Ancient Legion in battle-order, ch. 15–18)

15. How the lines of the legions are drawn up.[1]
Next, the manner in which the battle-array should be drawn up for imminent battle may be demonstrated from the example of one legion. This could be extended to more if need demands.

The cavalry are stationed on the wings. The infantry line begins to be ordered from the First cohort on the right wing. It is joined by the Second cohort. The Third cohort is placed in the middle of the line. The Fourth is placed next to it. The Fifth cohort holds the left wing. Those fighting before the standards, around the standards and (otherwise) in the front line were called *principes*[2] [i.e. the centurions[3] and the other under-officers].[4] This was the heavy armament, which had helmets, cataphracts, greaves, shields, large swords called *spathae*, and other smaller swords called *semispathia*,[5] five lead-weighted darts[6] slotted inside their shields, to be thrown at the first assault, and also two javelins, one of which was larger, with a triangular iron tip 9 in. long, and a shaft of 5½ ft.; it used to be called a *pilum*, and is now known as a *spiculum*. Soldiers were particularly trained at throwing this type, because when aimed with skill and force it often transfixes shield-bearing infantry[7] and heavy cavalry cuirassiers.[8] The other was smaller, with an iron tip 5 in. long and a shaft of 3½ ft.; it was once called a *vericulum*, and is now known as a *verutum*.[9]

---

[1]Essentially the same archaic manner as at I.20, except that there the light-armed are on the wings, and as at III.14, except that there the light lines are counted separately. V. also substitutes late-antique soldiers and weapons, creating anomalies.

[2]"frontlinesmen".

[3]*ordinarii*.

[4]*principales*. The bracketed text may be a marginal gloss that has become interpolated. V. or a scholiast mistakes *principes* for *principia* or *principales*. Cf. II.7 for *principia* = *principales*.

[5]The *spatha* and *semispathium* are late-Roman weapons substituted for the *gladius* and *pugio*. Cf. Isid. *Etym.* 18.6.4–5. The *spatha* or broadsword was an auxiliary weapon in the first century AD, cf. Tac. *Ann.* 12.35.

[6]*plumbatae*, cf. I.17.

[7]*scutati pedites*.

[8]*loricati equites*.

[9]The term *vericulum* or "little spit" is not otherwise attested as a weapon. The *pilum* and *vericulum* described are likely to be only nominally archaic. The *pilum* at I.20 had a head measuring 9 in. or 1 ft., and was also triangular. The special design "so that it could not be broken off" is paralleled by Polyb. 6.23.9, whereas later designs beginning with that with one wooden pin introduced by C. Marius at Vercellae, 101 BC (Plut. *Mar.* 25.1) and

The second line was similarly armed.[1] The soldiers who took up position in it were called *hastati*.[2] In the second line, the Sixth cohort was placed on the right wing. The Seventh joined it. The Eighth cohort held the middle of the line, accompanied by the Ninth. The Tenth cohort always held the left wing in the second line.

Such were the arms in which the first line of *principes* and the second line of *hastati* are considered to have been arrayed. Behind them were the light troops[3] and light armament, whom we now call *exculcatores*[4] and *armaturae*,[5] and *scutati*[6] equipped with lead-weighted darts, swords and javelins, just as almost all soldiers seem to be armed today.[7] There were also archers armed with helmets, cataphracts and swords, in

---

ones with variable hardness of steel described by Caes. *Bell. Gall.* 1.25, Arr. *Ect.* 17 ff., App. *Celt.* 1.1, were designed to bend at the joint upon impact. However the length of V.'s heads is much smaller than sizes prescribed for the old javelins by Polyb., Dion. Hal. 5.46, Appian loc. cit. It seems unlikely that soldiers normally carried the weight of arms prescribed by V.; cf. IV.44 for a similar weight given to marines, where it seems still more inappropriate if they fought in loose order. Probably V. exaggerates to counteract the alleged tendency to discard heavy armour, cf. I.20.

[1] This and the following paragraph are here transposed, after A. Gemoll, "Exercitationes Vegetianae", *Hermes* vi (1871) 113-118. The distribution of cohorts is the same as at II.6.

[2] "spearmen".

[3] *ferentarii.*

[4] skirmishers.

[5] Here and in II.17 apparently not meaning those versed in the special drill called *armatura*, but simply "light-armed"; cf. Amm. 14.6.17: *deinde leves armaturas, post iaculatores... Exculcatores (aux. pal.* in *Not. Dig. occ.* 5.173 = 7.20 *exculcatores seniores,* 5.175 = 7.122 *exculcatores iuniores,* 5.207 *exculcatores iuniores Britanniciani*), known as σκουλκάτορες in Byzantine sources (Maur. *Strat.* 1.3.20: σκουλκάτορες οἱ κατάσκοποι λέγονται, 2.10 (11): ΠΕΡΙ ΚΑΤΑΣΚΟΠΩΝ Η ΣΚΟΥΛΚΑΤΟΡΩΝ on scouting during the battle, 4.5.1 where σκούλκα is one of the activities for which the *drungus*-formation is best suited, 7. B 13: ΠΕΡΙ ΣΚΟΥΛΚΑΣ on scouting before the battle, 7.17a.6, 9.5.), are associated with *armaturae* and *funditores* in V. *Epit.* II.15–17, and clearly resemble Ammianus' *proculcatores* in both function and word-formation (Amm. 27.10.10, where they scout out routes like *excursatores,* cf. Amm. 24.1.2, also Maur. *Strat.* 9.5.18, 4.3.9: προσκουλκεύ ειν); cf. also Theophyl. 6.9, referring the term σκούλκα to the sentries of the watch. Etymologists are inclined to believe the word is of Germanic rather than Latin origin, cf. A. Walde, J.B. Hofmann, *Lateinisches Etymologisches Wörterbuch* (1938–54³) 502, s.v. *sculca,* A. Ernout, A. Meillet, rev. edn. J. André, *Dictionnaire Étymologique de la langue latine* (1979⁴) 606, s.v. *sculca.*

[6] shield-bearing (light) infantry.

[7] Cf. Procop. *Bell.* 1.1.8–16. where we learn of early Byzantine mounted archers equipped with shields attached to the shoulder, without encumbering the hand, cf. Scutarii Sagittarii, *scholae palatinae,* archers being a light-armed category which does not usually carry a shield. There is no reason to think that such archers could only perform from horseback. V.'s *scutati* also belong to both heavy and light lines. The modern equipment does not fit the organization of the array, which implies more distinct equipment for the different rôles.

addition to bows and arrows.[1] There were slingers who fired stones from slings[2] and "sling-staves".[3] There were *tragularii*[4] who shot bolts with catapults[5] and crossbows.[6]

16. How *triarii* and centurions were armed.

Behind all the lines were posted the *triarii*,[7] armed with shields, cataphracts, helmets, greaves, broadswords,[8] *semispathia*,[9] lead-weighted darts, and a pair of javelins. They waited in reserve on bended knee, so that in the event of the front lines being defeated, the battle could be restored by them as if anew, and victory retrieved.[10] All *antesignani*[11] and standard-bearers,[12] though infantry, received small cuirasses, and (leather) helmets covered with bearskins to frighten the enemy. Centurions, however, had cataphracts, shields and iron helmets with transverse silvered crests for swifter recognition by their men.[13]

17. When battle commences the heavy armament stands like a wall.[14]

This point should be noted and maintained by every manner of means: when battle commenced, the First and Second lines stood immobile. The *triarii* also sat inactive. Meanwhile the light troops,[15] *armaturae*,

---

[1]Cf. Procop. ibid.
[2]*ad fundas* = *fundis*, cf. II.23 *ad omne genus... armorum, ...ad palum*, III.24 *ad latiores lanceas*, IV.8 *ad fundas*, IV.18 *ad maiores ballistas*, examples of late-Latin instrumental *ad.*
[3]*fustibali.*
[4]catapultiers and crossbowmen.
[5]*manuballistae.*
[6]*arcuballistae. Tragularii* were probably archaic; V. is the sole source for these specialists, but cf. Livy 24.42.2: *Cn. Scipionis femur tragula confixum erat* (214 BC). "Cn. Scipio's thigh had been pierced by a *tragula.*" *Manuballistae* and *arcuballistae* were characteristic late-Roman weapons (cf. IV.22). V. simply updates a manipular legionary array derived from Cato *de Re Militari.*
[7]"thirdlinesmen".
[8]*gladii* = *spathae.*
[9]short swords or daggers.
[10]Polyb. 6.23.16 and Livy 8.8.10 arm *triarii* with the *hasta* or thrusting spear, but V. assimilates their arms to his plan for the *principes* and *hastati.*
[11] = *campidoctores*, cf. II.7, or simply infantry NCOs, cf. II.2.
[12]*signiferi.*
[13]Cf. II.13.
[14]Cf. the Homeric tactic, *Il.* 4.299. Cf. also I.20.
[15]*ferentarii.*

exculcatores, archers, and slingers, that is, the light armament,[1] provoked the opposition, going in front of the line. If they managed to put the enemy to flight, they pursued. If they came under pressure from the other side's resolve or numbers, they returned to their own men and took up position behind them.[2]

Then the heavy armament[3] took up the battle, and stood so to speak like a wall of iron, fighting it out with javelins and at close quarters with swords. Even if they routed the enemy, the heavy armament did not pursue, lest they disturb their own line and battle-order, and the enemy charge back on them while dispersed and overwhelm them when disordered, but the light armament, with slingers, archers, and cavalry, pursued the fleeing foe. By adopting this disposition and these precautions, the legion would win without incurring danger, or if overcome was preserved intact. For the rule of the legion is neither to flee nor pursue easily.

18. The names and ranks of soldiers are to be written on the face of their shields.

To prevent soldiers straying from their comrades at any time in the confusion of battle, they painted different signs for different cohorts on their shields, *digmata*[4] as they call them themselves, and it is customary to do this even now.[5] Also the name of each soldier was inscribed in letters on the face of his shield, with a note of which cohort or century he was from.[6]

It is clear from the above, then, that a well-trained legion was like a very well-fortified city, which carried all that was essential for battle

---

[1] *levis armatura.* Cf. II.15.
[2] Cf. Onas. 19.
[3] *gravis armatura.*
[4] Greek for "designs".
[5] On the designs in the *Notitia Dignitatum*, cf. R. Grigg, "Inconsistency and Lassitude: the shield emblems of the *Notitia Dignitatum*", *JRS* lxxiii (1983) 132–142, M.P. Speidel, "The Army at Aquileia, the Moesiaci Legion, and the Shield Emblems in the *Notitia Dignitatum*", *SJ* xlv (1990) 68–82, = *Roman Army Studies* II, 414–418.
[6] Cf. Cass. Dio 67.10.1 on the introduction of the custom of inscribing the soldier's name and the name of his centurion on the shield in *c.* AD 89 by Tettius Julianus, cos. 83. V. customarily fails to distinguish between cohorts and centuries, probably because there was no distinction observed by the small legions of his day.

around with it everywhere, and feared no sudden hostile assault:[1] even in the midst of plains it would fortify itself upon an instant with fosse and rampart; it contained within itself all types of soldier and arms. If anyone, therefore, desires the defeat of the barbarians in an open battle, let him seek in all his prayers, that by the will of God and the Invincible Emperor's policies, the legions may be reinstated with new recruits. Within a brief space of time, recruits carefully selected and trained every day, not just in the morning but even in the afternoon, in every skill of arms and art of warfare, will easily match those soldiers of old who conquered the entire terrestrial sphere. Let it not be a problem that customs which were thriving have long since changed. Your Eternity's good fortune and foresight are such as both to devise innovations for the safety of the State, and to restore ancient principles. Every work appears difficult before you attempt it, but if trained and careful men are put in charge of the levy, a company fit for war can soon be assembled and thoroughly drilled. Skills can achieve anything you wish, if adequate funding is not spared.[2]

(The administration of the Ancient Legion, ch. 19–25)

19. As well as physical strength, skills in short-hand writing and computation are required of recruits.

Since there are several administrative departments[3] in the legions which require literate soldiers, it is advisable that those approving recruits should test for tall stature, physical strength and alertness in everyone indeed, but in some the knowledge of "symbols"[4] and expertise in calculation and reckoning is selected. For the administration of the entire legion, including special services,[5] military services,[6] and money,

---

[1] The image of a city on the move is influenced by the wagon-city or *carrago* of the Goths, Huns and Alans in the late-fourth century AD. At III.10 fin. V. recommends imitation of the *carrago*.

[2] In this epilogue to the "ancient legion" in battle-order V. commends it as a model of self-sufficiency, training and tactical flexibility, in implied contrast to the contemporary field armies. The model is conceived by V. in terms of a late-Roman field army as it could become, not as an essay in antiquarian reconstruction.

[3] *scholae* = *officia* or *scrinia*, i.e. offices.

[4] *notae*, short-hand writing.

[5] *obsequia. Limitanei* might be lent on secondment to the staff of ducal commanders as serjeants and orderlies; typical duties involved acting as messenger, porter, and prison warder. *Comitatenses* might be seconded to the staff of *magistri militum*. Cf. Jones, 597–598.

is recorded daily in the Acts with one might say greater exactitude than records of military and civil taxation are noted down in official files.[1]

Daily even in peacetime, soldiers take it in turns from all centuries and 10-man sections[2] to do night-watch duties,[3] sentry duty,[4] and outpost-duties.[5] The names of those who have done their turn are entered in lists so that no one is unjustly overburdened or given exemption. When anyone receives leave of absence[6] and for how many days, it is noted down in lists. For in antiquity it was difficult to be given leave unless for very good approved reasons. Established soldiers were not seconded to any special services at all, nor were they employed for private business. It seemed incongruous that a soldier of the Emperor, maintained in uniform and pay and rations[7] at public expense, should have time to serve private interests.[8] Instead, soldiers

---

[6]*munera*, ordinary officers' services, water, fodder and firewood; see below, and cf. also III.8.

[1]G.R. Watson, "Documentation in the Roman Army", *ANRW* II.1 (1974) 493–507, R.O. Fink, *Roman Military Records on Papyrus* (Cleveland, Ohio, 1971) A.K. Bowman, J.D. Thomas, *The Vindolanda Writing-Tablets*, Tabulae Vindolandenses II (London 1994); cf. SHA *Alex. Sev.* 21, Rufinus *adv. Hieron.* 2.36, Isid. *Etym.* 1.24.1.

[2]*contubernia.*

[3]*vigiliae.*

[4]*excubitus.*

[5]*agrariae.*

[6]*commeatus.* The corrupt granting of leave was a standing abuse in the army of the late fourth century, cf. Jones, 633, 639, 644–645, 648–649, Grosse, 246–248. See also M.P. Speidel, "Furlough in the Roman army", *YClS* xxviii (1985) 283–293, = id., *Roman Army Studies* II (Stuttgart 1992) 330–341.

[7]*annona.*

[8]An abuse banned by Augustus but always practised; cf. Paternus apud Aem. Macer *de Re Mil.* I (*Dig.* 49.16.12 §1): *Officium regentis exercitum non tantum in danda sed etiam in observanda disciplina constitit. Paternus quoque scripsit, debere eum, qui se meminerit armato praeesse, parcissime commeatum dare, equum militarem extra provinciam duci non permittere, ad opus privatum piscatum venatum militem non mittere, nam in disciplina Augusti ita cavetur: "Etsi scio fabrilibus operibus exerceri milites non esse alienum, vereor tamen, si quicquam permisero, quod in usum meum aut tuum fiat, ne modus in ea re non adhibeatur, qui mihi sit tolerandus".* "The duty of an army general consists not only in enforcing discipline but also in observing it. Paternus also wrote that a conscientious leader of soldiers should grant leave very sparingly, should not permit a military horse to be taken outside the province, should not detail soldiers for private business, fishing or hunting, for in the Discipline of Augustus it is laid down: 'Although I am aware that it is not inappropriate for soldiers to be exercised in building operations, yet I am afraid that if I permit anything which may be done for my or your benefit, a due proportion may not be observed in that activity, which would be acceptable to me'." *CJ* 12.35.13 (AD 398) orders dismissal for soldiers caught pursuing their own or another's private interests (*vel sibi vacet vel aliena obsequia*) without permission of their commanding officer (*sine nutu principali*). Those found keeping soldiers for private purposes were fined 5lb. gold. Soldiers sent as couriers were to execute their commissions

called "extras"[1] were assigned to serve commanders,[2] tribunes and under-officers,[3]—so called because they had been added after the legion had been filled.[4] They are now called "supernumeraries".[5] However, even established soldiers would carry "bundles",[6] that is, firewood, hay, water and straw, into camp. They are called "service-men"[7] because they perform these services.[8]

---

directly and promptly or face arrest for being absent without leave. *CJ* 12.35.15 (AD 458) orders fines for soldiers caught pursuing private business and for their employers, as soldiers were supposed to be training daily (*sed propriae muniis insudare militiae... sed frequentes esse in numero suo iubeat, ut armorum quotidiano exercitio ad bella se praeparent*).

[1]*accensi.*

[2]*iudices.*

[3]*principales.*

[4]Cf. *accensi* in the Catonian battle-order at V. *Epit.* III.14, and the Servian "constitution", Livy 1.43, and Livy 8.8.10, Paul. Fest. 13.23 L. s.v. *adscripticii*, Festus 216.23 L.: *Optio qui nunc dicitur, antea appellabatur accensus. Is adiutor dabatur centurioni a tribuno militum...*, "the *optio* as he is now called was once termed *accensus*. He was given to a centurion as an assistant by the tribune of the soldiers..."; ibid. 506.26 L.: s.v. *velati, ...Cato eos ferentarios dixit, qui tela ac potiones militibus proeliantibus ministrabant,* "Cato called them *ferentarii*, who served weapons and drinks to the fighting soldiers"; Varro de *ling. lat.* 7.58: *Accensos ministratores Cato esse scribit* (Jordan p.81, Cato *de Re Mil.* fr. 8), "Cato writes that *accensi* are servants."

[5]*supernumerarii.* Attested in the late-Roman civil service in this technical sense of men performing menial service but not on the establishment of a unit, cf. Jones, 571, 585, 598; in the army other ranks in waiting were *adcrescentes.* Suet. *Claud.* 25.1: *instituit et imaginariae militiae genus, quod vocabatur supra numerum, quo absentes et titulo tenus fungerentur,* "he also instituted an imaginary type of military service, which was called 'supranumerary' and was performed titularly by absentees", describing merely honorary officer-status, offers essentially the same term in a sense apparently not exampled elsewhere. Cf. R.O. Fink, doc. 58, col. ii.12, recording a single *supranumerar[--]* belonging to a century of *legio III Cyrenaica, c.* AD 90, but his duties are obscure. At III.20 V. uses the term to denote reserve forces on the battle-field, again in a non-technical way. The term was also used in the third century AD to distinguish centurions assigned to special duties, cf. J.R. Rea, "Ordinatus", *ZPE* xxxviii (1980) 217–219.

[6]*fascicularia.*

[7]*munifices.*

[8]*munera,* cf. II.7 fin.

20. Soldiers ought to deposit half their donative "with the standards", to be kept in savings for them.[1]

It was a divinely inspired institution of the ancients to deposit "with the standards"[2] half the donative[3] which the soldiers received, and to save it there for each soldier, so it could not be spent by the troops on extravagance or the acquisition of vain things.[4] Most men, the poor especially, spend as much as they can get.

This depositing of savings is judged to be in the interest first of the troops themselves, for as they are maintained by the public remuneration,[5] half of each donative goes into increasing their personal savings.[6] Secondly, the soldier who knows that his spending money is deposited "with the standards" never thinks of deserting, has greater love for the standards, and fights for them more bravely in battle, since it is human nature to care most about things on which one's fortune is staked.

So ten money-bags,[7] that is, ten sacks, were laid down one for each cohort, and in them was stored this account. An eleventh sack was also added, into which the whole legion made a small contribution for burial expenses. If any of the soldiers died, the cost of his burial might thus be defrayed from this eleventh sack.[8] These accounts were preserved in

---

[1]On the regimental savings bank, cf. G.R. Watson, *The Roman Soldier* (London 1969) 104 ff., R.O. Fink, *Roman Military Records on Papyrus* (Cleveland, Ohio 1971) doc. 68, esp. p. 245, M.P. Speidel, "The pay of the *auxilia*", *Roman Army Studies* I (Amsterdam 1984) 83–89, J.F. Gilliam, "The *deposita* of an auxiliary soldier", *Mavors: Roman Army Researches* (Amsterdam 1986) 317–327, R.W. Davies, "A note on *lorictitis*", *BJ* clxviii (1968) 161–165. See also R. Alston, "Roman military pay from Caesar to Diocletian", *JRS* lxxxiv (1994) 113–123.

[2]*apud signa.*

[3]*donativum*, bounty distributed on imperial birthdays and accession days, which by the late-fourth century AD seems to have completely eclipsed the annual *stipendium* which was by now of nugatory value, cf. Jones, 623–624.

[4]Some soldiers got rich on the opportunities of army life, cf. Amm. 22.4.7: *ut per ambitiones otiumque opibus partis auri et lapillorum varietates discerneret scientissime, contra quam recens memoria tradidit* (speaking of the corrupt court troops of Constantius II), "so that having got rich as a result of corruption and idleness (the soldier) distinguished the varieties of gold and jewels with expert skill,—a far cry from the recent memory (of tough army life under Diocletian and Maximian)."

[5]*annona*, including food and drink, bedding and clothing, for which soldiers of the late Empire, unlike their predecessors, did not have to pay.

[6]*castrense peculium*, cf. *Dig.* 49.17, 37.6.1.15, 22; *Pauli Sent.* 3.4a.3.

[7]*folles.*

[8]Cf. Onas. 36.1–2 on the importance of proper burial arrangements.

a wicker coffer, "with the standard-bearers",[1] as they now say. For this reason, standard-bearers were chosen not just for their trustworthiness, but for being literate men too, who would know how to look after deposits and render account to each man.

21. Promotions in the legion are made in such a way that those promoted pass through all cohorts.

It was not by human counsel alone but by divine inspiration as well, in my opinion, that the Romans organized the legions. In them the ten cohorts were so arranged that they all seemed to be one body, one unity.[2] For soldiers are promoted as if in a circle through different cohorts and different administrative departments,[3] so that a man promoted from the First cohort to any grade goes to the Tenth cohort, and then comes back as his years of service increase with higher grades through the other cohorts to the First again. Therefore it is in the First cohort that the chief centurion[4] reaches this palm of honour in which he of all the legion gains unlimited privileges, after he has administered all cohorts in rotation through different departments, just as the First secretary[5] of the Praetorian Prefects' staff reaches an honoured and lucrative end to his service. In this way, through the bonds of the 10-man section,[6] the legionary cavalry honour their own cohorts even though horse are naturally inclined to be on bad terms with foot.[7] By means, therefore, of this interweaving in the legions of all cohorts and of cavalry and infantry, one harmonious spirit was preserved.[8]

---

[1] *apud signiferos.* Apparently meaningless pedantry?

[2] Cf. Thuc. 2.11.9 on the Spartan military ideal put into the mouth of Archidamas.

[3] *scholae.*

[4] *centurio primi pili.* Cf. II.8 init. for the *commoda primipilatus.*

[5] *primiscrinius.*

[6] *contubernium.* V.'s calculations do not allow for cavalry to be included among the *contubernia* at II.6 and II.8

[7] On the modern antipathy between cavalry and foot, which probably arose because they belonged to separate units, cf. Julian's demotion of a cavalry regiment to infantry rank, Amm. 24.5.10.

[8] The thought is that, unlike in the modern field armies, the infantryman promoted cavalryman normally remained a member of the same legion, and might pass through a succession of promotions within it. This was still true as late as the reign of Diocletian, cf. T. Drew-Bear, "Les voyages d'Aurélius Gaius, soldat de Dioclétien", in *La Géographie administrative et politique d'Alexandre à Mahomet,* Actes de Colloque de Strasbourg 14–16 juin 1979 (Univ. de Strasbourg, 1982) 97, 101–102. More particularly, V. may misunderstand a note that under the Principate legionary cavalry remained on the books of the century of first enrolment, as appears from surviving evidence, cf. D.J. Breeze,

22. The difference between trumpeters, hornblowers and the bugle call.[1]

The legion also has trumpeters,[2] hornblowers[3] and buglers.[4] The trumpeter calls soldiers to battle, and again sounds for a retreat. When hornblowers sound, it is not the soldiers as such but the standards that obey their signal. So when soldiers alone are due to go out to do some work, the trumpeters sound. When the standards are to be moved, the hornblowers sound. But when there is to be a battle, both trumpeters and hornblowers sound together. The *classicum* is the name for the signal sounded by the buglers on the "horn".[5] This is considered the sign of the High Command,[6] because the *classicum* is sounded when the Emperor[7] is present, or when capital punishment is being inflicted on a soldier, since this must be done according to the Emperor's laws.[8]

So when soldiers go out to perform night-watch duties and outpost duties, to do some work, or drill in the parade-ground, they start work at the call of the trumpeter, and stop again at the signal from the trumpeter. But when the standards are moved or, once moved, are to be planted, the hornblowers sound. The signals are observed in all exercises and marches, so that soldiers may obey more readily in actual battle, if ordered by the leaders to fight, stand their ground, pursue or retire. For

---

"The organization of the legion: the First cohort and the *equites legionis*", *JRS* lix (1969) 50–55. The ideal of promotion through all departments perhaps belongs to the civil service.

[1] *classicum.*

[2] *tubicines.*

[3] *cornicines.*

[4] *bucinatores.*

[5] *cornu = bucina*, i.e. bugle, but V.'s logic here is obscure.

[6] *imperium.*

[7] *imperator*, lit. Commander-in-chief, who was the Emperor.

[8] Cf. Caes. *Bell. Civ.* 3.82.1: *Pompeius... suum cum Scipione honorem partitur classicumque apud eum cani et alterum illi iubet praetorium tendi.* "Pompey divided his command with Scipio and ordered the *classicum* to be sounded at his headquarters and a second command-centre to be put up." Ps.-Hyginus 21: *Si longiora fuerint (sc. castra), classica dicentur nec bucinum in tumultu ad portam decimanam facile potuerit exaudiri.* "If the camp is too long, the *classica* will be sounded but in an uproar the bugle will not be easily able to be heard at the rear gate." The Emperor's laws will be military regulations, some of which may have been issued ad hoc as *constitutiones*. Cf. A. Neumann, "Das römische Heeresreglement", *CPh* xli (1946) 217–225, = ditto, *HZ* clxvi (1942) 554–562, but with addendum pp. 222–225, A. Neumann, "Das Augusteisch-Hadrianische Armeereglement und Vegetius", *CPh* xxxi (1936), 1–1. See also A.A. Schiller, "Sententiae Hadriani de re militari", in *Sein und Werden im Recht: Festgabe für Ulrich von Lübtow zum 70. Geburtstag am 21. August 1970* (Berlin 1970) 295–306, who argues *contra* Neumann that there may well have been no rule-book as such.

it is obviously a sound principle that they ought always to be doing in peacetime what it is deemed necessary to do in battle.[1]

23. The training of soldiers.

Now that the organization of the legion has been summarized, we return to the exercises from which, as has been said already,[2] the army took its name. Recruits and novice soldiers were trained morning and afternoon in all types of arms, but veterans and trained soldiers also exercised with their arms once a day without fail. For length of time or number of years does not transmit the art of war, but continual exercise. No matter how many years he has served, an unexercised soldier is forever a raw recruit.

Armatura,[3] which is displayed on festal days in the Circus,[4] used to be learned not just by *armaturae*[5] under the drillmaster,[6] but by all ordinary soldiers alike in daily practice. For speed is acquired through bodily exercise itself, and also the skill to strike the enemy whilst covering oneself, especially in close-quarters sword fighting. What is more, they learn how to keep ranks and follow their ensign through such complicated evolutions in the mock-battle itself. No deviation arises among trained men, however great the confusion of numbers.[7]

It is also very useful for them to exercise with the post and foils, because they learn to go for the flank, feet or head with the point and with the edge.[8] Let them grow used to executing jumps and blows at the same time, rushing at the shield with a leap and crouching down again,

---

[1] Cf. III.5.

[2] Cf. II.1.

[3] special drill, cf. I.13 note.

[4] i.e. Circus Maximus in Rome. Cf. Claud. *pan. de Hon. cons. VI* 621–640 for contemporary tournaments of the type celebrating the consular games of AD 404, and Livy 44.9.2–7 (169 BC) for the Republican tournaments in the Circus—*ludicro circensi*—put on by *iuvenes Romani*. Also under the Principate, cf. Suet. *d. Iulius* 39.3, *Claud.* 21.3, *Dom.* 4.1, both pedestrian and equestrian tournaments, and the *lusus Troiae* whose origin Vergil describes in *Aen.* 5.553–603.

[5] special light troops, trained in *armatura*; cf. Firm. Mat. *Math.* 8.6.3: *aut <qui in> dorso stans equorum mirifica se moderatione sustentet, atque adprime equo vectus militares armaturas exerceat.* "or <one who> balances himself with wonderful control standing on the backs of horses, and riding his horse best of all trains the military *armaturae*."

[6] *campidoctor*.

[7] Cf. I.13 and II.13.

[8] Despite I.11, Polyb. 18.30.7 shows that the Roman *ordinatio* had soldiers using swords for both cutting and thrusting, as here and at III.4.

now eagerly darting forward with a bound, now giving ground, jumping back.[1] Let them also practise hitting the same posts from a distance with javelins, to increase their skill at aiming and the strength of the right arm.[2]

Archers and slingers used to put up *scopae*, that is, bundles of brushwood or straw, for a target, removing themselves 600 ft. (= *c*.580 ft., 177 m.) from the target, to practise hitting it frequently with arrows, or stones aimed from a "sling-staff".[3] This enabled them to do without nerves in battle what they had always done in exercises on the training-field. They should also be accustomed to rotating the sling once only about the head, when the stone is discharged from it. All soldiers also used to practise throwing stones of 1 lb. weight by hand alone.[4] This was considered a readier method, because it does not require a sling.[5]

They were also made to throw javelins and lead-weighted darts in continual and perpetual exercises; so much so, that in winter-time they built riding-schools[6] for the cavalry and a kind of drill-hall[7] for the infantry, roofed with tiles or shingles or, failing these, thatched with reeds, sedge or straw. In them the army was trained in arms under cover, when the weather was disturbed by wind and rain.[8] But for the rest of the time, even in winter, so soon as snow and rain ceased, they were made to train on the exercise-field, so that no interruption to routine might weaken soldiers' minds and bodies.

It is advisable that they should very frequently be felling trees, carrying burdens,[9] jumping ditches,[10] swimming in the sea or rivers,[11]

---

[1]Cf. I.9. Serv. ad Verg. *Aen.* 11.284: *Quantus in clipeum adsurgat: aut "quantus" est quotiens in hostem pergens erigit scutum: aut pugnandi exsecutus est genus. Qui enim scripserunt de arte militari dicunt summum genus esse dimicandi, quotiens calcato umbone adversarii se in hostilem clipeum erigit miles et ita contra stantis vulnerat terga.* "'With what force (Aeneas) charges the shield': either *quantus* refers to when advancing against the enemy he puts up his shield; or he executed a type of combat. For those who have written on the art of war say that it is the best type of combat when a soldier steps on the boss of his adversary and raises himself on the enemy shield and from this position wounds the opponent's back."

[2]Cf. I.14.

[3]*fustibalus*, cf. III.14.

[4]1 Roman pound = 0·7219 lb. avp., or *c*.11½ oz. or 327·45 grammes, cf. I.19 note.

[5]Cf. I.15–16.

[6]*porticūs*.

[7]*basilicae*.

[8]Cf. I.18, III.2.

[9]Cf. I.19.

marching at full step or even running in their arms, with their packs on.[1]
The habit of daily labour in peace may not then seem arduous in war.
Whether they be legion or *auxilia*, let them be training constantly. As
a well-drilled soldier looks forward to battle, so an untrained one fears
it. Finally, note that technical skill is more useful in battle than strength.
If training in arms ceases, there is no difference between a soldier and
a civilian.

24. Examples to encourage military exercises, drawn from other arts.

Athletes, show-hunters and charioteers are accustomed to maintain and
improve their skills by daily practice for paltry profit or at least to gain
the favour of the populace. The soldier, by whose hands the State must
be preserved, ought to be keener in keeping up his knowledge of
fighting and practice of warfare by continual exercises. He wins not
merely a glorious victory, but even greater spoils, since the hierarchy of
the soldiers and the Emperor's judgement regularly exalt him to riches
and dignities.[2] Stage artists never stop rehearsing to win the praise of
the populace. The soldier, once he has been selected and sworn in,
ought not to stop exercising at arms whether a novice or even an old
hand. For he must fight for his own life and the liberty of all, and it is
above all the ancient and wise opinion that all arts depend on practice.

25. Catalogue of the legion's tools and machines.

The legion is accustomed to be victorious not only on account of the
number of soldiers but the type of its tools also. Above all, it is
equipped with ballista-bolts[3] which no cuirass or shield can withstand.
For each century customarily has its own carriage-ballista,[4] with mules
assigned to draw it and a section,[5] that is, eleven men, to arm and aim

---

[10]Cf. I.9.
[11]Cf. I.10.
[1]Cf. I.19, I.9, I.27.
[2]Cf. II.7 and II.8.
[3]*iacula.*
[4]*carroballista*, cf. the *ballista quadrirotis*—four-wheeled ballista—described and illustrated
by the Anon. *de Rebus Bellicis* 7, a design similar to those shown mounted on two-
wheeled mule-carts or wooden pillar-bases on Trajan's column, Cichorius Pl. XXXI, scene
xl, Pl. XLVII, scene lxvi, and also to the miniature model in (Ps.)-Heron's
Cheiroballistra, a late-Roman technical work. See further under IV.22.
[5]*contubernium.*

it.[1] The larger these machines are the farther and more violently they shoot projectiles. Not only do they defend a camp, but they are also placed on the battlefield behind the line of the heavy infantry. Faced with their attack, neither the cavalry cuirassiers nor the shield-bearing infantry of the enemy can stand their ground. In one legion there are traditionally 55 carriage-ballistas.[2] There are also ten mangonels,[3] one for each cohort. They are carried around ready-armed on ox-carts, so that should the enemy come to attack the rampart to storm it, the camp can be defended with darts and rocks.[4]

The legion also carries with it canoes[5] hollowed out of single logs, and a supply of very long ropes and sometimes iron chains too. By binding together these "single timbers",[6] as they are called, and throwing planks on top, rivers that lack bridges and cannot be forded may be crossed safely by both infantry and cavalry.[7]

The legion has grappling-irons[8] called "wolves",[9] and iron siege-hooks[10] fixed on the end of very long poles.[11] Also, for constructing earthworks, it has forks, mattocks, spades, shovels, troughs and baskets for carrying earth. There are also axe-picks, axes, adzes and saws for chopping and sawing timber and stakes.[12] It has craftsmen too, equipped with every tool, making siege-sheds, mantelets, rams, "vines",[13] as they call them, and mobile towers, for attacking enemy cities.[14] But to avoid my speaking at too great length by listing each item separately, the legion ought to carry with it everywhere all that is thought necessary to

---

[1]Cf. Maur. *Strat.* 12.B (8) 6, on the equipment (one wagon each) of each 10-man *contubernium.* Significantly, some apparently had wagons with revolving *ballistae* at each end. V.'s eleventh man is the "dean" or *decanus/caput contubernii,* cf. II.8.

[2]About the right number, according to Jos. *Bell. Iud.* 3.166, where Vespasian's three legions brought to bear 160 pieces of artillery against Jotapata in AD 67.

[3]*onagri,* "wild asses".

[4]Cf. IV.22.

[5]*scaphae.*

[6]*monoxyli,* cf. III.7.

[7]Cf. III.7.

[8]*harpagones.*

[9]*lupi.*

[10]*falces.*

[11]Cf. IV.23.

[12]Cf. I.24.

[13]*vineae,* i.e. penthouses.

[14]Cf. II.11, IV.14–17.

any kind of warfare, so that in whatever place it pitches camp, it makes an armed city.[1]

---

[1]Cf. II.18.

Book III

Preface.

The annals of old declare that the Athenians and the Spartans were masters of the world before the Macedonians. But among the Athenians throve the cultivation of other arts besides that of war, whereas the chief concern of the Spartans was war.[1] Indeed, they are credited with having been the first to collect evidence about the fortunes of battles and write an art of war; insomuch, that they reduced warfare, previously thought to be restricted to courage alone or at least luck, to a discipline and study of skills, and they instructed drillmasters, whom they called "tacticians",[2] to teach their youth the various fighting techniques.[3] O men worthy of the highest admiration and praise who wished to learn that art in particular without which the other arts cannot be![4]

Following these men's precedents the Romans maintained the principles of warfare in practice and transmitted them in writing. This material, dispersed through various authors and books, Invincible Emperor, you ordered my Mediocrity to summarize,[5] so that neither should boredom arise from excessive detail, nor complete confidence be lacking because of brevity. The extent to which military science was of benefit in the battles of the Spartans is made clear from the case of Xanthippus, not to mention the rest. When he brought help as an individual to the Carthaginians not by courage but by skill, using armies that had been utterly defeated, he captured and conquered Atilius Regulus and an often victorious Roman army. By triumphing in a single

---

[1] On the Spartans being interested in nothing more than improving their skills at war, cf. Plato *Laches* 182e–183b. On superiority of Spartan tactical training, Xen. *Const. Laced.* 11.510. On Spartan training, Arist. *Pol.* 8.4, 1338b.

[2] *tactici.*

[3] Cf. E.L. Wheeler, "The hoplomachoi and Vegetius' Spartan drillmasters", *Chiron* xiii (1983) 1–20. The identity of these *tactici* is unknown, unless the Arcadian (?) Aeneas Tacticus, by far the most significant early tactical writer, is meant.

[4] Ael. *Tact.* 1.7 quotes Plato *Leges* 625e–626b for the same in praise of Cretan lawgivers, there being by nature "undeclared war between all cities". Cf. also III.10 init.

[5] Cf. Amm. 23.4.1: *quantum mediocre potest ingenium*, "as far as a modest mind is able."

encounter, he concluded the entire campaign.[1] So also did Hannibal obtain the services of a Spartan tactician, when he was going to invade Italy. It was due to his advice that he destroyed so many consuls and legions, though inferior himself in numbers and strength.[2]

Therefore, he who desires peace, let him prepare for war.[3] He who wants victory, let him train soldiers diligently. He who wishes a successful outcome, let him fight with strategy, not at random. No one dares challenge or harm one who he realizes will win if he fights.[4]

(Logistics, commissariat, discipline, signals, castrametation, ch. 1–8)

1. The proper size of an army.

The First book set out the selection and training of recruits. The Second explained the formation of the legion and its military disciplines. This Third book sounds the *classicum*.[5] For the former matters were discussed first so that the present subject, which comprises the skills of engagement and the elements of victory, may preserve the order of the discipline, thus being more readily comprehensible and of greater assistance.

---

[1] A Spartan general called in as adviser by the Carthaginians after their defeat on African soil by M. Atilius Regulus, cos., in 256 BC, Xanthippus reformed the Carthaginian army and defeated and captured Regulus the following year, whereupon he left Carthaginian service; but the war was eventually won by Rome in 241 BC. Cf. App. *Lib.* 3, Cass. Dio fr. 43, 24, Polyb. 1.32 ff., Diod. Sic. 23.14 ff., Cic. *de Off.* 3.99, Florus 1.18.23: *nam conversis ad extrema auxilia hostibus, cum Xanthippum illis ducem Lacedaemon misisset, a viro militiae peritissimo vincimur.* "The enemy turned to desperate remedies, Sparta sent them Xanthippus as a general, and we were defeated by a man most expert in warfare."

[2] Identified by Wheeler, art. cit. 1, as Sosylus. The surviving fragment of his history of Hannibal shows deep historical knowledge of tactics, cf. U. Wilcken, "Ein Sosylus Fragment in der Würzburger Papyrussammlung", *Hermes* xli (1906) 141. F. Jacoby, *FGH* IIA (1930) no. 176, id., *RE* IIIA.1 (1929) 1204, seems to underestimate his status. Nepos *Hann.* 13.3 says that he taught Hannibal Greek.

[3] The most memorable phrase in all Vegetius, and the earliest expression in Latin of the classic paradox, *si vis pacem, para bellum.* "If you want peace, prepare war." W. Haase, "Si vis pacem, para bellum", in *Akten des XI. internationalen Limeskongresses* 1976 (Budapest 1977) 721–755, explains it as deterrence-theory, but the Thuc. 4.92.5 parallel suggests that it need not exclude the pre-emptive strike. Cf. also A. Otto, *Die Sprichwörter und sprichwörtlichen Redensarten der Römer* (Leipsig 1890) 54 s.v. "bellum", with refs.

[4] Cf. IV.31. Cf. also Jos. *Bell. Iud.* 3.72.

[5] bugle-call of the High Command, cf. II.22.

"Army"[1] is the name for a host of legions, *auxilia* and cavalry gathered together for the purpose of waging war.[2] Its proper size is discussed by military experts. For when one reads the examples of Xerxes,[3] Darius,[4] Mithridates[5] and other kings who armed countless populations, it is clearly apparent that over-large armies have been overcome more by their own size than the bravery of the enemy. For a greater multitude is subject to more mishaps. On marches it is always slower because of its size; a longer column often suffers ambush even by small numbers; in broken country and at river-crossings it is often caught in a trap as a result of delays caused by the baggage-train. Also it is an enormous labour to collect fodder for large numbers of animals and horses. Difficulties again with the grain-supply, to be avoided on any expedition, afflict larger armies sooner.[6] For however thoroughly rations may have been prepared, they run out more quickly, the more they are distributed to. Finally water itself sometimes hardly suffices for too large a number.[7] And if for some reason the battle-line should turn tail, more casualties must inevitably occur to more men, and those who escape, once terrified, thereafter fear battle.

[1]*exercitus.*

[2]The tripartite field army of the fourth century AD is meant, cf. Hoffmann, I.72, 397.

[3]Xerxes, king of Persia 486–465 BC, invaded Greece 480 with allegedly 1,700,000 infantry, 1,207 warships, 3,000 smaller ships and 80,000 cavalry, and obtained large additional forces en route from the Hellespont, cf. Hdt. 7.60 ff., 184 ff., but what modern historians estimate as totalling nearer 180,000 men in his army and 800 triremes, cf. J.B. Bury and R. Meiggs, *A History of Greece* (London 1975[4]) 169. They were defeated at sea at the battle of Salamis 480 and on land at the battle of Plataea 479 BC.

[4]Darius I, king of Persia 521–486 BC, father of Xerxes, sent an expedition to Greece 490, defeated on land at the battle of Marathon 490.

[5]Mithridates VI Eupator, king of Pontus, assembled a huge force against Lucullus in 73 BC but was defeated at Cyzicus by problems of supplies, exploited by his opponent; cf. App. *Mithr.* 69–78, Plut. *Lucull.* 7–13.

[6]Cf. Pac. *Pan. Lat.* 2 (12) 32.5, on Theodosius I's expedition against Maximus AD 388, notable for the unprecedented size of its barbarian contingents. According to Pacatus, they cheerfully shared out inadequate rations.

[7]Famously, Xerxes' army drank numerous rivers dry, cf. Hdt. 7.21.1, 43.1, 58.3, 108.2, 127.2, 196. Herodotus was less surprised that rivers ran dry than that grain-suppplies held out, 7.187.

But the ancients, who learned to remedy their difficulties from experience, wished to have armies that were not so much numerous as trained in arms. So for smaller wars they thought one legion with mixed *auxilia* could suffice, that is, 10,000 infantry and 2,000 cavalry; and this force was often led on campaign by praetors, like lesser generals.[1] But if the enemy's numbers were said to be large, a man of consular authority was sent with 20,000 infantry and 4,000 cavalry, like a greater "count".[2] But if a countless horde of the fiercest tribes had rebelled, then under press of extreme urgency two generals and two armies were sent, with the following instruction: "Let both consuls, jointly or severally, provide that the Republic take no harm".[3] For when the Roman People were fighting virtually every year in various regions against different enemies, supplies of troops were adequate only because they judged it more useful to have not so much large armies as more of them,—yet the principle was observed that there should never be a greater number of Allied auxiliaries in camp than Roman citizens.[4]

2. How the army's health is controlled.

Next I shall explain a subject to which special thought must be devoted—how the army's health is preserved; that is, by means of site, water-supply, season, medicine and exercise. By "site" I mean that soldiers should not camp in pestilential areas near unhealthy marshes,

---

[1] *velut minores duces*: *duces* often means limitanean area commanders ("dukes"), but here it is used non-technically, note *velut*, to denote lesser field-army generals—*comites rei militaris*. The latter could not have been called *minores comites* by V. since this technically denoted "dukes", who ranked as Counts of the Second class, cf. T. Mommsen, "Das römische Militärwesen seit Diocletian", *Hermes* xxiv (1889) 267 = id., *Gesammelte Schriften* VI (Berlin 1910) 272.

[2] A modern Field-Marshal or *magister militum* is meant, cf. also II.9. Cf. Polyb. 3.107.10–15 for the old consular armies of the Republic.

[3] The *senatus consultum de republica defendenda* or *SC "ultimum"*, allegedly used in 464 BC (Livy 3.4.9) and 384 BC (Livy 6.19.3). However, it cannot be traced reliably before 133 BC against Ti. Gracchus (Val. Max. 3.2.17, Plut. *Ti. Gracch.* 19), cf. *RE* Suppl. VI (1935) 756, and many would see its first certain use only in 121 BC by the consul L. Opimius. V. gets the formula right, cf. Cic. *Phil.* 8.14, Sall. *Cat.* 29.2, Caes. *Bell. Civ.* 1.5.3, but wrongly retrojects it into the context of Rome's foreign, rather than civil, wars. It would have been more correct to speak of the Republican dictatorship at this point. V., or a pro-senatorial source such as Frontinus, may have substituted the consular emergency powers.

[4] *sociales auxiliares*. Cf. Polyb. 6.26.7–8, 30.2.

nor in arid plains and hills, lacking tree-cover, nor without tents in summer. They should not move out too late in the day and fall sick from sunstroke and marching-fatigue, but rather start a march before dawn, reaching the destination in the heat of the day. They should not in severe winter weather march by night through snow and ice, or suffer from shortage of firewood or an inadequate supply of clothes. For a soldier who is forced to be cold is not likely to be healthy or fit for an expedition. Neither should the army use bad or marsh water, for bad drinking-water, like poison, causes disease in the drinkers. Besides, it requires constant vigilance on the part of officers[1] and tribunes and of the "count" who holds the senior command to see that ordinary soldiers who fall sick from this cause may be nursed back to health with suitable food[2] and tended by the doctors' art. It is hard for those who are fighting both a war and disease.

But military experts considered that daily exercises in arms were more conducive to soldiers' health than doctors. So they wished that the infantry be trained without cease, under cover when rainy or snowing, in the exercise-field on the rest of the days.[3] Similarly they gave orders that the cavalry should constantly train themselves and their horses not only on the flat, but also over precipitous places and on very difficult ways with gaping ditches, so that nothing unfamiliar might meet them in the stress of battle.[4] From this it is appreciated how zealously an army should always be trained in the art of war, since the habit of work may bring it both health in the camp, and victory in the field.

If a multitude of soldiers stays too long in autumn or summer in the same place, then drinking-water contaminated by pollution of the water-supply and air tainted by the foul smell itself give rise to a most deadly disease.[5] This can only be prevented by frequent changes of camp.

---

[1] *principia.*
[2] e.g. chicken, cf. IV.7.
[3] Cf. II.23.
[4] Cf. I.27. V. ought perhaps to have mentioned the indoor riding-schools again, as at II.23, cf. I.18, but his eye seems to have slipped over his source.
[5] i.e. cholera or typhoid. On the foul smell cf. Sall. *Jug.* 44.4, Onas. 9.1.

3. How much attention should be devoted to the procurement and storage of fodder and grain.

The order of subjects demands that I speak next about the provisioning-system for fodder and grain.[1] For armies are more often destroyed by starvation than battle, and hunger is more savage than the sword.[2] Secondly, other misfortunes can in time be alleviated: fodder and grain supply have no remedy in a crisis except storage in advance.[3]

On any expedition the single most effective weapon is that food should be sufficient for you while dearth should break the enemy. Therefore, before war is commenced, careful consideration should be given to supplies and their issue in order that fodder, grain and the other army provisions[4] customarily requisitioned from provincials may be exacted in good time, and quantities always more than sufficient be assembled at points well-placed for waging war and very well-fortified.[5] But if the taxes in kind be insufficient, everything (needed) should be compulsorily purchased from advance payments in gold. For there is no secure possession of wealth, unless it be maintained by defence of arms.[6]

Often an emergency is doubled and a siege becomes longer than expected,[7] when the opposition though hungry themselves do not give up besieging those whom they expect to be overcome by hunger. Also

---

[1]Cf. Jones, 626–629.

[2]Front. *Strat.* 4.7.1, cf. Caes. *Bell. Civ.* 1.72.1, Amm. 25.7.4.

[3]Cf. IV.30.

[4]*annonariae species.*

[5]e.g. the huge dépôt at Batnae, where 50 men were killed by a collapsing pile of bales of chaff, cf. Amm. 23.2.8. Provincials had to contribute a wide variety of foodstuffs and commodities as taxes in kind for delivery to government warehouses specifically to supply the army, in the system known as *annona militaris*, cf. Jones, 458–460, 626–630, etc.

[6]Cf. Amm. 17.3.1 ff. for *conquisita* or *incrementa*—special supplementary levies announced by the Praetorian Prefect Florentius, to make up what was lacking from the poll-tax and land-tax accounts. V. seems to envisage mandatory pre-payments of tax.

[7]V. unconsciously assumes that warfare will be defensive, that campaigns will be on Roman territory. This happened, for example, in AD 377 when Adrianople was besieged by Fritigern's Goths and the rich farmlands of Thrace overrun, cf. Amm. 31.6. The Romans responded by driving the marauders into the mountains, where they unsuccessfully attempted to starve them into submission or death, cf. Amm. 31.8.1, as they had the Isaurians in AD 354 and 367–368, cf. Amm. 14.2.13, 27.9.7.

all livestock, any sort of fruit and wine which the enemy invader can seize for his own sustenance should be collected into strong forts secured by armed garrisons, or into very safe cities, by landowners acting under the admonition of edicts or the compulsion of specially appointed escorts,[1] and the provincials impelled to shut themselves and their property behind fortifications before the invasion.[2] Repairs to all walls and torsion-engines should be taken in hand in advance too, for if the enemy once find you unready, everything becomes confused in panic and things needed from other cities are denied you through the roads being closed. Faithful stewardship of granaries and controlled issue usually provides for a sufficiency, especially if taken in hand from the outset. But economy comes too late to save (grain) when there is a deficiency.[3]

On arduous campaigns the ancients used to provide rations by heads of soldiers rather than by status, on the understanding that after the emergency there was restitution to these men[4] from the State.[5] In winter problems of firewood and fodder, in summer of water should be avoided. Shortages of grain, wine-vinegar, wine and salt should be prevented at all times. Therefore cities and forts should be defended by those soldiers who prove less useful in the field, equipped with arms, arrows, "sling-staves",[6] slings and stones, mangonels[7] and catapults.[8]

---

[1] *prosecutores.*

[2] Cf. measures taken in AD 359 in response to king Sapor's invasion of Mesopotamia: the compulsory movement of the population, rich and poor, into fortified strong-points, along with the stockpiling therein of supplies and collection of livestock, and the burning of the country abandoned; Amm. 18.7.3. Also cf. similar strategy against the Goths overrunning Thrace in AD 376–377, Amm. 31.81.1. The historic precedent was set by Q. Fabius Maximus (Cunctator), *dictator* in 217 BC, cf. Livy 22.11.4.

[3] Cf. IV.7.

[4] i.e., senior ranks.

[5] This step was taken by Julian's army in the middle of the Persian campaign in AD 363, cf. Amm. 25.2.1.

[6] *fustibali.*

[7] *onagri,* "wild asses".

[8] *ballistae.* V. may possibly refer to *limitanei* or frontier garrison troops, and *burgarii* or civil guard. The system of fortresses and staging-posts, themselves often doubling as cities, through which the expeditionary army would move until it reached enemy territory is described by SHA *Alex. Sev.* 45.1–3, 47.1 and Ambr. *Exp. Psalmi CXVIII* 5.2. The slingstaves are discussed at III.14, the mangonels and catapults at IV.22.

Especial care should be taken lest provincials in their unsuspecting simplicity be deceived by the treachery and perjuries of the enemy. Pretended trade and peaceful relations have more often caused harm to gullible people than arms. By this strategy the enemy if they collect together suffer famine, and if they disperse are easily beaten by frequent surprise attacks.[1]

4. Measures needed to ensure that soldiers do not mutiny.[2]

An army gathered together from different places occasionally raises a riot and, when in fact it is unwilling to fight, it pretends to be angry at not being led out to battle. This is chiefly the action of those who have lived at their home base in idleness and luxury. Taking offence at the harshness of the unaccustomed effort which it is necessary to endure on campaign, fearing battle besides, having shirked exercises in arms, they plunge headlong into a rash enterprise of this sort.

A compound treatment is usually applied to this wound. While they are still separate and in their base, (soldiers) should be held to every article of discipline by the strictest severity of tribunes, "vicars"[3] and officers,[4] and observe nothing but loyalty and obedience. They should be doing *campicursio*,[5] as they themselves term a review of arms, constantly, they should have opportunity for no leave of absence, they should continually be obeying the muster[6] and be present at the

---

[1]The strategy which Fritigern had to face in AD 377, Amm. 31.11.5, cf. 31.7.6. It was also that endorsed by Ammianus himself, 31.7.2.

[2]The chapter has some resonances with Polyb. 11.25–30, in which Scipio Africanus Maior quells a mutiny, cf. Livy 28.24–29. V. takes the opportunity to repeat again a summary of the training, cf. II.23.

[3]*vicarii*, acting tribunes.

[4]*principia.*

[5]parade-ground marching-manoeuvres. Cf. III.9 fin., where it seems to mean "field manoeuvres" as for a battle, and II.22 *decursio campi*, "parade-ground drill".

[6]*ad nomen observare*, cf. *ad nomen respondere* in Livy 7.4.2, 2.28.6, 28.29.12; cf. also Maur. *Strat.* 7 (A) 2, ἀδνουμιάζειν, v.l. for ἀγιάζειν (τὰ βάνδα). The Byzantine ἀδνούμιον denoted a meeting of the troops for a blessing, address, counting and distribution of pay, cf. H. Mihaescu, "Les éléments latins des Tactica-Strategica de Maurice-Urbicius et leur écho en Néo-grec", *RESE* vi (1968) 497. It could also be dangerous to the High Command to assemble the troops *en masse* so as to realize their strength, cf. Leo *Tact.* 9.4, 6.15. But there were also smaller assemblies for organizing training and manoeuvres, etc., such as V. must mean, cf. Du Cange (ed.), *Glossarium ad*

standards,[1] and be kept as frequently as possible shooting arrows,[2] throwing javelins,[3] throwing stones with the sling or by hand,[4] performing the gestures of the *armatura*,[5] fencing with foils made to imitate swords with the point and with the edge for most of the day until they are exhausted.[6] They should furthermore be trained at leaping over fosses by running and jumping.[7] If the sea or a river is near their base, in summer they should all be made to swim,[8] also to fell trees,[9] march through thickets and broken country,[10] hew timber, open a fosse,[11] occupy some point, and strive with shields mutually opposed not to be dislodged by their comrades.[12] Soldiers who have been so trained and exercised at their base, whether they are legionaries, *auxilia* or cavalry,[13] when they come together for a campaign from their various units inevitably prefer warfare to leisure in the rivalry for valour. No one thinks of mutiny, when he carries confidence in his skill and strength.

But the general should be careful to learn from tribunes, "vicars" and officers in all legions, *auxilia* and vexillations,[14]—not according to the malice of informers but the true facts—if there are any disorderly or mutinous soldiers. The more prudent policy is then to segregate them from camp to so some work which might seem to them almost desirable or else to allocate them to fortifying and guarding forts and cities, with such subtlety that they seem to have been specially selected although they are being cast off. For an army never breaks out in dissent with

---

scriptores mediae et infimae Graecitatis (Lyon 1688) s.v.
[1]Cf. Maur. and the ceremony alluded to above.
[2]Cf. I.15.
[3]Cf. I.14.
[4]Cf. I.16.
[5]special drill, cf. I.4. I.13.
[6]reading *ad vectes... feriendos.* Cf. I.11–12.
[7]Cf. I.9.
[8]Cf. I.10.
[9]Cf. II.23.
[10]Cf. I.9, I.27.
[11]Cf. I.21–25, III.8.
[12]Cf. I.9.
[13]The three divisions of the fourth-century field army; cf. Hoffmann, I.72, 397.
[14]"Vexillations" refers to the cavalry arm of the tripartite field army.

equal enthusiasm, but is incited by a few who hope to escape punishment for vices and crimes by involving large numbers in wrongdoing. But if extreme necessity urges the medicine of the sword, it is juster to follow ancestral custom and punish the ringleaders of crimes, so that fear extends to all, but punishment to few. However, those generals who have instilled discipline in their army through hard work and routine are more praiseworthy than those whose soldiers are forced into submission by fear of punishment.[1]

5. How many kinds of military signals there are.[2]

Many indeed are the orders to be given and obeyed in battle, since no remission is granted to negligence when men are fighting for their lives.[3] But of all the rest there is nothing so conducive to victory as heeding the warnings of signals. Since an army in the confusion of battle cannot be governed by a single voice, and many orders have to be given and carried out on the spur of the moment in view of the urgency of events, ancient practice of all nations devised a means whereby the whole army might recognize by signals and follow up what the general alone had judged useful.

So there are generally agreed to be three types of signals, voiced, semi-voiced and mute. Of these the voiced and semi-voiced are perceived by ear, whereas the mute are transmitted to the eye. Those called "voiced" are pronounced by the human voice, such as a watchword on night-watch duties or in battle, for example, "victory",[4] "palm",[5] "virtue",[6] "God with us",[7] "Triumph of the Emperor"[8] and whatever others the supreme commander in the army may choose to

---

[1]Sixth-century examples of such praiseworthy generals include Justinian son of Germanus (Theophyl. 3.12.7), Maurice (Men. Prot. fr. 23.2–3, Blockley), and Philippicus (Evagr. 6.3, Theophyl. 2.4.3–4).
[2]A traditional chapter in the *tactici*, cf. Arr. *Tact.* 27, Ael. *Tact.* 35.
[3]Cf. I.13 fin.
[4]*victoria.*
[5]*palma.*
[6]*virtus.*
[7]*Deus nobiscum.*
[8]*triumphus imperatoris.*

give. But note that these words should be changed daily, lest the enemy recognize the sign from familiarity and spies pass among our men with impunity.[1]

The "semi-voiced" are those given by the trumpet,[2] horn[3] or bugle.[4] The "trumpet" is the name for the straight instrument. The "bugle" is that which is bent back on itself in a bronze circle. The "horn" is that which is made from the wild aurochs, bound with silver, and when modulated with a skilful breath emits a note of singing wind.[5] By these means through unambiguous sounds the army recognizes whether it should halt, advance or retreat, whether to pursue fugitives into the distance or sound for a withdrawal.

The "mute" signals are eagles, dragons, ensigns, *flammulae, tufae* and plumes.[6] The soldiers accompanying their standard must go wherever the general directs them to be carried. There are also other mute signals which the general gives orders to be kept on horses, on clothes, or on the arms themselves, to distinguish them from the enemy. Besides this he may indicate something with his hand or, in barbarian fashion, with a whip, or even by a movement of the clothes he is wearing.[7] All this, in camp, on the march, in every field exercise, every soldier should learn to follow and understand. For continual practice is obviously

---

[1]Cf. Onas. 26, and III. 26.

[2]*tuba.*

[3]*cornu.*

[4]*bucina.*

[5]Cf. Hieron. *in Os.* 5.8: *bucina pastoralis est et cornu recurvo efficitur.* "The bugle is a shepherd's instrument made from a curving horn." R. Meucci, "Lo strumento del bucinator. A. Surus e il cod. Pal. Lat. 909 di Vegezio", *BJ* clxxxvii (1987) 259–272 proposes that in V. the words *bucina* and *cornu* have become transposed; cf. II.22. See also P. Barton, "On making a Roman cornu", in *Roman Military Equipment. The Accoutrements of War*, Procs. of the Third Roman Military Equipment Research Seminar, ed. M. Dawson, BAR Int. Ser. 336 (Oxford 1987) 28–37.

[6]Cf. II.1, and Ioh. Lydus *de Mag.* I.8: δόρατα ἐπιμήκη... ἀκροξιφίδας μὲν οὐκ ἔχοντα, ἠωρημένας δὲ λοφιάς· καλοῦσι δὲ αὐτὰς οἱ μὲν 'Ρωμαῖοι ἰούβας, οἱ δὲ βάρβαροι τούφας, βραχύ τι παραφθαρει'σης τῆς λέξεως· βήξιλλα πρὸς τούτοις οἱονεὶ δόρατα μακρὰ ἐξηρτημένων ὑφασμάτων—φλάμμουλα αὐτὰ ἀπὸ τοῦ φλογίνου χρώματος καλοῦσι, "long lances... having not bladed tips but crests rising in the air; the Romans call them *iubae*, the barbarians *tufae*, corrupting the word a little; and *vexilla* (ensigns) in addition to these, that is, long lances with cloths hanging from them—(the Romans) call them *flammulae* from their flame colour."

[7]Amm. 18.6.13 (movement of cloak), Claud. *pan. de Hon. cons. VI* 625 (whipcrack).

necessary in peacetime of a procedure which is to be maintained in the confusion of battle.

There is also a "mute" signal common to both sides, when dust is disturbed by an army as it marches, and rises up in clouds, betraying the approach of the enemy. Similarly when forces are divided, they use fires by night and smoke by day to signal to their comrades what cannot be announced by other means.[1] Some hang beams on towers of forts and cities, indicating what is going on by now raising, now lowering them.[2]

6. The degree of caution to be observed when an army moves in the vicinity of the enemy.

Those who have made a careful study of the art of war[3] assert that more dangers tend to arise on the march than in battle itself. For in battle everyone is armed, and they see the enemy at close quarters and come mentally prepared for fighting. On the march, the soldier is less armed and less alert; he is thrown into instant confusion by a sudden attack or concealed ambush. Therefore the general should take steps with all caution and prudence to ensure that the army suffer no attack on the march, or may easily repel a raid without loss.

First, he should have itineraries of all regions in which war is being waged written out in the fullest detail, so that he may learn the distances between places in terms of the number of miles and the quality of roads, and examine short-cuts, by-ways, mountains and rivers, accurately described. Indeed, the more conscientious generals reportedly had itineraries of the provinces in which the emergency occurred not just annotated but illustrated as well, so that they could choose their route when setting out by the visual aspect as well as by mental calculation.[4]

---

[1]Onas. 6.8, cf. Hanno's smoke-signal to Hannibal, Livy 21.27.7.
[2]Only very simple signals are meant, not a semaphore system. Cf. Onas. 25.3 on fire-signals.
[3]V. never claims expertise; cf. I.8, II.3.
[4]Note that the use of coloured maps was not a novelty in the time of V. Cf. O.A.W. Dilke, *Greek and Roman Maps* (London 1985) 112, 210, R. Sherk, "Roman geographical exploration and Military maps", *ANRW* II.1 (1974) 558 ff. Cf. Polyb. 9.13.6 on the second principle of generalship—accurate geographical knowledge.

In addition, he ought to find out everything from intelligent men, from men of rank,[1] and those who know the localities, individually, and put together the truth from a number of witnesses. Furthermore he should collect[2] at the risk of those responsible for choosing them[3] able guides, knowledgeable of the roads, and keep them under guard having given them a demonstration of punishment and reward. They will be useful when they understand that there is no longer any chance of escape for them, and that there is ready reward for loyalty and retribution for treachery. He should also make sure that men of discernment and experience are found, lest the error of two or three individuals put everyone at risk. Occasionally inexperienced rustics promise more than they can deliver and believe they know what in fact they do not.[4]

But the most important thing to be careful about is to preserve secrecy concerning the places and routes by which the army is to proceed. The safest policy on expeditions is deemed to be keeping people ignorant of what one is going to do. It is for this reason that the ancients had the standard of the Minotaur in the legions. Just as he is said to have been hidden away in the innermost and most secret labyrinth, so the general's plan should always be kept secret.[5] A safe march is that which the enemy least expect to be made.

Nevertheless, some words should be said about how one ought to go about meeting an attack, because scouts[6] sent from the other side can

---

[1]*honorati.*

[2]reading *percipere.*

[3]reading *eligentium*: V. may have in mind cases of collusion between false guides, working for the enemy, and barbarian Roman officers, such as was suspected of Latinus, *comes domesticorum*, Agilo, *tribunus stabuli*, and Scudilo, tribune of the Scutarii, with an unnamed Alaman guide in AD 354, cf. Amm. 14.10.8. Cf. Onas. 10.15, Polyb. 9.14.1–3.

[4]V. is consistently contemptuous of the intelligence of common people; cf. III.3 fin., IV.41 fin., I.3 fin.

[5]Paul. Fest. 135.21 L.: *Minotauri effigies inter signa militaria est, quod non minus occulta esse debent consilia ducum, quam fuit domicilium eius labyrinthus.* "The image of the Minotaur is included among the military standards, because the plans of the generals should be not less secret than was the labyrinth, his home." Cf. Onas. 10.22–24, Polyb. 9.13.2–5 on the first principle of generalship—secrecy, keeping one's plans to oneself. On the Minotaur and other early Roman standards, cf. Marquardt, 354 n. 4.

[6]*exploratores.*

detect an expedition by its tracks or by sighting it, and occasionally deserters and traitors are not wanting. When a general intends to set out with his army in column, he should send ahead very reliable and quick-witted men on excellent mounts to reconnoitre those places through which the army is due to march, both in advance and in the rear, and to right and left, to prevent the enemy laying ambushes. Scouts operate more safely at night than in daytime. In some measure a general betrays himself if his scout[1] is captured by the enemy.[2]

So let the cavalry take the road in front, then the infantry, with the baggage,[3] pack-horses,[4] servants[5] and vehicles placed in the middle, and the light-armed portion of the infantry and cavalry bringing up the rear. For attacks on a marching army are sometimes made at the front, but more usually in the rear. The baggage-train should also be enclosed on the flanks with equal strengths of soldiers, for ambushers frequently attack the sides. But the part which the enemy is expected to approach one should be particularly careful to reinforce with a screen of picked cavalry, light-armed infantry and foot-archers. If the enemy surround on all sides, reinforcements must be prepared on all sides. To prevent added losses from a sudden commotion, soldiers should be warned beforehand to be mentally prepared and have their arms in their hands. In an emergency sudden things are terrifying, things that are foreseen do not usually strike panic.[6]

The ancients took very thorough precautions against disturbance to the fighting troops by servants getting wounded on occasion or afraid or by pack-animals terrified at the din of battle, lest being extended too far or massed together more than expedient, (the troops) might impede their own side and help the enemy. Therefore they decided to marshall the baggage-train like the soldiers under certain standards. So they

---

[1] *speculator.*
[2] Cf. Maur. *Strat.* 7. B 13, 9.5.
[3] *impedimenta.*
[4] *sagmarii.*
[5] *calones.*
[6] Cf. Onas. 6.5–6, Arr. *Ect.* 1–10, Jos. *Bell. Iud.* 3.115–126.

selected men of ability and practical experience from among the servants, whom they call *galearii*,[1] and put them in charge of up to 200 pack-animals and grooms.[2] To them also they gave ensigns, so that they might know to which standards they should gather the baggage. But the fighting men were divided from the baggage-train by a certain interval, so that they were not pushed together and wounded in battle.

When an army is marching, the system of defence varies with changes in terrain. On open plains cavalry are more likely to attack than infantry, while on the contrary in wooded, mountainous or marshy country, infantry forces are more to be feared. One thing to avoid is the column being severed or thinned out through the negligence of one group setting a fast pace while another is moving more slowly, for the enemy immediately penetrate any gaps. Therefore the most experienced drillmasters,[3] "vicars"[4] and tribunes should be put in charge, with orders to slow down those who are too brisk and force those going too slowly to speed up. When an attack happens, those who have gone far ahead wish to get away rather than go back. Meanwhile those who are in the rear deserted by their comrades are overwhelmed by the violence of the enemy and their own despair.[5]

One should bear in mind that the enemy sets up concealed ambushes or engages in open battle only in places he thinks favourable to himself. The general's diligence provides against suffering damage from surprises, so it is advised that he reconnoitre everything in advance. Then if an ambush is detected and properly surrounded, it suffers more damage than it was preparing to inflict.[6] Again if an open battle is being prepared in mountain-country, the higher ground should be seized by

---

[1] Cf. I.10: *lixas, quos galearios vocant.* V. seems to mean a generic term for soldiers' servants, rather than specifically those put in charge of the pack-animals and grooms. Cf. M.P. Speidel, "The Soldiers' Servants", *Anc.Soc.* xx (1989) 239–248, = *Roman Army Studies* II, 342–352.

[2] *pueri*, "boys".

[3] *campidoctores.*

[4] *vicarii*, acting-tribunes.

[5] V. updates the centurions of the source to *campidoctores*, etc., as at III.8. Cf. Jos. *Bell. Iud.* 3.124, Arr. *Ect.* 9–10.

[6] Cf. Onas. 6.7.

sending forces ahead so that when the enemy arrives, he finds himself on lower ground, and dare not attack when he can see armed men in front of him and overhead. But if there are routes which are narrow but safe, it is better for soldiers to go ahead with axes and picks, opening a road with their toil, than to suffer peril on the best route.[1]

We ought also to know the habits of the enemy—whether they usually attack by night, at daybreak or during the rest-hour when men are tired—and avoid that which we think they will do from routine.[2] It is likewise in our interest to know whether they are stronger in infantry or cavalry, in pikemen or archers, and whether they are superior in numbers of men or military equipment, so that we may adopt the tactics which are judged[3] useful to ourselves and disadvantageous to them.[4] We should calculate whether it is advantageous to begin the march during the day or by night and how great are the intervals between places to which we wish to advance, so as to save the men on the march from being troubled by lack of water in summer, or faced with difficult or impassable morasses and great torrents in winter, or the army from being cut off before it can reach its destination through its march being impeded.[5]

Just as it is to our advantage to avoid these things by being prudent, so we ought not to let slip any opportunity which the enemy's inexperience or negligence offers to us. We should reconnoitre assiduously, sollicit traitors and deserters so we can find out the enemy's present and future plans and, with our cavalry and light armament in prepared positions, catch them in unforeseen ambushes while marching or seeking fodder and food.

---

[1]Cf. Jos. *Bell. Iud.* 3.118.

[2]Cf. III.9, IV.27.

[3]*Docetur* in this sense is a late-Latinism, also common in legal or official documents, cf. *TLL* s.v. *doceo*, 1708.59 ff., 1713.30 ff.

[4]Cf. III.9.

[5]Cf. III.2.

7. How to cross large rivers.[1]

When crossing rivers careless armies often get into serious difficulties. For if the current is too strong or the river-bed too wide it is likely to drown baggage-animals, grooms and sometimes even the weaker warriors. So when a ford has been reconnoitred two lines of horsemen on picked mounts are lined up in parallel with sufficient space between them for infantry and baggage-train to pass through the middle. The upper line breaks the force of the waters, while the lower line collects up any who may be snatched away or swept under, and brings them safely across.[2] But where the water is too deep to allow either infantry or cavalry to cross, if the river flows through flat country, it may be dispersed by digging multiple channels and easily crossed when divided. Navigable rivers, however, are made passable by driving in piles and boarding over the top, or else, for a temporary work, empty barrels may be tied together and timbers placed upon them to provide a passage.[3] Also the cavalry are accustomed to take off their accoutrements and make fascines from dry reeds and sedge and place upon them cuirasses and arms, so as not to get them wet. They and their horses swim across, drawing <on reins>[4] the fascines that they have tied to themselves.

But it has been found better for an army to carry around with it on carts "single timbers",[5] which are rather wide canoes, hollowed out of single trunks, very light because of the type and thinness of the wood. Planks and iron nails are also kept with them in readiness. The bridge

---

[1]Cf. *RE* XXI (1952) 2437–2452 s.v. "Pons" (Lammert), Maur. *Strat.* 1.9.8, 8.1.19, 9.1.11.

[2]The method was Caesar's, cf. id. *Bell. Civ.* 1.64.5–6.

[3]The latter, presumably, for a kind of pontoon-bridge. V. does not mention the use of inflated skins to buoy timber raft-bridges, cf. J. Hornell, "Floats and buoyed rafts in military operations", *Antiquity* xix (1945) 73–79, or the bridge of allegedly skins and cables alone described by the Anon. *de Rebus Bellicis* 16, carried on fifty packhorses or the backs of "very few men" (*praef.* 14). Amm. 24.3.11 mentions skins in conjunction with pontoon-bridges using wooden floats, cf. id. 25.6.15 and Zos. 3.39.5. Cf. the raft-bridge described and illustrated by Apoll. Dam. *Polior.* 191.5 W.

[4]Reading *loris*, an emendation by Stewechius. The MSS reading *sociis* would mean "for their comrades", cf. III.5 fin. Perhaps they were specially trained at swimming with rafts of arms across rivers, cf. the Batavi, Tac. *Agric.* 18.4, *Hist.* 4.12.3, Cass. Dio 69.9, M.W.C. Hassall, "Batavians and the Roman conquest of Britain", *Britannia* i (1970) 131–136.

[5]*monoxyli* (Greek). Cf. II.25.

thus speedily constructed, tied together by ropes which should be kept for the purpose, provides the solidity of a masonry arch in quick time.[1]

The enemy often launch rapid ambushes or raids at river crossings. Armed guards are stationed against this danger on both banks, lest the troops be beaten by the enemy because they are divided by the intervening river-bed. It is safer to build stockades along the bank on either side, and bear without loss any attack that is made. But if a bridge is needed not just for one crossing, but for returning and for supply-lines, broad fosses are dug around each bridgehead and a rampart constructed to receive soldiers to defend and hold it for as long as strategic needs require.[2]

8. How to lay out a camp.[3]

It seems fit, once the disposition of a march has been described, to move on to consider the camp in which one is to stay. For a walled city is not always available in wartime to provide a halting place[4] or night-quarters,[5] and it is reckless and full of danger for an army to bivouac at large without any fortification. For it is easy to contrive ambushes when soldiers are busy taking their meal or scattered to do their duties;[6]

---

[1]Cf. Amm. 24.7.4 (AD 363): *subiectis ignibus exuri cunctas iusserat naves praeter minores duodecim, quas profuturas pangendis pontibus disposuit vehi carpentis...* "he had ordered the burning of all the boats by fires placed under them, except twelve smaller ones to be used for constructing bridges, which he arranged to have transported on wagons..." 24.7.8: *maerebat tamen ob haec imperator et miles, quod nec contabulandi pontis erat facultas amissis navibus temere...* "both Emperor and soldier were aggrieved that there was not a chance of constructing a bridge, having lost the boats through carelessness..." Cf. Zos. 3.26.3. Note that "single timber" floats were taken over from the Gauls by Hannibal at the crossing of the river Rhone, 218 BC, cf. Livy 21.26.8–9.

[2]The Anon. *de Rebus Bellicis* 16.5 stationed *manuballistarii* on either bank to defend those building the bridge. Apoll. Dam. *Polior.* 191.5 W. attached hinged screens to his bridge to cover those defending it.

[3]A shorter version of largely the same material is given in I.21–25. See F. Lepper, S. Frere, *Trajan's Column* (Gloucester 1988) Pt. 4, pp. 260–266 "Roman Camps and Forts", D. Baatz, "Quellen zur Bauplannung römischer Militärlager", *Mavors* XI (Stuttgart 1994) 315–325.

[4]*stativa*, cf. SHA *Alex. Sev.* 45.2, where *stativae (stationes?)* seem virtually identical to *mansiones.*

[5]*mansio.*

[6]*munera.*

moreover the darkness of night, the need for sleep and the dispersal of grazing horses all provide opportunities for attack.

When surveying a camp, it is not sufficient to choose a good site unless it be so good that no other site better than it can be found. Otherwise a more advantageous site overlooked by us may then be occupied by the enemy, bringing danger. Also ensure that unhealthy water is not close by nor wholesome water too far away in summer, that there is no shortage of fodder and firewood in winter, that the site on which one is to camp is not liable to flooding after sudden rainstorms, that it is not in broken, remote country where the enemy may surround us and make it difficult to escape, and that missiles cannot be shot from higher ground by the enemy so as to reach it.[1]

When these conditions have been carefully and stringently investigated, you may build the camp square, circular, triangular or oblong, as required by the site. Appearance should not prejudice utility, although those whose length is one-third longer than the width are deemed more attractive. But surveyors[2] should calculate the square footage of the site-plan[3] so that the area enclosed corresponds to the size of the army. Cramped quarters constrict the defenders, whilst unsuitably wide spaces spread them thinly.[4]

There are potentially three sorts of fortification defined for a camp. The first is for the passage of one night or for brief occupation on a march. The raised turves are laid out in line, forming a rampart.[5] Above it, *valli*,[6] that is, stakes[7] or wooden spars[8] are ranged along its length. The turf is cut around with iron tools, retaining the earth in the grass roots, ½ ft. high, 1 ft. wide and 1½ ft. long. When the earth is too loose

---

[1] Cf. Ps.-Hyginus 57.
[2] *agrimensores.*
[3] *podismus mensurae.*
[4] Cf. I.26, III.6. The free shape of the Roman camp appears late-antique, cf. III.10, where V. recommends the Gothic (circular) *carrago* or "wagon-city". Contrast Ps.-Hyg. 21, Polyb. 6.31.10, 6.42.
[5] *agger.*
[6] stockades.
[7] *sudes.*
[8] *tribuli.*

for it to be possible to cut out the turf like a brick, the fosse is dug in "temporary style",[1] 5 ft. wide, 3 ft. deep, with the rampart rising on the inside. Thus the army is enabled to rest secure and without fear.

But a stationary camp[2] is fortified with greater care and effort, whether in summer or winter, when the enemy is near. For each century receives a footage[3] apportioned by the drillmasters and officers.[4] The men distribute their shields and packs in a circle around their own standards and, armed only with a sword, open a fosse 9 ft. wide, or 11 ft. or 13 ft. or, if a major hostile force is feared, 17 ft.—it is usual to keep to odd numbers. The rampart is then raised between lines of revetments or barriers of logs and branches interposed to stop the earth easily falling away. Above it a system of battlements and turrets is constructed like a wall. The centurions measure the work with ten-foot rods, checking that no one's laziness has resulted in digging too little or making mistakes. The tribunes also go round and, if they are conscientious, do not go away until it is completed in every part. However, to prevent a raid from being mounted on the men at work, all cavalry and that part of the infantry which through the privilege of rank does not labour take up position in front of the fosse in an armed cordon and repel enemy attack.

So first the standards are set up in their places inside the camp, because nothing is more revered by the soldiers than their majesty, the headquarters[5] is prepared for the general and his staff-officers[6] and the pavilions[7] are erected for the tribunes, who are served with water, firewood and fodder by privates[8] assigned to services.[9] Next, in order of

---

[1]*opere tumultuario*, cf. 1.24, where it is 9 ft. wide and 7 ft. deep. Obviously the first sort of fortification has regard only for the turf rampart, the second, "emergency work/fosse" and third, "proper work/fosse" for the rampart and fosse as a defensive system of differential sizes.

[2]*stativa castra.*

[3]*pedatura*, cf. Ps.-Hyginus *Castr.* 1, etc.

[4]*campidoctores et principia*,, here substituted for centurions and tribunes mentioned below; cf. III.6.

[5]*praetorium.*

[6]*comites*, "counts".

[7]*tabernacula.*

[8]*contubernales.*

rank, sites are appointed in camp for the legions and *auxilia*,[1] for cavalry and infantry, to pitch their tents.[2]

From each century four cavalrymen and four infantrymen undertake sentry-duty by night.[3] Because it was clearly impossible for individuals to remain constantly awake in their look-out posts, the night-watches[4] have been divided into quarters by the water-clock, ensuring that is necessary to be awake for no more than three hours a night.[5] All the watches are called by the trumpeter and at the end of their time recalled by the hornblower.[6] The tribunes select able and very reliable men to patrol the watches and report any fault that emerges. These used to be called *circumitores*; they have now been made a rank of service and are called *circitores*.[7] Note that the cavalry should do night watch-duties outside the rampart. During the day in the case of a stationary camp[8] they change guard (merely) for morning and afternoon shifts in the out-stations,[9] to avoid exhausting the men and horses.[10]

Among the things particularly incumbent upon a general, whether he is quartered in a camp or a city, is to see that the animals' pasturage,

---

[9]*munera.*

[1]palatine *auxilia.*

[2]*papiliones.*

[3]*excubitus.* V.'s usage of technical terminology is often non-technical, cf. Isid. *Etym.* 9.3.42: *excubiae autem diurnae sunt, vigiliae nocturnae,* "*Excubiae* are daytime, *vigiliae* are night-time." However, cf. Caes. *Bell. Gall.* 7.69.7: *haec eadem noctu excubitoribus ac firmis praesidiis tenebantur,* "The same (fortlets) were held at night by *excubitores* and strong garrisons."

[4]*vigiliae.*

[5]Cf. Aen. Tact. 22.24–25, Onas. 10.10–12, Ps.-Hyg. 1, Polyb. 6.35.1–5, Philo *In Flaccum* 3, J. Marquardt, *Römische Staatsverwaltung* II (1885[2]) 420.

[6]This conflicts with the signalling convention described in II.22, and the *bucina* was long identified with the watch-signal (and watch-period); cf. J. Marquardt, 421.

[7]"patrolmen". Of *circumitores*, Petronius 53.10, of a civilian, is the only attestation. Here it is perhaps V.'s etymologizing invention to explain *circitores*. Cf. Sall. *Jug.* 45.2, Polyb. 6.35.8–12, 6.36.1–9, Tac. *Hist.* 2.29, *Ann.* 15.30, Jos. *Bell. Iud.* 5.510. V.'s comment on *circitores* is confirmed by Fink, doc. 47.i.7 and 17, doc. 49.2. It was the legal duty of a commander *clavas portarum suscipere vigilias interdum circumire,* "to hold the keys to the gates and patrol the watches regularly", cf. *Dig.* 49.16.12.2. See R.W. Davies, "Minucius Iustus and a Roman Military Document from Egypt", *Aegyptus* liii (1973) 75–92, esp. 88–90.

[8]*castra posita.*

[9]*agrariae.*

[10]Cf. Livy 44.33.10–11 (168 BC), an innovation by L. Aemilius Paullus. Cf. III.22 note.

the transportation of grain and other provisions, and the ministration of water, firewood and fodder are rendered secure from hostile attack.[1] The only way to achieve this is to plant garrisons at suitable points through which our supply trains pass. These may be cities or walled forts. If no old fortifications are available, temporary forts are established in favourable positions and girded with broad fosses; such *castella*[2] are named after *castra*[3] by a diminutive word. A number of infantry and cavalry stationed in them on outpost-duty provide a safe passage for supplies. The enemy hardly dares attack points where he knows his adversaries are camped ahead and behind.[4]

(Pre-battle strategy, ch. 9–13)

9. What and how many things are to be considered when judging whether to engage the enemy in raids and ambushes or else in pitched battle.

Whoever will deign to read these commentaries on the art of war abridged from authors of the highest repute, wishes to hear first and foremost the science of battle and the recommended tactics. But a pitched battle is defined by a struggle lasting two or three hours, after which all hopes of the defeated party fall away. That being so, every expedient must be thought of previously, tried out in advance and implemented before matters come to this final pass. For good generals do not attack in open battle where the danger is mutual, but do it always from a hidden position, so as to kill or at least terrorize the enemy while

---

[1]On the duty of a commanding officer to ensure an adequate supply of food, see R.W. Davies, "Some notes on military papyri from Dura", *BASP* v (1968) 33 and nn.15–16.
[2]forts. A smaller size of *castella* are defined as *burgi* at IV.10.
[3]fortress-camp.
[4]The fortification of roads with *burgi* is attested in late-fourth-century Britain, Belgium, Spain and Pannonia; cf. R. MacMullen, *Corruption and the decline of Rome* (Yale 1988) 187.

their own men are unharmed as far as possible. In this connexion I shall describe the measures which the ancients found quite essential.[1]

An important art useful to a general is to call in persons from the entire army who are knowledgeable about war and aware of their own and the enemy's forces, and to hold frequent discussions with them in an atmosphere from which all flattery, which does so much harm, has been banished, to decide whether he or the enemy has the greater number of fighters, whether his own men or the enemy's are better armed and armoured and which side is the more highly trained or the braver in warfare.[2] A further question is which side has the better cavalry or infantry, bearing in mind that the strength of an army depends mainly on its infantry.[3] And, among the cavalry, which side has more pikemen or archers, which is wearing more cuirasses and which has brought better horses. Then he should consider whether the terrain itself in which one is to fight appears advantageous to the enemy or to ourselves. For if we are strong in cavalry, we should opt for plains; if in infantry, we should choose confined places, obstructed by ditches, marshes or trees, and sometimes mountainous.[4] Also, which side has more food or lacks it, for hunger, they say, fights from within, and often conquers without a blow.[5]

But most important of all, he should deliberate whether it is expedient for the crisis to be prolonged or fought out more swiftly. For sometimes the enemy hopes that the campaign can be ended quickly, and if it becomes long-drawn out, is either reduced by hunger, or called back to his own country by his men's homesickness, or through doing nothing significant is compelled to leave in despair. Then very many desert,

---

[1]V. was writing in the aftermath of a disastrous pitched battle with the barbarians (Adrianople, AD 378), and has a correspondingly high opinion of covert or guerilla actions. It seems from this chapter that he considered the Romans inferior in numbers and strength to the barbarians and did not trust the loyalty of the *auxilia palatina*. Cf. II.3, where he contrasts their looser discipline and readier privileges with the legions.

[2]Cf. I.2 fin., Onas. 3.1–3, 11.6, and Amm. 31.12.7 on the damage done by adulation in council.

[3]Cf. II.1.

[4]Cf. III.13.

[5]Cf. III.3.

exhausted by effort and weariness, some betray others and some
surrender themselves, since loyalty is less common in adversity, and the
enemy who came in great force begins to be denuded.[1]

It is also relevant to find out the character of the adversary himself,
his senior staff-officers[2] and chieftains.[3] Are they rash or cautious, bold
or timid, skilled in the art of war or fighting from experience or
haphazardly? Which tribes on their side are brave or cowardly? What
is the loyalty and courage of our *auxilia*?[4] What is the morale of the
enemy forces? What is that of our own army? Which side promises
itself victory more?[5] By such considerations is the army's courage
bolstered or undermined.

When the men despair, their courage is raised by an address from the
general, and if he appears fearless himself, their spirits are raised, if for
example you have brought off some exploit from an ambush or
opportunity, if the opposition have begun to suffer mishaps, or if you
have been able to overcome some of the weaker or poorly-armed
elements of the enemy.[6] Be careful never to lead a hesitant and
frightened army into a pitched battle. It matters whether you have an
army of recruits or veteran soldiers, and whether they were on active
service a short time before or have spent a number of years at peace.
For men who stopped fighting a long time ago should be treated as
recruits.

Indeed, when legions, *auxilia*[7] and cavalry[8] arrive from different
stations, the best general should have them trained by picked tribunes
of known conscientiousness in all types of arms separately as single
units, and after forming them into one body, he will often train them

---

[1]Cf. Claud. *pan. de Hon. cons.* VI 250–264, Alaric, defeated by Stilicho at Pollentia AD
402–403, suffers a wave of desertions.
[2]*comites.*
[3]*optimates.*
[4]i.e. palatine *auxilia.*
[5]*Repromitto*, cf. *relego* II.4, with late-Latin redundant prefixes.
[6]Cf. III.12.
[7]i.e. palatine *auxilia.*
[8]i.e. *vexillationes*, cf. III.10.

himself as if for fighting a pitched battle, and will test them to see what their potential skill and courage may be, how well they interact with one another and whether they obey promptly the warnings of trumpets, directions of signals and his own orders and authority. If they err in any respect, let them be trained and instructed for as long as it takes to become perfect. But if they become fully expert in field manoeuvres,[1] archery, throwing javelins and drawing up the line, they should not even then be lightly led into a pitched battle, but on a carefully chosen opportunity, and only after being blooded in smaller-scale conflicts.

So let the general be watchful, sober and discreet.[2] Let him call a council-of-war and judge between his own and the enemy's forces, as if he were to adjudicate between parties to a civil suit. If he finds himself superior in many particulars, let him be not slow to enter a battle favourable to himself. If he recognizes that the enemy is stronger, let him avoid a pitched battle, because forces fewer in number and inferior in strength carrying out raids and ambushes under good generals have often brought back a victory.

10. What to do if one has an army unaccustomed to fighting or newly recruited.

All arts and all works progress through daily practice and continual exercise. If this is true of small things, the principle should hold all the more true in great matters. Who can doubt that the art of war comes before everything else, when it preserves our liberty and prestige, extends the provinces and saves the Empire? The Spartans long ago abandoned all other fields of learning to cultivate this, and later so did the Romans.[3] Even today the barbarians think this art alone deserves their attention; they are sure that everything else either depends on this art or can be obtained by them through it.[4] It is essential to those whose

---

[1]*campicursio.*
[2]Cf. Onas. 1.1.
[3]Cf. III praef.
[4]Cf. Sen. *de Ira* 1.11.3–4.

business is war, for it is the means to hold on to life and win a victory.[1] So the general who has bestowed on him the insignia of great power, and to whose loyalty and strength are entrusted the wealth of landowners, the protection of cities, the lives of soldiers and the glory of the State, should be anxious for the welfare not just of his entire army, but for each and every common soldier also.[2] For if anything happens to them in war, it is seen as his fault and the nation's loss.[3]

Therefore if he is leading an army of recruits or of men long unaccustomed to bearing arms, let him thoroughly explore the strength and spirit of each legion, *auxilium*[4] and *vexillatio*.[5] Let him find out by name if possible the military potential of each "count",[6] tribune,[7] aide[8] and private.[9] Let him assume maximum authority and severity, punish all military crimes according to the laws, have a reputation for forgiving no errors and make trial of everyone in different places in diverse situations.[10] When he has seen to these things properly, let him choose

---

[1] Cf. II.24.

[2] Cf. I.7.

[3] Cf. SHA *Alex. Sev* 47.1: *dicens milites se magis servare quam se ipsum, quod salus publica in his esset*, "saying that he preserved the soldiers more than his own person, because the national salvation rested on them."

[4] palatine auxiliary regiment.

[5] cavalry vexillation.

[6] *comes rei militaris* or regimental commander.

[7] Also a regimental commander, properly a *comes*, but often the *vicarius* seems to have stood in for his boss as "tribune", usurping his title, cf. Jones 1278, n. 158; V. calls him the "lesser tribune" (II.7).

[8] *domesticus*, cf. Grosse, 120 ff. The *domesticus*, like the *vicarius*, was usually a *primicerius*, whose rank varied according as his boss's. V. likens his *centurio primi pili* to a *primiscrinius = primicerius* (II.21). As bureau-chief, the *domesticus* was often called a *princeps* (II.12); V. has difficulties visualizing an "ancient legion" having both a *primus pilus* and a *princeps* (II.8).

[9] *contubernalis*.

[10] Cf. M. Fronto *ad Verum Imperatorem Aurelium Caesarem* II.1.23 = Cato *Dierum Dictarum de consulato suo* fr. 13 (Jordan p.35): *Interea unamquamque turmam manipulum cohortem temptabam, quid facere possent; proeliis levibus spectabam cuius modi quisque esset; si quis strenue fecerat, donabem honeste, ut alii idem vellent facere, atque in contione verbis multis laudabam. Interea aliquot <p>au<ca> castra feci, sed ubi anni tempus venit, castra hiberna...* "Meanwhile I tested each and every troop, maniple and cohort, to see their potential. In small-scale encounters I observed each man's characteristics; if anyone acted bravely I rewarded him handsomely, so that others would wish to do the same, and I praised him at length in addresses. Meanwhile I constructed a number of small camps, and when the season of year came, a winter camp..."

a moment when the enemy are roving carelessly about, scattered for ravaging, to send in his well-tried cavalry or infantry accompanied by the new recruits or poor-quality soldiers. Routing the enemy at a favourable opportunity gives experience to the latter group, and raises the morale of the rest.

Let him set up ambushes in complete secrecy at river-crossings, mountain passes, wooded defiles, marshes and other difficult passages. Let him so regulate his march that, fully prepared, he attacks the enemy when they are suspecting nothing, when they are eating meals, sleeping or at any rate resting, when they are relaxed, unarmed, unshod and their horses unsaddled, to the end that his men may acquire self-confidence in battles of this kind. For those who have not for a long time, or never at all, seen men being wounded or killed are greatly shocked when they first catch sight of it, and confused by panic start thinking of flight instead of fighting. Also, if the enemy are ranging abroad, let him attack them when they are fatigued by a long march; let him harass the rear, or at least attack by surprise, and those who loiter at a distance from their people for fodder or plunder, let him attack suddenly with picked men. Those actions should be tried first which do less harm if they fail, and bring the most benefit if successful.[1]

It is (also) the mark of a skilled general to sow seeds of discord among the enemy. For no nation, however small, can be completely destroyed by its enemies, unless it devours itself by its own feuding. Civil strife is quick to compass the destruction of political enemies, but careless about the readiness of (the nation's) own defence.

There is but one premiss to this work: let none despair of the possibility of doing that which was done in the past.[2] One may say, it

---

[1] This strategy is illustrated by Sebastianus' raid on the marauding Goths on the eve of Adrianople, AD 378, in striking contrast to Valens' action in forcing a pitched battle. Cf. Amm. 31.10.4, and the historian's approval of guerilla tactics against the Goths, Amm. 31.7.2. Similarly Modares, a Gothic *magister militum* in Thrace AD 380–382, inflicted a crushing defeat on a Gothic band caught in the act of enjoying their plunder, cf. Zos. 4.25.2–4.

[2] V. reverts to the theme of I.21 ff. on the failure to build camps and the disastrous results thereof. There is some suggestion that Theodosius I's field armies did not always build camps on campaign when it was clearly advisable to do so, cf. Zos. 4.31.3-4, 4.49.

is many years since anyone enclosed an army encampment with a fosse, rampart and stockade. We shall respond, if that precaution had been taken, there is nothing that the enemy could have done to harm us by attacking by night or day. The Persians copy the Romans in building their camps with lines of fosses. And because almost all of them are in sandy areas, they build their rampart using sacks which they have brought empty with them, filling them up with the dusty earth dug out of the fosse, and forming them into a pile.[1] All barbarians spend nights secure from attack behind their wagons linked together in a circle like a military camp.[2] Are we afraid that we are unable to learn what others have learned from us?

These skills were formerly maintained in use, as well as in books, but once they were abandoned it was a long time before anyone needed them, because with the flourishing of peacetime pursuits the imperatives of war were far removed.[3] But lest it be thought impossible for an art to be revived whose use has been lost, let us be instructed by precedents. Among the ancients, military science often fell into oblivion, but at first it was recovered from books, and later consolidated by the authority of generals. Scipio Africanus took over our armies in Spain after they had been several times beaten under other commanders. By observing the rule of discipline, he trained these so thoroughly in every article of work and digging of fosses, that he said that they deserved to be stained by digging mud, because they had declined to be wetted by the enemy's blood.[4] With these same men, he eventually captured the

---

[1] Cf. baskets filled with sand and used to build temporary fortifications in Aen. Tact. 32.1, 8.

[2] The *carrago* or "wagon-city" of the Goths, Huns and Alans; cf. Amm. 31.7.7, cf. 7.5 (Goths), 31.2.18 (Alans, cf. Arr. *Anab.* 5.22.4, from autopsy?), Amm. 31.2.10 (Huns).

[3] Cf. I.28.

[4] So Flor. 1.34.10: *quippe adsiduis et iniustis et servilibus maxime operibus adtriti ferre plenius vallum, qui arma nescirent, luto inquinare, quia sanguine nollent, iubebantur,* "for worn out by continual, excessive and above all servile work, they were ordered all the more to carry stakes, since they did not know how to carry arms, and to be stained by mud, since they refused blood." Cf. I.20 ff. on the training-value of building encampments. The sixth-century Maurice was also credited with having restored this discipline to the army, after it had been forgotten, cf. Men. Prot. fr. 23.3 (Blockley).

city of Numantia, and so cremated the inhabitants that none escaped.[1] Metellus took over an army in Africa which had been sent under the yoke when Albinus was its commander. He reformed it on ancient principles, and later overcame the same men who had sent them under the yoke.[2] The Cimbri destroyed the legions of Caepio and Mallius inside Gaul. The remnants were taken up by Gaius Marius, who trained them in the knowledge and art of warfare. The result was that they not only destroyed an innumerable host of Cimbri, but of Teutones and Ambrones as well, in a general engagement.[3] But it remains easier to train new men in valour than to reanimate those who have been terrified out of their wits.[4]

11. Precautions to be taken on the day of engaging in a general action.[5]

After treating of the lesser skills of war, our analysis of military science invites us to consider the hazard of the general engagement, the fateful day for nations and peoples. For total victory depends upon the outcome of an open battle. Therefore this is the time when generals should exert themselves all the more, in proportion as the vigorous may hope for greater glory, and worse peril dogs the slack. This is the moment when application of skill, theory of warfare and planning dominate.[6]

---

[1]P. Cornelius Scipio Aemilianus (Africanus) (Numantinus), cos. 147 BC, defeated and destroyed Carthage in 146, took over command of the campaign at Numantia, Spain, as consul II in 134, retrained the army, and captured and destroyed the city in 133 BC.

[2]Q. Caecilius Metellus (Numidicus), cos. 109, took over command in the war against Jugurtha after the defeat of the army under A. Postumius Albinus, *legatus pro praetore*, in 110 BC. Sall. *Jug.* 44–45 tells the story of his retraining programme.

[3]C. Marius defeated the Cimbri at Vercellae in 101 BC and the Teutones and Ambrones at Aquae Sextiae in 102 BC avenging the defeat of the Roman armies of Q. Servilius Caepio, cos. 106, and Cn. Mallius Maximus, cos. 105, in 105 BC, and other defeats. These examples presuppose that V. was still writing in the aftermath of military defeat (cf. I.20), despite the victories praised in II praef.

[4]Cf. I.13 fin.

[5]The material on the battle (III.11–22) is stylistically distinct. The frequent use of the verbal 2nd pers. sing. and of *tuus-a-um* is marked; cf. D. Schenk, 60–61. There are other grounds (cf. III.17, III.20) for thinking parts of the section are based largely on Cato's lost *de Re Militari*, and this appears to be the best explanation of the style, too.

[6]Cf. Colum. 1.1.16: *usus et experientia dominantur in artibus*, "method and experience in the arts and sciences dominate."

In ancient times it was customary to lead soldiers into battle after they had been treated to a light meal, so that the food ingested might give them strength,[1] and in a prolonged fight they might not grow tired from hunger.[2] You should also take care if you lead your men to battle from a camp or a city when the enemy are present, lest, while the army is marching out in defile through narrow gates, it may be worsted by massed and prepared hostile forces. Therefore one should ensure that all soldiers get clear of the gates and form a battle-line before the enemy arrives. But if he arrives prepared for battle while your men are still inside the city, postpone your exit or at least pretend to. Then when the enemy troops start hurling insults at men they do not expect to come out, when they turn their attention to booty or withdrawal, when they break ranks, that is the moment for your crack troops to sally forth against the stunned enemy and attack them in force unexpectedly.[3]

Beware also not to force to a pitched battle soldiers who are tired after a long march or horses that are weary from galloping. Men who are going to battle lose much of their strength from marching-fatigue. What is one to do, if he reaches the line exhausted?[4] This is something the ancients avoided, and in the recent past[5] it was the armies, to say no more, who learned the lesson after Roman generals had through lack of expertise failed to provide against it.[6] For when a tired man enters battle with one who has rested, or a sweating man with an alert, or one who has been running with one who has been standing, he fights on unequal terms.

---

[1] Cf. Onas. 12.

[2] Cf. Front. *Strat*, 2.1.1, 2.1.5, and Belisarius' defeat with a hungry army at Callinicum AD 531, Procop. *Bell. Pers*. 1.18.13 ff.

[3] Cf. Onas. 10.20.

[4] Cf. Onas. 6.9.

[5] *superiore vel nostra aetate*, cf. I.28.

[6] A reference to the battle of Adrianople, AD 378, where the Emperor Valens was killed along with two-thirds of the Eastern field army by the Goths, Huns and Alans, commanded by Fritigern; cf. Goffart, 83, and Sabbah, 142. V. uses hyperbaton to emphasize the words *hoc... exercitus didicerunt*; cf. I.10 fin. for a similar figure in a possible allusion to the Tigris disaster, AD 363. Amm. 31.12.10–13.7 stresses that the battle followed upon an exhausting forced march in the heat of the day from Adrianople itself to the Gothic camp, where the battle took place, the troops not having been fed or watered. At 31.14.5 he says that Valens was skilled in neither military nor liberal studies.

12. One should find out how soldiers are feeling before battle.
Explore carefully how soldiers are feeling on the actual day they are
going to fight. For confidence or fear may be discerned from their facial
expression, language, gait and gestures. Do not be fully confident if it
is the recruits who want battle, for war is sweet to the inexperienced.[1]
You will know to postpone it if the experienced warriors are afraid of
fighting. An army gains courage and fighting spirit from advice and
encouragement from their general, especially if they are given such an
account of the coming battle as leads them to believe they will easily
win a victory. Then is the time to point out to them the cowardice and
mistakes of their opponents, and remind them of any occasion on which
they have been beaten by us in the past. Also say anything by which the
soldiers' minds may be provoked to hatred of their adversaries by
arousing their anger and indignation.[2]

It is a natural reaction in the minds of nearly all men to be fearful as
they go to do battle with the enemy. But those whose minds are
panicked by his actual appearance are without doubt the weaker sort.
Their fears may be lessened by the following remedy. Before the battle,
repeatedly draw up your army in safe positions from which they can get
used to seeing and recognizing the enemy. Let them also try their hand
now and then when an opportunity arises: let them put to flight or kill
their opponents; let them learn to recognize their adversaries'
characteristics, arms and horses,[3] for familiar things are not frightening.[4]

13. How a suitable place is chosen for battle.
The good general should know that a large part of a victory depends on
the actual place in which the battle is fought. Be at pains therefore when

---

[1]Cf. Pindar fr. 110: γλυκὺ δὲ πόλεμος ἀπείροσιν, ἐμπείρων δέ τις | ταρβεῖ
προσιόντα νιν καρδίᾳ περισσῶς. "War is sweet to the inexperienced, but an experienced
man fears it as it approaches with all his heart, extraordinarily."
[2]Cf. III.9. Aeneas Tacticus appears to have written a whole book—*Akousmata*—on things
to say to the troops, cf. Aen. 38.5. Cf. also Caes. *Bell. Gall.* 1.40.4 ff.
[3]Cf. III.10. Cf. the strategy of Q. Fabius Maximus (Cunctator) for the demoralized
survivors of the battle of Lake Trasimene in 217 BC, Livy 22.12.8–10.
[4]Cf. Plut. *Mar.* 16. V. is unaware of Tac. *Agr.* 30.4: *omne ignotum pro magnifico est.*
"Every unknown is assumed to be great."

you are going to engage in combat, to get help first from the place. This is judged the more advantageous, the higher the ground occupied. For weapons descend with more violence onto men on a lower level, and the side which is higher dislodges those opposing them in greater force. He who struggles uphill enters a double contest with the ground and with the enemy. But there is this distinction: if you are hoping for victory from your infantry over enemy horse, you should choose rough, broken and mountainous country; but if you are looking for victory from your cavalry over opposing infantry, you should go for positions that are, indeed, on a slightly higher level, but flat and open, unobstructed by woodland or morasses.[1]

(Battle tactics and strategies, ch. 14–26)

14. How the line should be drawn up to render it invincible in battle.[2]

When the general is ready to draw up his line, he should attend first to three things, sun, dust and wind. When the sun is in front of your face, it deprives you of sight. Head-winds deflect and depress your missiles, while aiding the enemy's. Dust thrown up in front of you fills and closes your eyes. Even inexperienced generals usually avoid these things at the time of ordering the lines, but the provident general should take care of the future lest, a little while later as the day wears on, the changed position of the sun may be harmful or a head-wind may habitually arise at a regular time, during the fighting. Therefore let the lines be ranged with these problems behind our backs, and if possible so that they may strike the faces of the enemy.[3]

---

[1] Cf. III.9.

[2] Essentially the same material as II.15–17 (and assumed in I.20), except that the light lines are here differentiated by their own ordinal number. The material is based on Cato; cf. Livy 1.43, 8.8, Dion. Hal. 4.16, for similar arrays. Developments under the Principate did not render the basic patterns obsolete, cf. Arr. *Ect.* 12–26, Amm. 14.6.17.

[3] This was above all the problem to which the Romans attributed their defeat by Hannibal at Cannae in 216 BC. Cf. Flor. 1.22.16: *callidus imperator (sc. Hannibal) in patentibus campis observato loci ingenio, quod et sol ibi acerrimus et plurimum pulvis et eurus ab oriente semper quasi ex constituto, ita instruxit aciem, ut, Romanis adversus haec omnia obversis, secundum caelum tenens vento pulvere et sole pugnaret,* "The cunning

"Line"[1] means the army drawn up for battle. The "front"[2] is the part that looks towards the enemy. If wisely deployed it is very useful in a general engagement. If unskilfully, however excellent the warriors may be they are weakened by bad ordering. The rule of drawing up an array is to place in the first line the experienced and seasoned soldiers, formerly called *principes*, and to rank in the second line archers protected with cataphracts and crack soldiers armed with javelins[3] and light spears,[4] formerly called *hastati*.[5] Individual infantrymen regularly occupy 3 ft. each. Therefore in a mile[6] 1,666 infantrymen are ranked abreast, without light showing between them but leaving room to handle their weapons. Between line and line, they wished to have a space 6 ft. in depth behind them to give the fighting men room to move forward and back, missiles being more forcibly thrown from a running jump.[7] In these two lines are posted those older in years, confident and experienced, and protected by heavy armour. Their rôle is to act like a wall;[8] at no time should they be made to retreat or pursue lest they disturb their ranks. They should receive oncoming adversaries and repel or rout them by standing their ground and battling it out.

---

commander-in-chief (Hannibal) observed the character of the place, that both the sun was very fierce there and there was much dust, and that the east wind blew always from the east as if by covenant, so he drew up his battle-line in the spreading plain in such a way, that the Romans might be facing all these disadvantages while he himself, keeping the sky in his favour, would be fighting along with the wind, dust and sun." Cf. 1.38.15, Front. *Strat.* 2.2.7. Cf. Aug. *civ. Dei* 5.26 D, Oros. 7.35.17–18 for a "miraculous wind" helping Theodosius I against Eugenius at the battle of the river Frigidus, AD 394.

[1] *acies*, literally "cutting edge".

[2] *frons*.

[3] *spicula*, cf. II.15.

[4] *lanceae*.

[5] V. intends to follow his source in that the first and second line were heavy-armed, but the contemporary cataphract archers and spearmen he substitutes appear to have been something in between the old heavy and light categories, cf. Procopius cited at II.15.

[6] 1 Roman mile = *c*.1,617 yds., 1,478·5 m., cf. I.9 note.

[7] Cf. Polyb. 18.30.6–7, who suggests the more individualistic style of combat used by the Roman lines required minima of 3 ft. between man and man in both directions. V. wrongly assumes no space at all laterally, as in the Macedonian phalanx, because this is incompatible with the generous forward-and-back movement he also allows.

[8] Cf. II.17, I.20.

The third line is formed from very fast light infantry,[1] young archers and good javelinmen. They were formerly termed *ferentarii*.[2] The fourth line is similarly constructed from very light "shield-bearers",[3] young archers and those who fight briskly with light javelins[4] and lead-weighted darts called *plumbatae*.[5] They used to be termed "light armament".[6] It should be noted that whereas the front two lines stand their ground, the third and fourth lines always go out to challenge the enemy with missiles and arrows, in the forward position. If they can put the enemy to rout, they set off in pursuit themselves with the cavalry. But if they are driven back by the enemy, they return to the first and second lines and retire between them to their own stations.[7] The first and second lines bear the full brunt of the battle when it comes to what is called "to broadswords and javelins".[8]

In a fifth line were sometimes placed carriage-ballistas,[9] and *manuballistarii*,[10] "sling-staff men"[11] and slingers. "Sling-staff men" are those who cast stones from a "sling-staff".[12] The "sling-staff" is a staff[13]

---

[1] *armaturae.*

[2] Used by Cato fr. 6 *de Re Mil.* and Sallust *Cat.* 60.2, archaic by the time of Livy and Caesar. Cf. Varro apud Non. Marc. 520.10 M.: *vocabant ferentarios, qui depugnabant fundis et lapidibus,* "They called *ferentarii* those who fought with slings and stones." Paul. Fest. 506.26 L: *Cato eos ferentarios dixit, qui tela ac potiones militibus proeliantibus ministrant.* "Cato called them *ferentarii,* who served weapons and drinks to the soldiers as they fought."

[3] *scutati,* i.e. again probably late-Roman archers or spearmen with shields attached to their body-armour. Cf. Procop. *Bell.* 1.1.8–16 for similar horse-archers in the early Byzantine army; cf. at II.15 V.'s identification of these light *scutati* with modern soldiers.

[4] *veruta,* cf. II.15.

[5] Variatio for *plumbatae* called *mattiobarbuli,* cf. I.17, showing the possible extent of manipulation of technical terms for stylistic effect.

[6] *levis armatura.*

[7] Cf. I.20, II.17.

[8] *ad spathas et ad pila.* Obviously the close-quarters phase of battle is intended. The technical phrase is not otherwise attested, however. Cf. I.20 fin. where it is called *ad pila.*

[9] *carroballistae.* Cf. Arrian's array, *Ect.* 19, for the positioning of artillery behind all the lines and on the flanks. Cf. also II.15, II.25, III.24.

[10] crossbowmen or catapultiers.

[11] *fundibulatores.*

[12] *fustibalus.*

[13] *fustis.*

4 ft. long, attached to the middle of which is a sling[1] made of leather, and operated with either hand, it discharges stones almost like the mangonel.[2] Slingers[3] discharge stones from slings made of flax or hair—the latter are said to be better—by whirling the arm about the head. Those not issued with shields fought in this line, throwing stones and missiles by hand.[4] They were called "extras", as being recruits, added afterwards.[5]

The sixth line behind all the others was held by very reliable warriors, armed with shields and every type of arms. These the ancients called *triarii*. They would wait in reserve behind the last lines, to attack the enemy more violently, being themselves rested and intact. If anything happened to the lines in front, all hope of recovery depended on their bravery.[6]

15. Counting the square-footage, how much space in the line should be left abreast between each man, and in depth between each rank. Now that it has been explained how the lines should be drawn up, I shall discuss the square footage[7] and plan of the formation itself. In a mile of field,[8] a single line will contain 1,666 infantry, since individual fighting men take up 3 ft. each.[9] If you wish to draw up six lines in a mile of field, 9,996 infantry are needed. If you wish to deploy this

---

[1]*funda.*

[2]*onager*, "wild ass". The "sling-staff" is known from mediaeval art also, cf. T.G. Kolias, *Byzantinischen Waffen* (Vienna 1988) 255, with refs. The sling was actually attached to the top end, not the middle as V. says. At IV.22, q.v., V. refuses to describe the *fustibalus, arcuballista* and *funda* on the grounds of their familiarity, evidently forgetting that he had described two of them here.

[3]*funditores.*

[4]Cf. I.16, II.23. Cf. also Arr. *Ect.* 25 on throwing stones.

[5]*accensi*, cf. II.19. They belong in the third and second centuries BC, but they are likened to the modern category of *tiro* or "recruit", which was a rank in itself at the bottom of the pay-scale, cf. Anon. *de Rebus Bellicis* 5.7 and Hieron. *c. Ioh. Hierosol.* 19.

[6]Cf. I.20, II.16.

[7]*podismus.*

[8]1 Roman mile, consisting of 1,000 Roman paces or 5,000 Roman feet, *c.*1,617 yds., 1,478·5 m., cf. I.9 note.

[9]Cf. III.14.

number in three lines, it takes up two miles; but it is better to make additional lines than to thin the soldiers out.

We said that 6 ft. ought to lie between each line in depth from the rear,[1] and in fact each warrior occupies 1 ft. standing still. Therefore, if you draw up six lines, an army of 10,000 men will take up 42 ft. in depth and a mile in breadth. [If you decide to draw up three lines, an army of 10,000 will take up 21 ft. in depth and two miles in breadth.][2] In accordance with this system, it will be possible to draw up even 20,000 or 30,000 infantry without the slightest difficulty, if you follow the square footage for the size.[3] The general does not go wrong when he knows what space can hold how many fighting men.

They say that if the field is too narrow, or if numbers are sufficient, the lines can be drawn up ten-deep or more. For it is more useful that they should fight in close order than too far separated. If the line is too thinly deployed, it is quickly broken through when the enemy make an assault, and after that there can be no remedy.[4] The units which should be deployed on the right wing, the left and in the middle, are either distributed according to their traditional ranking, or else changed to match the ability of the enemy.

---

[1] Cf. III.14.

[2] This sentence is included in MSS ΠV and recentiores, but was rejected as an interpolation by Stewechius, followed by Lang. There seems no obvious reason to make up such a sentence, which describes a valid permutation of V.'s system, and so is probably genuine.

[3] Cf. the same man–space mentality for the size of the camp, I.22, III.8. For armies of these sizes, cf. III.1. V.'s figures are over-generous in depth, allowing 6+1 ft. for each line, as compared with Polybius' 3(+1?) ft., and too mean in breadth, allowing 3+0 ft. for each man, as compared with Polybius' 3(+3?) ft., thus no room to move at all, cf. III.14 note.

[4] Cf. Onas. 21.1–2.

16. On deploying cavalry.[1]

When the infantry line has been formed up, the cavalry are posted on the wings, so that all cuirassiers[2] and pikemen[3] are next to the infantry, and mounted archers and those not issued with cuirasses range farther afield. For the heavy cavalry should be used to protect the infantry's flanks, while the swift light cavalry are for overwhelming and throwing into disorder the enemy's wings.

The general should know against which *drungi*,[4] that is, "groups"[5] of the enemy he should set which of the cavalry. For some obscure, or indeed, one might say, divine reason, some men fight better against others, and those who have conquered the stronger are often themselves defeated by the weaker.[6] But if the cavalry are outnumbered, the ancient custom should be adopted of mixing in with them very swift infantry with light shields, specially trained for the purpose, once called *velites*. If this is done, no matter in what force the enemy cavalry turn out, they cannot match the mixed formation.[7] All ancient generals found this to be the only answer. They trained young men who were outstanding

---

[1]V. says relatively little about cavalry or mixed formations of horse and light infantry, because these tactics were highly developed and successful in his own day, cf. I.20 init., III.26 fin. He intends his legionary cavalry to include both light and heavy divisions, and the latter at least seem to comprise two types, *loricati* and *contati*. Note the variety of Arrian's auxiliary cavalry, id. *Ect.* 21.

[2]*loricati*.

[3]*contati*.

[4]This word is identified as Celtic by philologists, cf. Kempf, 369–370, who explained it as Celtic, cf. Old Irish "drong", and this is preferred by Walde–Hofmann, 374, and declared "sans doute" by Ernout–Meillet, 185. The loose cavalry formation or *globus* was adopted by the Romans, too (cf. III.19), and the barbarian term δρούγγος became standard for units or formations in the early Byzantine army, cf. Maur. *Strat.* 1.3.10 etc., Leo *Tact.* 16.6. V. is the earliest author apart from the probably contemporary SHA *Prob.* 19.2 to use the word.

[5]*globi*, flying platoons.

[6]Thuc. 2.11.4: ἄδηλα γὰρ τὰ τῶν πολέμων, καὶ ἐξ ὀλίγου τὰ πολλὰ καὶ δι' ὀργῆς αἱ ἐπιχειρήσεις γίγνονται· πολλάκις τε τὸ ἔλασσον πλῆθος δεδιὸς ἄμεινον ἠμύνατο τοὺς πλέονας διὰ τὸ καταφρονοῦντας ἀπαρασκεύους γενέσθαι. "Events in war are unforeseen, and attacks usually happen swiftly and in anger; often too the smaller force with its fear fights better against the greater force because their arrogance makes them unprepared." Cf. Sall. *Jug.* 107.1: *saepe antea <a> paucis strenuis advorsum multitudinem bene pugnatum.* "Often before now a few strong men have fought successfully against a whole host." The divinity V. alludes to is presumably fickle Fortune, cf. III.22. V. is coy about the pagan religion, cf. IV.39.

[7]*mixtum agmen*.

runners, placing them one between two horsemen, on foot and armed with light shields, swords and javelins.[1]

17. On reserves,[2] which are posted behind the line.[3]

The best principle, and that which contributes most towards victory, is for the general to hold in readiness behind the line the pick of the infantry and cavalry, together with unattached "vicars", "counts" and tribunes,[4] some about the wings, and some about the middle. Then wherever the enemy attack strongly, they may rapidly move in to prevent the line being broken, reinforce any weak points and, with their additional strength, break the enemy's onset.

This tactic was first discovered by the Spartans, imitated by the Carthaginians, and later used everywhere by the Romans. No disposition has been found better than it. For the straight battle-line ought to and can only repel or rout the enemy.[5] If a "wedge"[6] or "pincer"[7] is to be formed, you will need to hold reserves behind the line, from which to

---

[1]There were contemporary kinds of mixed formation to which V. is perhaps assimilating the *velites* of the middle Republic, cf. Amm. 16,11.9, 19.3.1, 21.12.9, 24.1.13; Caes. *Bell. Gall.* 1.48.5–7 describes a similar German mixed formation to that described by Amm. 16.12.21 at the battle of Strasbourg, AD 357. Caesar later used a similar tactic at the battle of Pharsalus, 48 BC, cf. Front. *Strat.* 2.3.22. The *velites* are further described in action against elephants at III.24, as at the battle of Zama, 202 BC. The original *velites* were probably abolished by Marius' reforms, cf. Festus 274.21 L.: *parmulis pugnare velites* (*milites*, codd.) *soliti sunt; quarum usum sustulit Marius datis in vicem earum Bruttianis*, "*Velites* (*milites*, 'soldiers', codd.) were accustomed to fight with small round shields; Marius phased out their use, giving instead Bruttian shields", or at least soon after. Cf. M.J.V. Bell, "Tactical Reform in the Roman Republican Army", *Historia* xiv (1965) 421, who argued from Front. *Strat.* 2.3.17, mentioning Sulla's deployment of *velites et levem armaturam* at Orchomenus in 85 BC, that Festus meant that Marius merely gave the *velites* bigger shields.

[2]*subsidia.*

[3]Cf. Onas. 22.

[4]*vicarii, comites tribunique vacantes*, i.e. all staff-officers, cf. III.10. Note that Ammianus applies *vacans* only to tribunes.

[5]Cf. III praef. on Spartan tactics mediated to the Carthaginians by Xanthippus and Sosylus in the First and Second Punic Wars. Cato was said by Pliny *Hist. Nat.* praef. 30 to have learned his soldiering under Scipio Africanus and even Hannibal also. Each developed and refined the offensive reserve over the Second Punic War, cf. H.H. Scullard, *Scipio Africanus in the Second Punic War* (Cambridge 1930) 212, 270, after Hannibal had used it at Cannae, 216 BC, cf. Livy 22.47.6–10.

[6]*cuneus.* Cf. I.26.

[7]*forfex.*

make your wedge or pincer. If a "saw"[1] is to be drawn up, it is likewise drawn from reserves. Once you start transferring soldiers of the line from their stations, you will throw everything into confusion. If a detached "group"[2] of the enemy begins to press your wing or some other part, unless you have reserves which you can send against the "group", you will have to remove foot or horse from the line, and in so doing you will denude one part at your peril in your desire to defend another.[3]

When an abundant supply of soldiers is not available to you, it is better to have a shorter line, provided you place a very large number in reserve. In the middle of the field you need to hold the pick of your heavy-armed infantry in reserve, with which to form a "wedge" and suddenly break through the enemy line; whereas on the flanks you should keep in reserve cavalry pikemen and cuirassiers, with the light-armed infantry, for surrounding the enemy wings.[4]

18. In what position the commander-in-chief, the second- and third-in-command should stand.[5]

The general who holds the chief command usually stands between the infantry and cavalry on the right flank. This is the position from which the whole line is commanded, and from which there is direct and unobstructed forward movement. He stands between the two arms so as to be able to direct with his advice and exhort by his authority both cavalry and infantry to battle. It is his task to use his cavalry reserves[6]

---

[1]*serra.*

[2]*globus*, flying platoon.

[3]These special tactics were described in Cato's lost *de Re Militari*, cf. fr. 11 = Fest. 466.30 L.: *sive opus sit cuneo aut globo aut forcipe aut turribus aut serra, uti adoriare,* "whether there is need of a 'wedge', 'flying platoon', 'pincer', 'towers' or 'saw' in order to attack." They are further discussed in III.18–20. Arr. *Ect.* 30 proposed to lengthen the lines to deal with Alan flying platoons.

[4]This contradicts III.16 init., where only light cavalry are said to be for this purpose.

[5]This system of command may refer to the rotation-system followed for example at Cannae. Cf. Livy 22.45.8.

[6]*supernumerarii*, probably merely one of V.'s non-technical word for reserves, drawn from the usage of the civil service; cf. II.19 n. In III.17 he uses *superflui, abundantes, reservati* for the same, and in III.18, *superflui* and *supernumerarii.*

with light infantry mixed in with them to surround the enemy's left wing, which stands opposite himself, and press it constantly from the rear.

The second-in-command is posted in the middle of the infantry line to sustain and encourage it. He should have about him very strong and heavy-armed infantry from the said reserves, from which to make a "wedge" and break through the enemy line or, if the enemy form a "wedge", to make a "pincer" so he can counter their "wedge".

On the left flank of the army the third-in-command should be found, a suitably warlike and resourceful officer because the left flank is more awkward and stands as though maimed[1] in the line. He should have about him good reserve cavalry and very swift light infantry, with which he can constantly extend the left wing to prevent it being surrounded by the enemy.

The war-cry, which they call *barritus*, should not be raised until both lines have engaged each other. It is a mark of inexperienced or cowardly men if they cry out from a distance. The enemy are more terrified if the shock of the war-cry is made to coincide with the blows of weapons.[2]

Always strive to be first to draw up the line, because you can do at your pleasure what you judge useful to yourself, while no one is obstructing you. Secondly, you increase the confidence of your men and diminish the courage of the enemy, because the side which does not hesitate to challenge appears the stronger. The enemy, by contrast, begin to be afraid when they see lines being drawn up against them. Thirdly, it allows of the greatest advantage in that you may attack first while you are drawn up and prepared and the enemy is still ordering his forces and

---

[1] *Mancus*, technically denoting one forced to use his left hand because of damage to his right, cf. Ulp. *Dig.* 21.1.12.3. Cf. Thuc. 5.71 on the tendency of opposing battle-lines to shunt respectively to the right.

[2] Originally the tribal war-cry of the Cornuti, either a tribe or a collective noun for "Germans", enrolled by Constantine I, the *barritus* quickly spread to the whole field army; cf. Amm. 31.7.11, 26.7.17, 16.12.43, Lact. *Plac. in Stat. Theb.* 4.394 J., Kempf, art. cit. 372; A. Alföldi, "Cornuti: A Teutonic contingent in the service of Constantine the Great", *DOP* xiii (1959) 169–179. Cf. also SHA *Alex. Sev.* 53.8–9, Arr. *Ect.* 25, Onas. 29; and Arr. *Tact.* 44.1 on the various ethnic war-cries in use in the Roman army of Hadrian.

unsteady. For part of victory consists in throwing the enemy into confusion before you fight.

19. Remedies to counter the strength and stratagems of the enemy in battle.[1]

With the exception of raids and surprises, undertaken at some moment of advantage which an experienced general never misses—for when soldiers are marching wearily, divided while crossing a river, bogged down in marshes, struggling over mountain-passes, dispersed and unsuspecting in fields or sleeping in a night camp,[2] an attack is always made on favourable terms, as the enemy is preoccupied with other business and is killed before he can prepare himself,[3]—[but] if the opposition are careful and present no opportunity for ambush, then one fights on equal terms, in the full presence, knowledge and view of the enemy. However, the art of war is not less useful to the proficient in the open field of battle than it is in covert operations. Take care above all that your men be not surrounded on their left wing or flank, as often occurs, or indeed on their right, although this happens rarely, by a mass of the enemy or by mobile "groups",[4] which they call *drungi*.[5] If this occurs there is one remedy: fold back and round off your wing or flank, until your men who have wheeled round may defend the backs of their comrades. At the salient angle of the end itself let a very strong force be posted, because that is where the main attack is usually made.[6]

---

[1]Further discussion of tactics originally described by Cato; cf. III.17. The use of the modern term *drungi* shows V. is updating, as usual. Lang moved the rubric for III.19 down to the sentence beginning *Tamen*, "however", against the unanimous witness of the MSS, and in violation of the best sense of V.'s words, which involve an anacoluthon after the long parenthesis by way of stressing the point that a pitched battle ought to be a last resort. Stelten restored the capitulation but incongruously kept Lang's punctuation.

[2]*mansio.*

[3]V. hammers home the importance of opportunities for guerilla-tactics; cf. III.6, III.8, III.10, III.22, and Polyb. 9.12.7–8 on the third principle of generalship, the mastery of timing.

[4]*globi.*

[5]flying platoons.

[6]The ἐπικάμπιος τάξις, "angular line," of Greek tactics, described by Ael. *Tact.* 45–46, Onas. 21.1–2.

Likewise there are appointed methods of countering a "wedge" of the enemy. A "wedge" is the name for a mass of infantry who are attached to the line, which moves forward, narrower in front and broader behind, and breaks through the enemy lines, because a larger number of men are discharging missiles into one position.[1] Soldiers call this tactic a "pig's head".[2] Against this is deployed the formation known as a "pincer". A body of crack troops is formed into a letter V, and this receives the "wedge", shutting it in on either side. Once this is done, it cannot break through the line. The "saw" is the name of a formation which is ranged by crack troops before the front, facing the enemy, so that a disordered line may be repaired.[3] The "group"[4] is a body of men who separate off from their own line, and charge into the enemy in a mobile attack. A more numerous and stronger *globus* is sent against it. Beware also of deciding to change your ranks or transfer certain units from their stations to others at the moment when battle is being joined. Uproar and confusion instantly ensue, and the enemy more easily press upon unready and disordered forces.

---

[1]See F. Lammert, "Der Keil in der Taktik des Altertums", *Gymnasium* li (1940) 15–31, identifying it as a double linear formation only vaguely resembling a wedge. Hannibal used a *cuneus* at Cannae, cf. Livy 22.47.5 and 8.

[2]*caput porcinum.* Cf. Amm. 17.13.9: *desinente in angustum fronte, quem habitum caput porci simplicitas militaris appellat*, "a front tailing off to a corner, which formation simple soldiers call a 'pig's head'", Agathias 2.8.8 (Keydell, 51): συὸς κεφαλή, "pig's head", and Kempf, 369, citing Germans in Scandinavia who had a *svínfylking* = *acies porcina.*

[3]Cf. Festus 466.28 L.: *SERRA PROELIARI dicitur, cum assidue acceditur recediturque, neque ullo consistitur tempore.* "'To fight in saw-formation' is said when there is a constant advancing and withdrawing, and no standing still at any time."

[4]*globus*, flying platoon.

20. How many modes for engaging in a pitched battle there are, and how the side that is inferior in numbers and strength may prevail. There are seven types or modes of general actions,[1] when hostile standards engage from two sides. The first action has the army in rectangular formation with an extended front, just as even now it is usual to do battle almost always.[2] However, experts in military science do not consider this type of action best, because when the line is extended over a wide area, it does not always meet with even ground. If there are any gaps in the middle, or a bend or curve, that is the point at which the line is often breached.[3] Further, if the enemy has the advantage of numbers, he envelops your right or left wing from the sides. There is great danger in this unless you have reserves who can move up and hold back the enemy. Only he who has more numerous and strong forces should engage in this formation. He should envelop the enemy on both wings and enclose him as it were in the embrace of his army.

The second action is oblique, and better in very many respects. With this, if you draw up a small strong force in the proper position, you will be able to bring off a victory even though you are impeded by the numbers and strength of the foe. The method is as follows. When the drawn lines advance to the encounter, you will remove your left wing farther from the enemy's right, so that neither missiles nor arrows can reach it. You should fasten your right wing to the enemy's left, and start the battle there first, while using your best cavalry and most reliable infantry to attack and surround the enemy's left flank, on which you have fastened, and by dislodging and outflanking them, reach the enemy's rear. If once you begin to rout the enemy from then on, with

---

[1]*depugnationes.*

[2]The contents of this chapter are probably largely based on Cato *de Re Militari*; cf. Jordan fr. 10 = Non. Marc. 204.32 M.: *una depugnatio est fronte longo, quadrato exercitu,* "A first mode of general action is with an extended front, the army in rectangular formation", and Vegetius: *una depugnatio est fronte longa quadro exercitu.* The archaic usage (?) whereby *unus* seems here to head a list *secundus, tertius, etc.,* thus containing the idea *primus,* is reproduced by Vegetius, but not the archaic masculine gender of *frons,* and *quadratus* is replaced by the late-Latin *quadrus.*

[3]Cf. Polyb. 18.31.5–7 on the similar problem of finding suitable ground for the Macedonian phalanx to operate.

those of your men who are attacking you will undoubtedly gain a victory, while the part of your army which you moved away from the enemy will remain undisturbed. The lines in this mode of battle are joined in the shape of a letter A or a mason's plummet-level.[1] If the enemy does this to you first, you should assemble on your left wing those cavalry and infantry we said should be placed behind the line as reserves,[2] and then resist the adversary with maximum force to avoid defeat through tactics.[3]

The third action is similar to the second, but inferior insofar as you begin by engaging his right from your left wing. For its attack is as it were maimed;[4] the men fighting on the left wing are clearly in difficulties when attacking the enemy. I shall explain this more clearly. If you find that your left wing is far superior, reinforce it with your strongest cavalry and infantry, and in the encounter attach it first to the enemy right wing and make as much haste as you can to defeat and surround the right flank of the enemy. But the other part of your army, in which you know you have inferior warriors, remove as far as possible from the enemy left, so that it is not attacked with swords or reached by missiles. With this formation, care must be taken that your transverse line shall not be harmed by wedge-formations of the enemy. It will only be useful to fight in this mode in the case where your adversary has a weak right wing, and you have a far stronger left.

The fourth action is as follows. When you have ordered your line, at 400 or 500 paces[5] before you reach the enemy, suddenly spur on both your wings when he is not expecting it, in order to turn the enemy to flight by catching him unprepared on both wings and win a quick victory. But although this type of battle may overcome quickly, provided you deploy highly experienced and brave men, it is nevertheless risky, because he who uses this formation is forced to

---

[1] i.e. the lines meet at an acute angle at one end; the cross-bar of the A is ignored.
[2] Cf. III.18.
[3] Cf. Onas. 21.8.
[4] Cf. III.18
[5] i.e. 2,000 or 2,500 Roman feet = c.647 yds. (591 m.) or c.808 yds. (739 m.), cf. III.15 note.

denude the middle of his line and divide his army into two halves. Moreover if the enemy is not beaten at the first assault, he has opportunity to attack the divided wings and undefended middle line.[1]

The fifth action is like the fourth, but with the sole refinement of placing the light armament and archers before the front line, so it cannot be breached while they defend it. The general is then free to use his right wing to attack the enemy left and his left wing to attack the enemy right. If he can turn him to flight, he wins at once; if not, his middle line does not come under pressure, being defended by the light armament and archers.

The sixth action is the best, being very similar to the second. It is used by those generals who despair of the numbers and bravery of their men, and if they draw up their men well, they always win a victory even with fewer forces. For when the drawn line nears the enemy, apply your right wing to the enemy left, and start the battle there using very reliable cavalry and very swift light infantry. Remove the remaining part of your army as far as possible from the enemy line, and extend it in a straight line like a spit. Once you begin cutting down the enemy left wing from the flank and rear, you will certainly put them to flight. But the enemy is prevented from assisting his men in trouble either from his right flank or from the middle of his line, because your line is extended and projects as a whole like a letter I, and recedes a very long distance from the enemy. This formation is often used in encounters on marches.

The seventh action aids the combatant by using the terrain. This also allows you to hold out against the enemy with fewer and less brave forces. For example, if you have on one side of you a mountain, sea, river, lake, city, marshes or broken country, so that the enemy cannot approach from that direction, draw up the main part of your army in a straight line, but on the side which does not have protection place all your cavalry and light infantry. You may then safely engage the enemy

---

[1] Cf. Onas. 21.5–7. The tactic was used by the elder Scipio Africanus against Hasdrubal at the battle of Ilipa, 206 BC, cf. Livy 28.14, Polyb. 11.20–24, cf. Seneca *de Vit. Beat.* 4.1.

at your pleasure, because on one side the nature of the terrain protects you, and on the other there is roughly double cavalry posted.[1]

But note this—nothing better has been found: if you intend to fight with your right wing alone, place your strongest men there. If with your left, station the most effective there. If you wish to form "wedges" in the middle to breach the enemy lines, draw up your most experienced soldiers in the "wedge". Victory is usually owing to a small number of men:[2] so important is it for picked men to be ranged by a highly skilled general in those positions which judgement and utility demand.

21. An escape-route should be offered to the enemy so that they may be more easily destroyed in full flight.[3]

Most people ignorant of military matters believe the victory will be more complete if they surround the enemy in a confined place or with large numbers of soldiers, so they can find no way of escape. But trapped men draw extra courage from desperation, and when there is no hope, fear takes up arms. Men who know without a doubt that they are going to die will gladly die in good company.[4]

For this reason Scipio's axiom has won praise, when he said that a way should be built for the enemy to flee by.[5] For when an escape-route is revealed, the minds of all are united on turning their backs, and they are slaughtered unavenged, like cattle.[6] Nor is there any danger for the pursuers once the defeated have turned round the arms with which they

---

[1] Cf. Onas. 21.3–4.

[2] Cf. the *triarii*, I.20.

[3] This chapter has echoes of Sall. *Cat.* 58, Catiline's speech to his men when finally surrounded by the senatorial forces in 63 BC.

[4] Cf. Sen. *Contr.* 9.6.2: *morientibus gratissimum est commori.* "It is most gratifying to the dying to die in good company."

[5] Front. *Strat.* 4.7.16: *Scipio Africanus dicere solitus est hosti non solum dandam esse viam ad fugiendum, sed etiam muniendam,* "Scipio Africanus used to say that a way should not merely be given to the enemy to flee by, but even built for them", cf. ibid. 2.6.5,—the "golden bridge" of later tradition.

[6] Sall. *Cat.* 58.21: *cavete inulti animam amittatis, neu capti potius sicuti pecora trucidemini...* "Be warned not to lose your lives unavenged, nor be taken instead and butchered like cattle." Cf. Livy 25.16.19.

could have defended themselves.[1] In this tactic, the greater the numbers, the more easily is a mass cut down. For there is no need of numbers in a case where the soldiers' minds, once terrified, wish to avoid not just the enemy's weapons but his face.[2] Whereas trapped men, though few in number and weak in strength, for this very reason are a match for their enemies, because desperate men know they can have no other recourse. "The only hope of safety for the defeated is to expect no safety."[3]

22. How to retreat from the enemy if the plan to fight is rejected.
Now that I have summarized everything that military science preserved from experience and theory, one matter remains for me to explain—how to retreat from the enemy. For those learned in the art of war and historical precedent affirm that nowhere is the threat of danger greater. The general who retreats from the line before the encounter both diminishes confidence among his own men and gives courage to the enemy. But since this must often happen, the means of safely achieving it need exposition.

First, your men should not know that you are retreating because you refuse to enter battle, but believe they are being called back as part of some strategy to attract the enemy onto more favourable ground and overcome him more easily, or at least to set up a concealed ambush for the enemy troops who follow. For men are ready to take flight if they feel that their general is in despair. The enemy must also be prevented from noticing your retreat and attacking at once. To this end many generals have placed their cavalry in front of the infantry, manoeuvring about so that the enemy might not see the infantry retiring. They then

---

[1]Sall. *Cat.* 58.16: *nam in fuga salutem sperare, quom arma quibus corpora tegitur ab hostibus avorteris, ea vero dementia est,* "For to hope for safety by taking flight, when you have turned away from the enemy the arms by which bodies are protected,—that truly is madness."

[2]Cf. Caes. *Bell. Gall.* 1.39.1: *saepe numero sese cum his congressos ne vultum quidem atque aciem oculorum dicebant ferre potuisse,* "They would say that often in their encounters with these men they could not bear even their face and the gaze of their eyes."

[3]Verg. *Aen.* 2.354; it is preserved only in the ε group of MSS. Since V. likes to quote Vergil, however, Lang was wrong to excise it.

removed and called back each line piecemeal, beginning with the foremost, while the remainder stayed in their ranks. These were gradually pulled back later to join those removed first.[1]

Some would retire with the army by night along routes they had reconnoitred; when the enemy realized at dawn, they were unable to overtake those who had gone ahead. Or else, the light armament were sent ahead to the hills to which the whole army was withdrawn suddenly, and if the enemy wished to pursue, they were routed by the light armament who had occupied the place beforehand, aided by the cavalry. For nothing is thought more perilous than for careless pursuers to be attacked by men lying in ambush or who have prepared themselves in advance.

This is a time when ambushes may be opportunely set, because over-confidence and too little caution are used against fugitives. Necessarily, more freedom from fear generally brings with it graver danger.[2] Attacks are usually made on those who are unready, whilst they are eating a meal, wearily marching, grazing their horses and suspecting nothing of the kind. This should be avoided by us and damage inflicted on the enemy on such occasions. For neither bravery nor numbers can assist those caught in such a case. He who is beaten in battle in a general engagement, though there too art is of very great advantage, can nevertheless in his defence accuse Fortune; he who suffers sudden attack, ambushes or surprises cannot acquit himself of blame, because he could have avoided these things and discovered them beforehand through good scouts.[3]

On retreats the following stratagem is often used.[4] A few cavalry pursue by the direct route, while a strong force is sent secretly through other localities. When the cavalry reach the enemy column, they skirmish lightly with them and depart. Their general thinks he has passed whatever ambush there had been and, freed from care, relaxes

---

[1]This is a stratagem of L. Aemilius Paullus, employed in 168 BC; cf. Livy 44.37.1–3.
[2]Cf. Thuc. 2.11.3–5.
[3]*speculatores*, cf. III.6.
[4]i.e. against the retreating party.

into incaution. Then the force sent by the secret route attacks and destroys them unexpectedly. Many generals retreating from the enemy, if they are to go through forests, send men ahead to occupy defiles and precipitous places, to avoid falling into ambush there. They also block roads behind them by felling trees, in what they call a *concaedes*,[1] depriving the enemy of the facility to pursue.[2]

Opportunities for ambush on the march are pretty well equally shared between both sides, for the (adversary) in front leaves traps behind him in suitable valleys and wooded mountains, and when the enemy falls into them returns himself to assist his own men. The pursuer for his part sends light troops far ahead by back paths and prevents the adversary up ahead from getting past, closing him in, trapped in front and behind. If the opposition sleep at night either the (adversary) in front can double back, or the pursuer can attack by surprise, although there is a distance between them. At the crossing of rivers let the party in front try to rout the division that crosses first, while the rest are still separated by the river-bed, or let the pursuer arrive by forced marches to discomfit those who have not yet been able to cross.[3]

23. On the camels and armoured cavalry.[4]
Some nations in ancient times led forth camels into battle, and the Urcilliani in Africa and the other Mazices lead them forth even today.[5] It is a type of animal well-adapted to sands and enduring thirst, and is said to keep straight on roads without error even when they are

---

[1]"abattis".

[2]Cf. Tac. *Ann.* 1.50, Amm. 16.11.8, 17.1.9, 17.10.6.

[3]Cf. Caes. *Bell. Civ.* 3.75.3–5, Maur. *Strat.* 4 ΠΕΡΙ 'ΕΝΕΔΡΑΣ. "On Ambush."

[4]Antiochus III, king of Syria, appears to have been first to field cataphract cavalry and camels against the Romans at the battle of Magnesia, 190 BC, cf. Livy 37.40.5, 11, 12, 37.42.2: *alii propter gravitatem tegumentorum armorumque oppressi sunt*, "others were overcome because of the weight of their armour and weapons", 37.40.12: *cameli, quos appellant dromadas, his insidebant Arabes...* "camels called dromadaries, on these sat Arabs..."

[5]The *Urcilliani* are otherwise attested only by Corippus *Iohann.* 5.390, in the sixth century AD.

obscured by dust in the wind. However, apart from its novelty when it is seen by those not used to it, it is ineffective in battle.[1]

Armoured cavalry[2] are safe from being wounded on account of the armour they wear, but because they are hampered by the weight of their arms are easily taken prisoner and often vulnerable to lassos.[3] They are better in battle against loose-order infantry than against cavalry, but posted in front of legionaries or mixed with legionaries they often break the enemy line when it comes to *comminus*, that is, hand-to-hand, fighting.[4]

---

[1] It is claimed that the Romans later made some use of camels in battle as *dromadarii*, as well as for transport; cf. Ps.-Hyg. 29, R.W. Davies, "Ratio and Opinio in Roman military documents", *Historia* xvi (1967) 117, M.P. Speidel, *Guards of the Roman armies*, Antiquitas Reihe I, Bd. XXVIII (Bonn 1978) 26; as used for transporting heavy or bulky supplies, cf. Davies, *BASP* v (1968) 33–34. However, the arch of Galerius reliefs show only transportation, cf. H.P. Laubscher, *Der Reliefschmuck des Galeriusbogens in Thessaloniki*, Deutsches Arch. Inst. Archaologische Forschungen I (Berlin 1975) Taf. 28.3 camels carrying booty (?), Taf. 14.1 dromadaries carrying captive Persian royal harem-ladies.

[2] *cataphracti equites.*

[3] *laquei.* A Hun tactic, according to Amm. 31.2.9. The Parthians also had mounted soldiers who fought using a lasso, cf. *Suda* Σ.278 s.v. σειραῖς, and were themselves famous for their cataphract cavalry, cf. *Suda* Θ .439 s.v. θώραξ. Cf. IV.23 where it means "nooses".

[4] M.P. Speidel, "Horsemen in the Pannonian Alae", *SJ* xliii (1987) 61–65, = *Roman Army Studies* II 62–66, id., "Catafractarii clibanarii and the rise of the later Roman mailed cavalry: a gravestone from Claudiopolis in Bithynia", *EA* iv (1984) 151–156, with further refs., = *Roman Army Studies* II 406–413, J.R. Rea, "A Cavalryman's Career, A.D. 382 (?)–401", *ZPE* lxvi (1984) 80.

24. How scythed chariots and elephants may be resisted in battle.[1]

Scythed chariots[2] were used in battle by king Antiochus[3] and Mithridates.[4] Although at first they caused much alarm, they soon became a laughing-stock. For it is difficult for a scythed chariot to find a field that is constantly flat, and it is hindered by a slight impediment and captured if a single horse is stricken or wounded.[5] But most of all they fell victim to the following tactic of the Roman soldiers. When they came to battle, the Romans suddenly threw caltrops[6] over the whole field. The speeding chariots were destroyed as they encountered them.[7] A caltrop is a defensive weapon made out of four spikes; whichever way you throw it, it stands on three spikes and is armed by the fourth which is erect.

Elephants in battle cause men and horses to panic because of the size of their bodies, the horror of their trumpeting and the novelty of their very form. King Pyrrhus in Lucania was the first to use them against the Roman army,[8] and later Hannibal in Africa,[9] king Antiochus in the

---

[1]V. summarizes a traditional chapter. Arrian *Tact.* 2.5, cf. 19.1, found in his sources along with elephants various kinds of scythed chariot, with armoured and unarmoured horses, with a single pole and with two or more poles, but did not think the material worth transmitting because of its obsoleteness. Servius *ad Aen.* 1.476, writing in the late-fourth century, knew of scythed chariots only from ancient history. SHA *Alex. Sev.* 55.2, 56.4, on the capture by Severus Alexander during the Persian campaign of AD 232 of 1,800 scythed chariots, is apocryphal.

[2]*quadrigae falcatae*, according to tradition invented by Cyrus the great, king of Persia, Xen. *Cyr.* 6.1.29, cf. Arr. *Tact.* 22, Anon. *de Rebus Bellicis* 12.1.

[3]Antiochus III, king of Syria, used scythed chariots at the battle of Magnesia, 190 BC, cf. Livy 37.41.5, Florus 1.24.16.

[4]Mithridates VI Eupator, king of Pontus, whose general Archelaus used scythed chariots at the battle of Chaeronea, 86 BC, cf. Front. *Strat.* 2.3.17, Plut. *Sulla* 15.1, 16.3, and Mithridates himself used them in northern Asia Minor against Lucullus in 73 BC, cf. Plut. *Lucull.* 7.5. His son Pharnaces used them against Julius Caesar at Zela in 47 BC, cf. A. Hirtius *Bell. Alex.* 75.2, the last reliable use of this weapon.

[5]The Anon. *de Rebus Bellicis* 12–14 attempted to solve these problems by means of hinged blades and armoured horses, in his highly fanciful military reforms proposed to a late-fourth- or early-fifth-century AD Emperor.

[6]*tribuli.*

[7]The reference appears unknown. On *tribuli* cf. Philo Byz. *Bel.* 100.7, Polyaen. 1.39.2, 4.3.17, Herodian 4.15.2–3.

[8]At the battle of the river Siris, at Heraclea, Lucania, 280 BC, cf. Plut. *Pyrrh.* 16–17, Dion. Hal. 19.4–12, and Florus 1.13.7–8 who wrongly says Heraclea in Campania and the river Liris.

[9]At the battle of Zama, 202 BC, cf. Livy 30.33.1–3, 14–16.

Orient,[1] and Jugurtha in Numidia[2] had them in large numbers. Various methods of resistance have been worked out against them.—

A centurion in Lucania cut the hand off one with his sword,—what they call the *proboscis*.[3] Pairs of cataphract horses were harnessed each to a chariot; mounted on (the horses) were cataphract cavalrymen[4] who aimed *sarisae*, that is, very long pikes,[5] at the elephants. Being covered in iron they were not harmed by the archers riding on the beasts, and avoided their charges thanks to the speed of their horses. Others sent against elephants cataphract infantrymen;[6] on their arms, helmets and shoulders huge iron spikes were set, so that the elephant could not use its trunk to catch hold of the soldier coming against him. But especially the ancients deployed *velites*[7] against elephants. *Velites* were young men lightly armed and able-bodied, who sent spears with marvellous skill from horseback. While the horses ran past, they brought the beasts down using broad lances[8] or large javelins;[9] then, with increasing boldness, larger numbers of soldiers would combine together to cast *pila*, that is, javelins, into the elephants, destroying them with wounds. Another method was for slingers with "sling-staves"[10] and slings to shoot round stones at the Indians controlling the elephants, knock them off, turrets

---

[1]At the battle of Magnesia, 190 or 189 BC, cf. Livy 37.40.2–4, Florus 1.24.16.

[2]At the battle of the river Muthul, 109 BC, cf. Sall. *Jug.* 49.1, 53.3–4.

[3]i.e. trunk. The word is misspelled *promuscis* in the MSS, as also in the MSS of Florus 1.13.9. The allusion is to an incident at the battle of Asculum, in Apulia not Lucania, 279 BC, cf. Florus ibid.

[4]*clibanarii.* V. uses a late-Roman (from Persian) term for them; cf. *RE* IV (1900) 21–22 s.v. (Fiebiger), M.P. Speidel, "Catafractarii clibanarii and the rise of the later Roman mailed cavalry: a gravestone from Claudiopolis in Bithynia", *EA* iv (1984) 151–156 = id., *Roman Army Studies* II 406–413.

[5]*conti.* Presumably the chariot was used to screen the backs of the attackers, cf. Anon. *de Rebus Bellicis* 12–14. On the *saris(s)a*, see M.M. Markle, "The Macedonian Sarissa, Spear, and related armor", *AJA* lxxxi (1977) 323–339; P.A. Manti, "The Macedonian Sarissa, Again", *AncW* xxv (1994) 77–91.

[6]*cataphracti milites.*

[7]light troops.

[8]*lanceae.*

[9]*spicula.* The size of the weapons is explained below by that of the ballista-bolts as matching the elephants. The rôle of *velites* is also described at III.16, where they perform on foot; the material obviously belongs to the middle Republic.

[10]*fustibali*, cf. III.14.

and all, and slay them; no safer method has been found than this.[1] Or else, as the beasts charged, the soldiers yielded ground to them as if they had broken into the line. When they reached the midst of the formation, they were surrounded on all sides by massed groups[2] of soldiers and captured with their drivers, intact and free from wounds.[3] It is advisable to post behind the line carriage-ballistas[4] of a somewhat larger model—these shoot bolts farther and with greater force—mounted on cars with pairs of horses or mules; then, when the beasts come within the weapon's range they are pierced by ballista-bolts.[5] A broader and stronger iron head is fitted so as to make larger wounds in large bodies. Against elephants we have listed several examples and devices, so that if the need ever arise it may be known what should be deployed against such monstrous beasts.[6]

25. What to do, if part or if all of the army is routed.

Note that if part of the army is victorious and part is routed, one should be hopeful, because in a crisis of this type the steadfastness of the general can reclaim the whole victory for himself. This has happened in countless battles, and those who have despaired the least have been taken for the winners. Where their situations are similar, he is judged the stronger who is not dismayed by his adversities. Let him be first, therefore, to take spoils from the enemy slain—as (the soldiers) themselves say, "collect the field".[7] Let him be seen to be first to celebrate with shouts and bugles. By this show of confidence he will terrify

---

[1] The mahouts were called "Indians" by the Romans regardless of whether they controlled Indian or African elephants. Cf. Polyb. I.40.15, Livy 38.14.2. See also Apoc. 1 *Macc.* 6.38.

[2] *globi*, massed platoons.

[3] The stratagem was Scipio's at Zama, 202 BC, cf. Livy 30.33.1–3, 14–16, Polyb. 15.9.6–10, 15.12.1–4, Front. *Strat.* 2.3.16.

[4] *carroballistae*, cf. III.14 for *carroballistae* behind the lines.

[5] *sagittae ballistariae.*

[6] Arr. *Tact.* 19 dismissed chariots and elephants as obsolete, diverging from Ael. *Tact.* 22. But the Persians fielded elephants (but not chariots) regularly in the fourth century AD, cf. Amm. 19.2.3, etc., who also finds them formidable.

[7] *colligat campum.* This piece of soldiers' slang is not otherwise attested; cf. Kempf, 376.

the enemy and double the confidence of his own men, as if he had come off victor in every part of the field.

But if for some reason the whole army be routed in battle, the disaster can be mortal; yet the chance to recover has existed for many, and a remedy should be sought. Let the provident general therefore engage in pitched battle only if he has taken precaution that, should something go wrong owing to the variability of wars and the human condition, he may still get the defeated away without great loss. For if there are hills nearby, if there are fortifications to the rear,[1] or if the bravest troops resist while the rest retreat, they will save themselves and their comrades. Often a previously routed army has recovered its strength and destroyed those in loose order and pursuing at random. Never does greater danger tend to arise for the side that is celebrating, than when over-confidence is suddenly turned to panic.[2]

But in any event survivors should be collected up, stiffened for war by means of appropriate exhortations and restored with new arms. Then new levies of legionaries[3] and new *auxilia*[4] should be sought and, what is more important, opportunities to attack the victors themselves through concealed ambushes should be exploited, and morale regained in this way. There is no lack of opportunity, since human minds are carried away by success to become so much the more arrogant and careless. If anyone shall think this his last chance, let him reflect that the results of all battles in the early stages (of a war) have been more against those destined to ultimate victory.[5]

---

[1]Cf. I.21.
[2]Cf. Onas. 36.3–6, Thuc. 2.11.4.
[3]*dilectûs.*
[4]palatine *auxilia.*
[5]Cf. Polyb. 3.4.4–5.

26. General rules of war.[1]

In all battles the terms of campaign are such that what benefits you harms the enemy, and what helps him always hinders you. Therefore we ought never to do or omit to do anything at his pleasure, but carry out only that which we judge useful to ourselves. For you begin to be against yourself if you copy what he has done in his own interest, and likewise whatever you attempt for your side will be against him if he chooses to imitate it.

In war, he who spends more time watching in outposts and puts more effort into training soldiers, will be less subject to danger.[2]

A soldier should never be led into battle unless you have made trial of him first.[3]

It is preferable to subdue an enemy by famine, raids and terror, than in battle where fortune tends to have more influence than bravery.[4]

No plans are better than those you carry out in advance without the enemy's knowledge.[5]

Opportunity in war is usually of greater value than bravery.[6]

In solliciting and taking in enemy soldiers, if they come in good faith, there is great security, because deserters harm the enemy more than casualties.[7]

It is preferable to keep additional reserves behind the line than to spread the soldiers too widely.[8]

It is difficult to beat someone who can form a true estimate of his own and the enemy's forces.[9]

---

[1]V.'s "general rules" were much the most popular part of the Epitome in the Middle Ages, and Maurice at the end of the sixth century translated a number of them into Greek in his *Strategica* 8.2, as well as adding many more, some taken from elsewhere in V.'s Epitome, others from Onasander and other sources.

[2]Cf. I.3.

[3]Cf. III.9, III.10.

[4]Cf. III.3, III.9, III.22.

[5]Cf. III.6, III.18.

[6]Cf. III.18 fin.

[7]Cf. III.6 fin.

[8]Cf. III.15.

[9]Cf. III.9.

Bravery is of more value than numbers.[1]

Terrain is often of more value than bravery.[2]

Few men are born naturally brave; hard work and good training makes many so.[3]

An army is improved by work, enfeebled by inactivity.[4]

Never lead forth a soldier to a general engagement except when you see that he expects victory.[5]

Surprises alarm the enemy, familiarity breeds contempt.[6]

He who pursues rashly with his forces in loose order is willing to give the adversary the victory he had himself obtained.[7]

He who does not prepare grain-supplies and provisions is conquered without a blow.[8]

He who has the advantage in numbers and bravery, let him do battle with a rectangular front, which is the first mode.[9]

He who judges himself unequal, let him rout the left wing of the enemy with his right, which is the second mode.[10]

He who knows he has a very strong left wing, let him attack the right wing of the enemy, which is the third mode.[11]

He who has very experienced soldiers should begin battle on both wings together, which is the fourth mode.[12]

He who commands an excellent light armament, let him attack both wings of the enemy after posting the light troops before the line, which is the fifth mode.[13]

---

[1]Cf. I.8, III.16, III.20 fin.
[2]Cf. III.13.
[3]Cf. I.1, I.2, and passim.
[4]Cf. II.23 fin., III.4.
[5]Cf. III.12.
[6]Cf. III.6, III.12.
[7]Cf. III.22, III.25.
[8]Cf. III.3, III.9.
[9]Cf. III.20.
[10]Cf. III.20.
[11]Cf. III.20.
[12]Cf. III.20.
[13]Cf. III.20.

He who has confidence neither in the numbers of his soldiers nor their bravery and is to fight a pitched battle, let him repel the left wing of the enemy with his right having extended the rest of his men in the form of a spit; which is the sixth mode.[1]

He who knows he has fewer and inferior forces, in the seventh mode let him have on one flank a mountain, city, sea, or river, or some (other) support.[2]

He who has confidence in his cavalry should find places more suited to horsemen and wage war more by means of cavalry.[3]

He who has confidence in the infantry forces should find places more suited to infantry and wage war more through infantry.[4]

When an enemy spy[5] is wandering secretly in camp, let all personnel be ordered to their tents in daylight, and the spy is immediately caught.[6]

When you discover that your plan has been betrayed to the enemy, you are advised to change your dispositions.[7]

Discuss with many what you should do, but what you are going to do discuss with as few and as trustworthy as possible, or rather with yourself alone.[8]

Soldiers are corrected by fear and punishment in camp, on campaign hope and rewards make them behave better.[9]

Good generals never engage in a general engagement except on some advantageous occasion, or under great necessity.[10]

It is a powerful disposition to press the enemy more with famine than with the sword.[11]

---

[1] Cf. III.20.
[2] Cf. III.20.
[3] Cf. III.9, III.13.
[4] Cf. III.9, III.13.
[5] *explorator*.
[6] Not mentioned elsewhere in the text. Maur. *Strat.* 9.5.20 records the same tactic.
[7] Not mentioned elsewhere in the text.
[8] Cf. III.6, III.9.
[9] Cf. III.4.
[10] Cf. III.9.
[11] Cf. III.3, III.9.

The mode in which you are going to give battle should not become known to the enemy, lest they make moves to resist with any counter-measures.[1]

On cavalry there are many precepts, but since this branch of the military has progressed in its training practices, type of armour[2] and breed of horses, I do not think there is anything to be gained from books, for the present state of knowledge is sufficient.

I have set out, Invincible Emperor, the principles which the noblest authors handed down to posterity as having won the approval of different ages in the test of experience. To your skill at archery which the Persian admires in Your Serenity, to the skill and grace of your horsemanship which the nation of the Huns and Alans would like to imitate if it could,[3] to your speed in the charge which the Saracen and Indian cannot match, to your expertise in *armatura*[4] even part of whose routines the drillmasters[5] are delighted to have appreciated (as connoisseurs),[6] may now be joined a Rule-book of Battle, or rather an Art of Victory, in order that by the valour coupled with the strategy of your glorious State, you may manifest your rôle of both Commander-in-chief (Emperor) and Soldier.[7]

---

[1]Cf. III.19, III.20.

[2]Cf. I.20 init. on the improvements due to the Goths, Huns and Alans, and cf. *Mulomedicina* 3.6.5, where the Hunnic breed of warhorse is given pride of place, and a full description.

[3]The junction of these two peoples is reported by Amm. 31.3.1, cf. Ps.-Victor *Epit. de Caess.* 47.3.

[4]special drill, cf. I.13 note, II.23.

[5]*campidoctores.*

[6]The presence of these barbarians in the context of feats of arms including *armatura*, and the emulation ascribed to them in the same breath as to the Roman drillmasters, may suggest tournaments, i.e., friendly competition. In any event, the particular combination of names suits best the reign of Theodosius I, who concluded peace-treaties with the king of Persia, and with the Saracens and people called "Indians", cf. Pac. *Pan. Lat.* 2 (12) 22.2–5, as well as with the Huns and Alans, cf. ibid. 32.4, in the AD 380s.

[7]Cf. Sall. *Cat.* 60.4: *strenui militis et boni imperatoris officia simul exequebatur*, "he fulfilled at once the duties of an energetic soldier and a good commander-in-chief."

Book IV

Preface.

The wild and uncivilized life of man at the beginning of time was first separated from communion with dumb animals and beasts by the founding of cities. In them the common utility discovered the idea of the State. And so the most powerful nations and consecrated Princes thought that there was no greater glory than the foundation of new cities or the transfer of those founded by others to their own name under some expansion.[1] In this enterprise the Clemency of Your Serenity wins the palm. For by others few or single cities, by Your Piety countless cities have been completed with such continuous activity that they appear not so much built by human hands as sprung up by divine will.[2] You surpass all Emperors in felicity, moderation, morality, displays of indulgence and love of studies.[3] We see the good things of your reign and mind and we hold what both the past age wished to anticipate and the future longs to be perpetuated for ever.[4] We rejoice that in these things as much has been granted to the whole world as human mind could ask or divine favour bestow. But the value added to the dispositions of Your Clemency by the elaborate construction of walls is demonstrated by Rome, who saved the lives of her citizens through the defences of the Capitoline citadel, to the end that she might later win a more glorious Empire of the whole world.[5] To complete, then, a work undertaken by command of Your Majesty, I shall summarize in order from various authors the measures by which either our cities should be

---

[1] i.e. of the cities.

[2] Symm. *II laud. in Val.* 20 uses *civitates* of towers. Julian *Ep. ad Athen.* 297A claimed to have rebuilt 45 "cities", probably including forts on the German frontier as well as Gallic towns, cf. Amm. 16.11.11, 17.9.1; Themistius' description of Valens building the fort of Charsovo in Thrace 368–9, *Or.* 10.136a–138b: forts "rose as if by magic". But Theodosius I seems to have founded or renamed a significant number of cities in the East, e.g. Theodosiopolis-Resaina in Osrhoene, Theodosiopolis in Armenia, Theodosiana in Arcadia, Aegyptiaca, perhaps two other Theodosiopoleis in Egypt, Arcadiopolis-Bergula in Thrace, etc. Other examples of "Theodosiopolis" or "Theodosiana" may have been founded by Theodosius II. The historical exegesis seems based partly on Sall. *Cat.* 1–2; cf. also Hor. *Serm.* 1.3.99–112.

[3] Cf. Ps.-Victor *Epit. de Caess.* 48.11–12 on Theodosius I.

[4] Cf. Aus. *Grat. actio* 16 (75): *bonitatis et virtutis exempla, quae sequi cupiat ventura posteritas et, si rerum natura pateretur, adscribi sibi voluisset antiquitas,* "examples of goodness and virtue, such as future posterity will desire to imitate and, if the nature of things would allow, the past would have wished to be ascribed to itself."

[5] One of three references to the siege of the Capitol by the Gauls in 390 BC (traditional date), cf. IV.9 and IV.26. Rome is a strong symbol of inviolability for V., which strongly suggests he was writing before it was sacked by Alaric the Goth in AD 410.

undertaken by command of Your Majesty, I shall summarize in order from various authors the measures by which either our cities should be defended or the enemy's destroyed. Nor shall I regret my labour since foundations are being laid for the benefit of all.

(Fortifications, ch. 1–6)

1. Cities should be fortified either by nature or by works.

Cities and forts are either fortified by nature or by human hand, or by both, which is considered stronger. By "nature" is meant places which are elevated, precipitous, surrounded by sea, morasses or rivers; by "hand", fosses and a wall. In places enjoying the safest natural advantages, judgement is required of the selector; in a flat place, effort of the founder. We see cities of very great antiquity so built in the midst of spreading plains that in the absence of help from the terrain they were rendered invincible by art and labour.[1]

2. Walls should be built not straight, but with angles.

The ancients refused to build the circuit of their walls in straight lines, fearing that it might be exposed to the blows of rams. Instead they enclosed cities within foundations laid out in sinuous windings,[2] and put more frequent towers precisely at the angles so that if anyone tried to move up ladders or machines to a wall constructed on this system, he would be shut in before, on the flanks and virtually behind as though in an embrace, and destroyed.[3]

---

[1] e.g. Zama, Numidia, cf. Sall. *Jug.* 57.1: *id oppidum, in campo situm, magis opere quam natura munitam erat, nullius idoneae rei egens...* "that settlement, situated in the plain, had been fortified more by labour than by nature, was short of no needful thing..."

[2] Cf. Vitr. 1.5.2: *Curandumque maxime videtur ut non facilis aditus sit ad oppugnandum murum, sed ita circumdandum ad loca praecipitia et excogitandum uti portarum itinera non sint directa sed scaeva,* "One should take particular care that access to the wall for an attack should not be easy, but (the wall) should be so disposed around steep places and so designed that the roads to the gates should be not straight but bending to the left"; cf. Philo Byz. *Polior.* 86.2–11, 79.7–16; Amm. 20.7.17, describing a fort in Mesopotamia (Virta) thought to have been built by Alexander the Great: *muris velut sinuosis circumdatum et cornutis instructioneque varia inaccessum,* "surrounded by walls almost sinuous and cresent-shaped and made inaccessible by various construction."

[3] Cf. Vitr. 1.5.2: *Item turres sunt proiciendae in exteriorem partem uti, cum ad murum hostis impetu velit adpropinquare a turribus dextra ac sinistra lateribus apertis telis vulnerentur,* "Likewise towers are to project forward into the exterior side so that when the enemy wishes to approach the wall for an attack, they may be wounded by missiles from the towers, which have openings in their right and left flanks"; cf. Philo Byz. *Polior.* 79.11–16, 82.43–50.

3. How a terreplein[1] is attached to the wall from ground-level.

The wall is completed so that it can never be knocked down, on the following plan. Two internal walls are built at intervals of twenty feet each. Then earth which has been dug out of the fosses is dumped between them and rammed solid with piles, the first internal wall from the outer wall being built proportionately lower, the second far smaller, so that one can ascend from the ground-level of the city as if by stairs on a gentle slope up to the battlements. For no rams can breach a wall that is strengthened by earth, and if for some reason the masonry should be demolished the mass that has been compacted between the internal walls resists intruders in the wall's stead.[2]

4. On portcullises and gates, protecting them from fire.

Take care also that gates may not be burned by fires placed against them. To counter this they should be covered with hides and iron. But it is more useful, as antiquity discovered, to add a barbican[3] before the gate, and place in its entrance a portcullis,[4] which hangs on iron chains and ropes. Then if the enemy enter, it is let down, and they are shut in and exterminated.[5] The wall above the gate should be so designed as to admit openings through which water may be poured from the upper storey to quench a fire below.

5. On making fosses.

Fosses before cities should be made as wide and as deep as possible,[6] so that they cannot easily be levelled and filled in by besiegers and, once they begin to overflow with floodwater, hardly permit a sap to be continued by the enemy. A subterranean work is prevented from being constructed in two ways, by the depth and by the flooding of fosses.

---

[1]*adgestus*, talus or terreplein; more commonly means a siege-mound.
[2]Cf. Vitr. 1.5.5–7, on which account V. does not draw.
[3]*propugnaculum*, fortification, bastion.
[4]*cataracta*, Greek for cataract, waterfall, portcullis.
[5]On portcullises, cf. Aen. Tact. 39.3–4, Livy 27.28.10–12, describing the capture and massacre of 600 Roman deserters at Salapia, 208 BC, Appian *Bell. Civ.* 4.78 (328) on Xanthus besieged by Brutus in 42 BC, Amm. 30.5.17 on Valentinian I's inability to leave by a gate blocked probably by a jammed iron portcullis at Savaria in AD 375.
[6]Cf. Vitr. 1.5.6, Philo Byz. *Polior.* 85.4–6, 91.19–24; neither mentions moats.

6. On preventing men on the walls from being injured by enemy arrows.

There is a risk of defenders being frightened off the fortifications by a mass of archers, who then set up ladders and occupy the wall. Against this as many as possible in cities should have cataphracts and shields.[1] Secondly double-thickness cloaks and goat's hair mats[2] are strung up along the battlements to absorb the impact of arrows. For darts do not easily pass through material which yields and swings.[3] Another remedy was invented where they made frames of wood which they called *metallae*,[4] filled them with stones, and set them up between pairs of battlements in such a way that if an enemy climbed up a ladder and touched any part of one, he tipped the rocks onto his own head.[5]

(Preparations for a siege, ch. 7–11)

7. Measures to be taken so that the besieged do not suffer famine.

There are many forms of defence and attack, which we shall introduce at the appropriate place. For the present, note that there are two kinds of siege warfare; in one of them the adversary deploys pickets in suitable positions and[6] either prevents those under blockade from getting water, or hopes for a surrender through famine once he has stopped all transportation of supplies. By this strategy he himself remains at leisure and safe, while he wears down the enemy.

---

[1] Cf. I.20.

[2] *cilicia*, literally "Cilician (fabrics)", cf. IV.14.

[3] V.'s explanation resembles Heron *Mech.* 2.34q (Nix–Schmidt II.1, Teubner edn. 1900 p.186). Cf. Amm. 24.2.10: *per propugnacula ciliciis undique laxius pansis, quae telorum impetus cohiberent*, "goat's hair mats were spread loosely everywhere along the battlements, which might stop the impact of missiles", cf. Livy 38.7.10, Sisenna *Hist.* fr. 107. Cf. also Aen. Tact. 32.1, 9–10 sails and thick curtains, Philo Byz. *Polior.* 95.34 skins or curtains, Dexippus *Scyth.* fr. 29.3, F. Jacoby (ed.), *FGH* IIA p.474 cloaks and fleeces, Jos. *bell. Iud.* 3.172–173 raw hides, Thuc. 2.75.5 skins and hides.

[4] Perhaps *matella*, chamber-pot. *Metalla* is unattested, cf. *TLL* s.v.

[5] Cf. Anon. Byz. *Parang. Polior.* 205.3, wicker baskets filled with rubble or compacted earth, but thrown from walls. Cf. also Apoll. Dam. *Polior.* 139.11–12.

[6] A lacuna is noted here in the editions and supplemented in MS Parisinus 7232 (fourteenth century), *continuis insultibus impugnat obsessos, alteram cum*, "attacks the besieged by means of unremitting assaults, the other (is) when (he)..." As V. does not expressly talk about the other kind of siege warfare, the violent assault, until IV.12 ff., it is possible that there is no lacuna here, especially when IV.7–11 are all about the problem of the interruption of supplies.

Against these calamities landowners, prompted by the least suspicion, should as thoroughly as possible collect all means of sustaining life within walls so that they may have an abundance of supplies for themselves, and shortages force the adversaries to withdraw. Not only pork, but every kind of animal which cannot be kept enclosed should be sent for curing,[1] so as to eke out the grain with the aid of meat. Farmyard fowls, however, are fed without cost in cities and are needed for the sick. Fodder for horses above all should be stockpiled, and what cannot be carried in should be burned; stocks of wine, wine-vinegar, and other crops and fruits should be collected, and nothing which may be of use left for the enemy. Considerations of both utility and morale urge that gardening (for food) be conducted in the pleasure-grounds of town-houses and (public) open spaces.[2] But there is little point in having collected large stocks without sensible issue from the outset by competent officials: men who began to keep a frugal diet while there was still plenty have never been in danger of starving.[3] Also those unfit for fighting by reason of age or sex were often shut out of the gates because of the need to conserve food, lest hunger oppressed the soldiers guarding the walls.[4]

8. What supplies should be procured for the defence of walls.[5]

It is advised to procure bitumen, sulphur, liquid pitch and the oil which they call "burning-oil",[6] for burning the machines of the enemy.[7] For

---

[1] *laridum*, "bacon". Cf. Macr. *Sat.* 7.12.2: *saepe adposita salita carne, quam laridum vocamus, ut opinor quasi large aridam, quaerere mecum ipse constitui qua ratione carnem ad diuturnitatem usus admixtio salis servet.* "Often when salt meat has been served which we call 'larida' (bacon) as 'largely arid', I suppose, I have resolved to ask myself by what principle the admixture of salt preserves meat for prolonged use."

[2] Cf. the siege of Cremna, AD 278, where houses were razed and the sites sown with grain, Zos. 1.79.2.

[3] V. largely repeats material from III.3. Since in the epilogue at IV.30 he draws attention to his pronouncements on the subject of supplies, he may well have added his own ideas. Certainly the background is contemporary, cf. Amm. 18.7.3, and the details are circumstantial. But the basic strategy was that of Q. Fabius Maximus (Cunctator), *dictator*, 217 BC, cf. Livy 22.11.4.

[4] Cf. Thuc. 2.78.3, Onas. 42.23, Front. *Strat.* 3.4.5.

[5] Cf. a similar chapter by Philo Byz. *Polior.* 89.46–90.24.

[6] *oleum incendiarium*, cf. Amm. 23.6.37 on the military use of "Medic oil" in fire-darts (cf. IV.18), and 20.11.15 on the Persians pouring boiling pitch onto the Roman ram at Bezabde, AD 360.

[7] Cf. Jos. *Bell. Iud.* 3.228, Amm. 20.11.18–19, 22–23.

making arms, iron of both tempers[1] and coal are kept in magazines.[2] Wood, needed for spear-shafts and arrows, is also laid in. Round stones are very carefully collected from rivers, because they are heavier in proportion to their density and more suitable for throwing. The walls and towers are filled with them, the smallest for casting by slings and "sling-staves",[3] and by hand,[4] the larger are shot by mangonels,[5] and the biggest in weight and of a rollable shape are laid out on the battlements, so that, sent headlong below, they not only overwhelm hostile forces but smash their machines too. Huge wheels are also made out of green wood, and cylindrical sections, which they call *taleae*,[6] are cut from very stout trees and smoothed to make them roll.[7] These falling down with sudden impetus usually deter soldiers and horses. It is also necessary to have in readiness beams and planks, and iron nails of different sizes. Besiegers' machines are usually resisted by means of other machines, in particular when height needs to be added to walls and battlements by emergency works, so that the mobile towers of the enemy may not overtop and take the city.[8]

9. What to do if the supply of sinews runs out.

It is advisable to collect supplies of sinews[9] with the utmost vigour, because mangonels, catapults and other torsion-engines are of no use unless strung with ropes made of sinew, although horsehair taken from the tail and mane is said to be useful for catapults. Indubitably, however, women's hair has no less virtue in such kinds of torsion-engines, as was demonstrated in Rome's hour of need. For at the siege of the Capitol, the torsion-engines broke down from continuous and long fatigue after supplies of sinews ran out. But the matrons cut off

---

[1] i.e. iron and steel; it remains unclear whether Roman blacksmiths knowingly added carbon to harden iron into steel, although they managed to produce it.

[2] *condita*, cf. *CTh* 7.4.3.

[3] *fustibali*, cf. III.14.

[4] Cf. I.16. Cf. *saxorum manualium*, "stones for throwing by hand", Amm. 24.2.14, Livy 38.21.6.

[5] *onagri*, "wild-asses", cf. IV.22.

[6] "grafts" or "sticks".

[7] Described by Athen. Mech. 37.3 as σφόνδυλοι or "vertebrae", perhaps the *cylindri* mentioned by Amm. 31.15.13.

[8] i.e. by means of hoarding, cf. IV.17. Also see generally IV.22–23, and D. Baatz, "Town walls and defensive weapons", *Mavors* XI (Stuttgart 1994) 86–90.

[9] *nervi*.

their hair and presented it to their husbands as they fought, the machines were repaired and they repelled the hostile attack. For women of the highest character preferred to disfigure their heads for the moment in order to live in freedom with their husbands, than become slaves to the enemy with their beauty intact.[1] It is also advantageous to collect horns and raw hides for weaving cataphracts and other machines and armour.[2]

10. What to do to ensure that the besieged suffer no shortage of water.

It is a great advantage for a city when its wall includes perennial springs within it. But if nature does not provide, wells have to be dug to whatever depth and draughts of water extracted by rope. Sometimes places are too dry if built upon mountains and rocks. Fortifications erected on such places may discover sources of water outside the wall, lower down, and protect them with missiles shot from battlements and towers so as to allow free access to waterbearers. But if a source is beyond the range of missiles but on the hill below the city, it is advised to build a small fortification which they call a *burgus*[3] between the city and the spring, and station there catapults and archers to defend the water from the enemy. Also, under all public and many private buildings cisterns should be constructed very assiduously to provide reservoirs for rainwater that flows off roofs. It has proved difficult to overcome with thirst those besieged who used water only for drinking, however little there was.

---

[1]Cf. Serv. ad Verg. *Aen.* 1.720, as an explanation of the name Venus Calva. The Roman matron who set the example which V. praises was Domitia. On women's hair used in catapults, cf. Flor. 1.31.10 at Carthage *c.* 149 BC, Caes. *Bell. Civ.* 3.9 at Salonae 49–48 BC. On the siege of the Capitol, cf. IV praef. note.

[2]Cf. Tac. *Hist.* 1.79.3: *ferreis lamminis aut praeduro corio consertum* (of Sarmatian cataphract *contati*), "woven with iron scales or very tough leather."

[3]According to Kempf, 364, adopted by Roman soldiers from Germans in the first to second centuries AD. So Ernout–Meillet, 78, s.v., "mot évidemment germanique", citing Orosius 7.32.12: *crebra per limitem habitacula constituta burgos vocant (sc. Burgundiones qui inde dicti putantur).* "(The Burgundians, thought to be named therefrom), call *burgi* the dwelling-places built frequently along the frontier." According to Walde–Hofmann, 124, s.v., originally borrowed from Greek πύργος = "small fort, watch-tower", but later took on the meaning and (e.g. in Sidon. Apoll.) feminine gender of Germanic **burgs* = "fortified settlement". On both wells and *burgi*, cf. D. Baatz, *Mavors* XI (Stuttgart 1994) 79–85.

11. If salt runs out.

If a city is on the coast and salt runs out, water is taken from the sea and poured into troughs and other flat vessels; in the heat of the sun it hardens to salt. But if the enemy denies access to the sea, as does happen, people sometimes collect up sand which the sea stirred up by the wind has flowed over. They then wash it in fresh water, and this evaporated in the sun equally well turns to salt.

(Siege-strategies of attack and defence, ch. 12–30)

12. What to do when the first assault is pressed to the walls.

When however a violent assault is prepared against forts and cities, deadly battles are fought with mutual danger to both sides but greater bloodshed for the assailants.[1] For the side wishing to enter the walls doubles the sense of panic in hopes of forcing a surrender by parading its forces equipped with terrible apparatus in a confused uproar of trumpets and men.[2] Then because fear is more devastating to the inexperienced, while the townspeople are stupefied by the first assault if unfamiliar with the experience of danger, ladders are put up and the city invaded. But if the first attack is repelled by men of courage or by soldiers, the boldness of the besieged grows at once and the war is fought no longer by terror but by energy and skill.[3]

13. List of machines used in storming walls.

Machines moved up are "tortoises", rams, siege-hooks, penthouses, screens, mantelets and mobile towers. For each of them I shall describe how they are constructed, and how they are used in attack or repelled.

14. The ram, siege-hook and "tortoise".

The "tortoise"[4] is made from timbers and planks with a covering of hides, goat's hair mats[5] and fire-blankets[6] to save it from destruction by

---

[1]Cf. Amm. 19.9.9 on Persian losses at Amida, Nisibis and Singara, AD 359. Cf. Onas. 42.7–13, Livy 37.5.5, Tac. *Hist.* 5.13.4. This is the second kind of siege warfare foreshadowed at IV.7 init.

[2]e.g. by king Sapor (Shapur) II at Amida, Amm. 19.2.1 ff., and by Constantius II at Bezabde, Amm. 20.11.8.

[3]Cf. Livy 38.5.3–4.

[4]*testudo*, siege-shed.

[5]*cilicia*, cf. IV.6.

fire.[1] It holds within it a beam which is either tipped with an iron hook and called a *falx*[2] because it is curved for tearing stones out of the wall, or else the head of the beam itself is covered in iron and called a "ram".[3] This is either because it has an extremely hard brow for undermining walls, or because it backs off like a ram in order to strike harder at speed. The "tortoise" takes its name from its resemblance to the real tortoise. Just as it now withdraws, now thrusts out its head, so the machine at one moment withdraws its beam, at another sends it out to strike more strongly.[4]

15. "Vines", screens and the siege-mound.

The ancients called "vines"[5] what are now called in military and barbarian parlance *cau<s>iae*.[6] The machine is made of light wood, 8 ft. wide, 7 ft. tall and 16 ft. long. The roof is constructed with a double protective covering of boards and hurdles. The sides also are fenced with wicker against penetration by impact of stones and missiles. To avoid combustion from fire-darts the outside is covered with raw and freshly flayed hides[7] and fire-blankets.[8] When a number have been made, they are joined together in a line,[9] and under their shelter

---

[6]*centones*, cf. *centonarius*, a "fireman who used mats for extinguishing fires", *OLD* s.v.

[1]Cf. Caes. *Bell. Civ.* 2.9.4, 2.10.6.

[2]literally "sickle", i.e. siege-hook.

[3]*aries*. Cf. the Roman ram with its shed-timbers covered against fire-attack with wet hides, fire-blankets and alum at Bezabde, AD 360, Amm. 20.11.13, and the Ostrogothic rams used in the siege of Rome AD 536–537, Procop. *Bell. Goth.* 1.21.5–12.

[4]Cf. Varro *de ling. lat.* 5.161: *testudo dicebatur ab testudinis similitudine, ut est in praetorio et castris*, "'tortoise' was said after its likeness to the tortoise, as it is in the military headquarters and in the camp"; cf. Jos. *Bell. Iud.* 3.213–218.

[5]*vineae*, penthouses.

[6]So Lang, meaning literally a kind of Macedonian hat, but the word is garbled in the MSS; *cautiae, cauciae* and *cautib*– are the best evidence we have. Kempf, 365 n.3, suggested *cautia* may be Germanic, related to Anglo-Saxon *cyte* or cote, cottage. See O. Lendle, *Texts und Untersuchungen zum technischen Bereich der Antiken Poliorketik*, Palingenesia XIX (Wiesbaden 1983) 139–141.

[7]Cf. Jos. *Bell. Iud.* 3.173.

[8]Cf. IV.14.

[9]i.e. in a line roughly perpendicular to the wall; cf. Caes. *Bell. Civ.* 2.10.1, Livy 21.7.5. They were also used with rams (ibid. 21.7.5), mobile towers (8.16.8) and siege-mounds (37.26.8).

besiegers make openings to undermine the foundations of walls in safety.[1]

"Screens"[2] refers to apse-shaped structures made from wicker, covered with goat's hair mats and hides, and fitted with three wheels, one in the middle and two at the ends, so that they can be moved up in whatever direction you wish, like a wagon. Besiegers bring them up to walls and sheltering under their cover dislodge all defenders from fortifications by means of arrows, slings and missiles, so as to provide easier opportunity to mount by ladders.[3]

The siege-mound[4] is built from earth and timbers against the wall, and from it missiles are shot.[5]

16. Mantelets.[6]

They call *musculi*[7] the smaller machines which shelter soldiers who remove a city's stockade;[8] they also fill the fossework[9] with stones, timber and earth that they bring up, even making it solid so that mobile towers can be joined to the walls without obstruction. *Musculi* are named after the sea-creatures; for as they, though quite small, provide continuous support and assistance to whales,[10] so these diminutive

---

[1]Cf. Livy 23.18.8, 38.7.6; and cf. Amm. 24.4.13, 21–22, Zos. 3.22.2 for the same at Maozamalcha AD 363.

[2]*plutei*, cf. Amm. 21.12.6 at Aquileia AD 361, where the *pluteus* is indistinguishable from the *vinea* and is used to cover sappers. The triangular chassis with three wheels which are illustrated on Trajan's column, Cichorius Pl. LXXXV scene cxiv, may be intended to represent *plutei*.

[3]Also described by Athen. Mech. 38.9–13. The *tichodifrus* of the Anon. *de Rebus Bellicis* 8, 19.5–6, resembles it in size and purpose. See Lendle, 144–146.

[4]*agger*.

[5]Cf. Amm. 19.8.1–2 at Amida AD 359, Amm. 20.11.12 at Bezabde AD 360; Procop. *Bell.* 2.26.29, Maur. *Strat.* 10.1.14 know it as an ἄγεστα, derived from the Latin *aggestus*, a term also used by Amm.

[6]Cf. Caes. *Bell. Civ.* 2.10–11, a detailed description of a *musculus* indistinguishable from a *vinea*, and used to cover sappers. Cf. Athen. Mech. 15.12 ff. See Lendle, 141–144.

[7]"mice, mussels, muscles", i.e. mantelets.

[8]*sudatum*, cf. Maur. *Strat.* 12.8.22. This is the earliest occurrence of *sudatum* in Latin literature. Cf. F. Lammert, "Suda, die Kriegsschriftsteller und Suidas", *Byz.Z.* xxxviii (1938) 27.

[9]*fossatum*, cf. SHA *Gord.* 28.3, *CTh* 7.15.1. Cf. F. Lammert, loc. cit. For the process of levelling ditches by filling with faggots, cf. Procop. *Bell. Goth.* 1.21.13.

[10]Cf. Pliny *Hist. Nat.* 9.186, 11.165, Claud. *In Eutrop.* 2.425–431, apparently describing pilot-fish, and certainly not what we call "mussels".

machines are assigned to the big towers and prepare the way for their advance, building roads ahead.[1]

17. Mobile towers.[2]

"Towers"[3] refers to machines constructed from beams and planks looking like buildings. They are very thoroughly armoured with raw hides and fire-blankets, lest all this work be burnt by enemy fire. Their width increases in proportion to the height, for sometimes their dimensions are 30 ft. square, sometimes 40 ft. or 50 ft.[4] Their height is sufficient to overtop not only walls but even towers built of stone. Many wheels are placed under them by mechanical skill, so that by their rolling motion such a great bulk may be moved. The danger to a city is immediate once a mobile tower is moved up to the wall. For it holds within it many ladders, and attempts to make a breach in different ways. In the lower storey it contains a ram, whose impact destroys walls. About the middle storey it holds a bridge, made from two beams and fenced with wicker.[5] This is suddenly thrust out between the tower and wall and made secure, and soldiers emerging from the machine cross over by it into the city and occupy the walls. In the upper storey of the tower are stationed pikemen and archers, who cut down the defenders of the city from above with pikes, javelins and stones.[6] When this happens the city is captured without delay. What help is there left when those who were counting on the height of their walls suddenly spy a higher wall of the enemy above their heads?[7]

---

[1]The colourful etymology is not attested elsewhere, and may well be V.'s. More likely the machine is named after the diminutive of *mus* or mouse, whose shape it vaguely resembled.

[2]*turres ambulatoriae*, see Lendle, 101–105.

[3]*turres.*

[4]Vitr. 10.16.4 says that the breadth of the famous *helepolis* of Demetrius was 60 ft., and the height 125 ft.

[5]Cf. IV.21, where it is identified as the *exostra*, "thrust-bridge".

[6]At Julian's siege of Aquileia AD 361, three mobile towers were constructed with a drawbridge in the lower storey and soldiers shooting from the upper, and were conveyed to the city-walls on rafts, cf. Amm. 21.12.9–10. The Ostrogothic king Vittigis built mobile towers drawn on wheels by oxen for the siege of Rome AD 536–537, cf. Procop. *Bell. Goth.* 1.21.3–4.

[7]At the siege of Pirisabora AD 363, the sight of Julian's *helepolis* under construction was enough to induce the besieged to offer acceptable terms of surrender, cf. Amm. 24.2.18 ff.

18. How a mobile tower may be fired.

This very obvious peril is averted by a number of methods. First, if there are brave men or a force of soldiers on hand, a sortie is made in which a group[1] of armed men goes out and, violently repelling the enemy, pulls the hides off the woodwork and burns the huge machine. But if the townspeople dare not go out, they shoot from larger catapults[2] lighted fire-darts and fire-spears, so that piercing through the hides and fire-blankets the flame may be planted inside it. Fire-darts[3] are like arrows, and wherever they lodge they burn everything, because they come blazing.[4] The flaming spear[5] is like a spear in that it is fitted with a strong iron head; between the tube and the spearshaft is a wrapping of sulphur, resin, bitumen and tow, steeped in the oil which they call "burning-oil".[6] It is sent by the force of the catapult, pierces through the armour, is fixed blazing in the wood, and often burns up the tower-shaped machine.[7] Men are also let down on ropes while the enemy are asleep; carrying lights in lanterns they set fire to the machines and are hoisted up onto the wall again.[8]

19. How height is added to the walls.

Besides this the part of the wall which the machine attempts to reach is made higher by building it up with cement and stones, or mud or bricks, and finally with hoarding,[9] so that the machine cannot destroy the defenders of the walls by attacking the city from above.[10] Naturally the

---

[1]*globus*, platoon.

[2]*ad maiores ballistas*: V. occasionally lapses into late-Latin instrumental *ad*, cf. II.15 n.

[3]*malleoli.*

[4]Cf. Amm. 23.4.14–15, 20.11.13, 21.12.10, 24.4.16; Eusebius *Hist.* 9 fr. 2.2–4, F. Jacoby (ed.), *FGH* IIA p.480 (Gothic siege of Thessalonica, probably AD 253 or 269); Paul. Fest. 135 M.; Sisenna *Hist.* IV fr. 83; see S. James, "Archaeological evidence for Roman Incendiary Projectiles", *SJ* xxxix (1983) 142–143 with further refs.

[5]*falarica.*

[6]*oleum incendiarium*, cf. IV.8. Amm. 23.6.37 describes "Medic oil", a Persian product and perhaps a kind of petroleum, as used in fire-darts.

[7]Cf. Livy 21.8.10–12.

[8]Cf. Dexippus *Scyth.* fr. 27.9, F. Jacoby (ed.), *FGH* IIA p.471 (Gothic siege of Philippopolis, probably AD 250–251), and the Persian sorties at Bezabde AD 360 described by Amm. 20.11.18, 22–23.

[9]i.e. wooden boarding erected on stone fortifications to screen the defenders. Cf. Caes. *Bell. Gall.* 7.22.3.

[10]An allusion to Verg. *Aen.* 2.46–47: *aut haec in nostros fabricata est machina muros | inspectura domos venturaque desuper urbi*, "or else this is a machine constructed to harm our walls, to spy out our homes and to attack the city from above."

machine is rendered ineffective if it is found to be lower. But besiegers are in the habit of using the following kind of stratagem. First they build a tower in such a way that it looks smaller than the battlements of the city. Then they secretly make another turret inside out of planks and, when the machine is joined to the walls, suddenly the turret is pulled up from the middle on ropes and pulleys. From it emerge soldiers who, because it is found to be higher, at once capture the city.[1]

20. How the ground may be undermined so that the machine can be rendered harmless.

Sometimes very long iron-clad beams are opposed to an approaching machine and push it away from the vicinity of the wall. But when the city of Rhodes was under attack by enemies and a mobile tower higher than all the walls and towers was in preparation, the following remedy was invented by the genius of an engineer. During the night he dug a sap under the foundations of the wall and, removing the earth without any of the enemy realizing, hollowed out inside the place to which the tower was to be advanced on the following day. When the mass was moved on its wheels and reached the place that had been undermined, the soil gave way under such great weight and it subsided and could not be joined to the walls or moved farther. So the city was liberated and the machine abandoned.[2]

21. Ladders, drawbridge, "thrust-bridge" and swing-beam.

When mobile towers have been moved up, men are cleared from the walls by the action of slingers with stones, archers with darts, hand-catapultiers[3] and crossbowmen[4] with arrows, and darters[5] with lead-weighted darts[6] and javelins. This done, they put up ladders[7] and occupy

---

[1]Cf. Lendle, 105–106.

[2]The siege of Rhodes was conducted by Demetrius I Poliorcetes, in 305–304 BC. The tower was the famous *helepolis*, cf. Diod. Sic. 20.91.2 ff., Plut. *Dem.* 21, Athen. Mech. 27.2 ff., Vitruv. 10.16.4–8, Amm. 23.4.10. V. diverges from the version of the story in Vitruvius in which the Rhodians drenched the ground in front of the *helepolis* with sewage, so that it sank into the mire when moved forwards. V.'s tactic is that recommended by Aen. Tact. 32.8, writing earlier in the fourth century BC (cf. D. Whitehead, 8–9).

[3]*manuballistarii*, cf. IV.22.

[4]*arcuballistarii*, cf. IV.22.

[5]*iaculatores.*

[6]*plumbatae*, cf. I.17.

the city. But those climbing up ladders are often put in peril. For
example, Capaneus—reputedly the first to discover storming by
escalade—was slain with such violence by the Thebans that it was said
he had been blasted by a thunderbolt.[1]

For this reason besiegers get across onto the wall of the enemy by
means of the drawbridge, "thrust-bridge" and swing-beam. The
sambuca[2] is named after its likeness to the zither. For corresponding to
the strings on the zither, there are ropes on the beam which is placed on
the side of the mobile tower, and these let the drawbridge down from
the upper storey on pulleys, to descend onto the wall.[3] Warriors
immediately exit from the tower and cross over by it to invade the walls
of the city. The *exostra*[4] denotes the bridge we described earlier,[5]
because it is suddenly thrust out onto the wall from the tower.[6] The
tolleno[7] is the term for a very tall pole planted in the ground, which has
attached to its top end a cross-beam of longer dimensions, balanced at
the middle so that if you depress one end, the other is raised. On one
end is constructed a machine made from hurdles and boards, and in it
a few soldiers are placed. Then as the other end is pulled and lowered
by ropes, they are lifted up and deposited on the wall.[8]

22. Catapults, mangonels, "scorpions", crossbows, "sling-staves" and slings, torsion-engines by which the wall is defended.

The besieged normally defend themselves against these contrivances
using catapults, mangonels, "scorpions", crossbows, "sling-staves" and
slings. The catapult[9] is strung with ropes of sinew, and the longer arms

---

[7]*scalae.*

[1]V. offers a Christian(?) rationalizing account of the story from the mythical war of the
Seven against Thebes which is the central episode of Statius' *Thebaid* at 10.837–939, in
which Jupiter kills Capaneus with a thunderbolt.

[2]literally "lute", i.e. drawbridge.

[3]See Lendle, 104. Cf. Polyb. 8.4.11 and Lendle, 176 on the etymology. There is only a
vague resemblance to a musical instrument.

[4]"thruster-out" in Greek, i.e. "thrust-bridge".

[5]Cf. IV.17.

[6]See Lendle, 101–104.

[7]swing-beam.

[8]See Lendle, 117–127, cf. Polyb. 8.5.8–11, 8.6.1–4, Livy 24.34.10–11 (used to lift ships
up on end), 38.5.4 (used to drop weights onto rams).

[9]*ballista.*

it has, that is, the bigger the machine is, the farther it shoots darts.[1] If it is tuned in accordance with mechanical art and aimed by trained men who have worked out its range in advance, it penetrates whatever it hits. But the mangonel[2] shoots stones, and throws various weights in proportion to the thickness of the sinews and size of stones. The larger the machine, the bigger the stones it hurls like a thunderbolt.[3] No type of torsion engine more powerful than these two types is found.[4]

They used to call "scorpions" what are now called *manuballistae*;[5] they were so named because they inflict death with tiny, thin darts.[6] I think it superfluous to describe "sling-staves",[7] crossbows[8] and slings,[9] which are familiar from present-day use.[10] Heavy stones thrown by the mangonel destroy not only horses and men, but also the machines of the enemy.

---

[1] *spicula.*

[2] *onager,* literally "wild ass".

[3] Cf. IV.29.

[4] Cf. Amm. 23.4.1–7, Procop. *Bell. Goth.* 1.21.14–19. Note that V., like all authors of the late Empire, uses *ballista* for an arrow-firer, which would have been called a *catapulta* in the early Empire, and *onager* for a stone-thrower, which would have been called a *ballista,* no doubt because of technological changes—on which see E.W. Marsden, *Greek and Roman Artillery: Historical Development,* 188 ff., id. *Greek and Roman Artillery: Technical Treatises,* ch. VII–VIII.

[5] hand-catapults.

[6] *spicula.* Amm. 23.4.7 says *scorpio* was the old name for the *onager.* D.B. Campbell, "Auxiliary Artillery Revisited", *BJ* clxxxvi (1986) 128 n.82, listing earlier ancient sources which apply the term exclusively to static arrow-firing field-artillery, says that Ammianus and V. are both wrong. The *manuballista* is probably (Ps.-)Heron's *Cheiroballistra,* on which see E.W. Marsden, *Tech. Tr.* 236, 209, D. Baatz, "Recent finds of ancient artillery", *Britannia* ix (1978), 1–17, = *Mavors* XI 224–245, Campbell, 130. Torsion-engines of this type, though much larger, first appear on Trajan's column, Cichorius Pl. XXXI scene xl, Pl. XLVII scene lxvi.

[7] *fustibali.*

[8] *arcuballistae.*

[9] *fundae.*

[10] V. forgets that he earlier (at III.14 fin.) described the *fustibalus* and *funda.* The *arcuballista* was invented by the early Empire, at least, cf. Arr. *Tact.* 43.1, D.B. Campbell, art. cit., 131–132, and the *manuballista* may have differed from it principally in the means of propulsion, using torsion not tension. Such at any rate seems to have determined the thirteenth-century illuminator of MS Marley Add.1 *Vegetius De Re Militari,* f.86 (Fitzwilliam Mus., Cambridge), to draw one "crossbow" with a thick, twisted sinew, and the other with a fine bowstring. See also D. Baatz, art. cit., 14–15.

23. Mattresses, nooses, grapnels and heavy columns are useful against rams.

There are also a number of remedies against rams and siege-hooks. Some people let down[1] on ropes quilted blankets[2] and mattresses,[3] putting them in front of the places where the ram strikes, so that the impact of the machine, weakened by the soft material, may not destroy the wall.[4] Others catch the rams in nooses[5] and, using gangs of men, drag them from the wall [up][6] at an angle, overturning them sheds and all.[7] Many attach ropes to a toothed iron instrument like a pair of pincers, which they call a "wolf",[8] and catching the ram they either overturn it or they hang it up so it loses the impetus to strike.[9] Sometimes marble bases and columns launched with great impetus from walls smash rams.[10] But if such force is used that the wall is pierced by rams and, as often happens, it falls down, one hope of safety remains, and that is to demolish houses and build another wall inside.[11] The enemy may then be wiped out between the two walls if they attempt to enter.

24. On saps, whereby the wall is undermined or the city penetrated.[12]

Another method of assault is subterranean and secret, which they call a "burrow",[13] after the hares which dig tunnels underground and hide in them. A gang is set to work digging the earth with great labour as in the mines where the industrious Bessi explore veins of gold and silver,[14] and by means of the excavated cave an underground route to the city's

---

[1]*Chalo, -are*, a graecism, already in Vitr. 10.8.1; cf. *chalatorios* (IV.46).
[2]*centones.*
[3]*culcitae.*
[4]Cf. Aen. Tact. 32.3, bales of chaff, woolsacks, freshly-flayed oxhides inflated or stuffed, Jos. *Bell. Iud.* 3.223, bales of chaff.
[5]*laquei*, cf. III.23 where it means "lassos".
[6]I insert the reading *sursum*, "up", from MS Π, which seems to explain *in obliquum.*
[7]Cf. Aen. Tact. 32.4, Thuc. 2.76.4, Caes. *Bell. Gall.* 7.22.2, Amm. 20.11.15.
[8]*lupus*, i.e. grapnel.
[9]Cf. Lendle, 194–196; cf. Livy 28.3.7.
[10]Cf. Amm. 20.11.10, 31.15.14, Tac. Hist. 2.22.2.
[11]e.g. Thuc. 2.76.3, at Plataea, 429 BC., and Diod. Sic. 20.93.1, 97.4, at Rhodes, 304 BC.
[12]Cf. Aen. Tact. 37.
[13]*cuniculus*, i.e. sap.
[14]Cf. II.11.

destruction is sought.[1] This stratagem is effected by two methods of attack. Either they penetrate beneath the city and, emerging by the burrow at night unbeknown to the townspeople, open the gates to admit a column of their own side who kill the enemy in their own homes taking them unawares;[2] or else when they reach the foundations of the walls, they excavate the largest possible part of them, placing dry timber there and holding up the collapse of the wall by temporary works. They also add brushwood and other inflammable tinder. Then, when the soldiers are ready, fire is introduced to the work and, all the wooden props and boards having burned, the wall suddenly collapses, opening a way for invasive action.

25. What the besieged should do if the enemy break into the city.[3]

Countless examples demonstrate that enemies have often been slain to a man after they had invaded a city. This is the certain result, if the citizens hold on to the walls and towers and occupy the higher ground. For then from windows and rooftops people of all ages and both sexes overwhelm the invaders with stones and other kinds of missiles. To avoid this fate, the besiegers frequently open the city gates in order to induce resistance to stop by conceding the chance to escape. For necessity is a desperate kind of courage.[4] In this case there is only one help for the besieged, whether the enemy enters by day or night, and that is to hold the walls and towers, climb the higher ground, and overwhelm the enemy from all sides by fighting it out in the streets and squares.[5]

26. What precautions should be taken to prevent the enemy occupying the wall by stratagem.

Besiegers often think up a stratagem in which they take themselves far off in feigned despair. But when all fear has gone and the town relaxes

---

[1]Cf. Caes. *Bell. Gall.* 7.22.2, linking Gallic skill at saps with their iron-mining.
[2]Cf. Amm. 24.4.21–23, Zos. 3.22, siege of Maozamalcha, AD 363.
[3]Cf. Onas. 42.18–22.
[4]Cf. III.21.
[5]Cf. Front. *Strat.* 2.6.9: *Pyrrhus Epirotarum rex, cum quandam civitatem cepisset clausisque portis ex ultima necessitate fortiter dimicantes eos, qui inclusi erant, animadvertisset, locum illis ad fugam dedit.* "When Pyrrhus, king of the Epirotes, had taken some city and, having closed the gates, noticed that those shut inside were fighting strongly on account of their extreme peril, he gave them the chance to escape." Cf. Polyaen. 3.9.3, Leo *Tact.* 15.21.

into careless complacency, abandoning the watches on the walls, they seize their chance in the darkness of night to come stealthily with ladders and climb the walls. Against this increased security should be used when the enemy withdraws, and small huts[1] should be placed on the walls and towers themselves, in which sentries may be protected in winter months from rain and cold, in summer from sun.[2] Experience also discovered the trick of keeping very keen-scented and alert dogs in towers, which can anticipate the arrival of the enemy by their scent and reveal it by barking.[3] Geese also by their clamour indicate night-attacks with equal skill. For having attacked the Capitoline citadel the Gauls would have destroyed the the very name of Rome, had not Mallius been roused by the clamour of the geese to stop them. Marvellous was the watchfulness or good fortune, whereby one bird saved the men destined to send the whole world under the yoke.[4]

27. When surprise attacks are made on the besieged.
Not just in sieges but in every kind of warfare it is deemed of the highest importance to spy out and get to know thoroughly the habits of the enemy.[5] For an opportunity for a surprise attack cannot otherwise be found unless you know the times when the adversary leaves off attending to his work, when he is rendered less careful, sometimes at mid-day, sometimes in the evening, frequently at night, otherwise at the meal-times, when soldiers on both sides disperse to rest or look after the body. When this starts to happen in a city, the besiegers cunningly remove themselves from the action to give free rein to their adversaries' negligence. When this has increased as it goes unpunished, suddenly they move up machines or put up ladders and capture the city.[6] For that reason stones and the other torsion artillery are placed in readiness on the walls,[7] so that when a surprise attack is detected those running to

---

[1]*teguriola*, also spelled *tuguriola*, π class MSS, and Apul. *Met.* 4.12.
[2]Cf. II.23.
[3]e.g. at the siege of the Capitol, 390 BC, cf. Livy 5.47.3.
[4]M. Mallius (Capitolinus), hero of the siege of the Capitol. For the story, cf. Livy 5.47, Florus 1.7.15, Ambrose *Ep.* 18.4. V. aligns himself with the Christian rationalizing tradition. Cf. also Ovid *Met.* 11.599: *sollicitive canes canibusve sagacior anser*, "nervous dogs or, more alert than dogs, a goose."
[5]Cf. III.6.
[6]Repeats IV.26, a sign that V. is elaborating on jejune source-material.
[7]Cf. IV.8.

resist may have to hand the material to roll and shoot down onto the heads of the enemy.

28. What the besiegers do to avoid suffering surprise attacks from the besieged.[1]

When negligence intervenes, besiegers are equally subject to surprise attack. For whether they are preoccupied with food or sleep, or dispersed to rest or on some other necessity, then is the time when the citizens suddenly break out and kill them unawares, setting fire to the rams, machines and even the siege-mounds, and overthrowing all the works constructed for their own ruin.[2] Against this the besiegers make a fosse beyond the range of missiles, and equip it with a rampart, stockade and turrets, so that they can resist sorties from the city; they call this work a "breastwork".[3] Often in descriptions of sieges in historical works one finds that a city has been surrounded with a breastwork.[4]

29. The type of torsion-engines with which a city is defended.

Spears, lead-weighted darts, lances, longer javelins,[5] and shorter javelins[6] fall more violently on those below when aimed from a height. Also arrows shot from bows and stones thrown by hand, slings or "sling-staves" penetrate farther the higher the point of origin.[7] But catapults and mangonels, provided they are tuned very carefully by experts, surpass everything else. No amount of courage or armour can defend soldiers from them. For like a thunderbolt, they generally either smash or pierce whatever they hit.[8]

---

[1]Cf. Onas. 40, which may well have influenced Frontinus' *De Re Militari,* and hence indirectly V.

[2]e.g. Jos. *Bell. Iud.* 3.227–228, cf. also Livy 5.7.2.

[3]*loricula.*

[4]Cf. Polyb. 9.41.1–3. The term is usually *lorica* in Latin, cf. Caes. *Bell. Gall.* 5.40.6, Florus 1.34.13, Amm. 24.5.2, 31.3.7, 31.15.4; but the *TLL* cites for the diminutive *loricula,* as well as V., A. Hirtius *Bell. Gall.* 8.9.3, Itala Biblia *Deut.* 22.8, and Hieron. *in Is.* 26.1.

[5]*veruta.*

[6]*spicula.*

[7]Cf. III.13.

[8]Repeats IV.22. Cf. the *ballista fulminalis*—"thunderbolt" catapult—described by the Anon. *de Rebus Bellicis* 18 as able to shoot over the Danube. Jos. *Bell. Iud.* 3.243 ff. gives a vivid account of the power of torsion-engines in attacking cities, as does Amm. 19.5.6, 19.7.4–7, 31.15.12, in defending them. Cf. Amm. 24.4.28 for the gruesome death

30. How the measurement is obtained for making ladders and machines.

Ladders and machines are most useful for capturing walls if they are made to such a size that they surpass the height of the city.[1] The measurement is worked out by two methods. Either a thin, light thread is tied at one end to an arrow, and when it reaches its mark having been aimed at the top of the wall, the height of the walls is found from the length of thread. Or else when the slanting sun casts a shadow of the towers and walls on the ground, the length of the shadow is measured without the knowledge of the enemy. At the same time a ten-foot rod is fixed upright in the ground and its shadow measured in the same way. With this information, the height of the city is undoubtedly revealed by the shadow of the ten-foot rod, as it is known what height casts what length of shadow.[2]

Both the recommendations of the authors of arts of war for attacking and defending cities and what the experience of recent emergencies has discovered, I have summarized for the public benefit, as I believe, making the point again and again that the most thorough precautions should be taken against shortage of drinking-water or food arising at any time, since such troubles cannot be ameliorated by any stratagem. Therefore, so much the more should be stockpiled within walls, in proportion to the length of blockade known to be within the capability of the besiegers.[3]

---

of an engineer—*architectus*—caused by the misfiring of one of his own mangonels.

[1] Cf. Amm. 20.11.20 (siege-mounds), 21.12.6 (ladders), Procop. *Bell. Goth.* 1.21.5 (ladders).

[2] Cf. Polyb. 9.19.5–20.4; Jul. Afr. *Cest.* 1.15 recommends using a *dioptra* or alidade on the end of the measuring-rod. For counting courses of bricks or stones to calculate the height of walls, cf. Thuc. 3.20.3–4, Procop. *Bell. Goth.* 1.21.3–4.

[3] V. singles out IV.7 for special emphasis, as it was particularly relevant to contemporary conditions of barbarian invasion and attacks on civilian communities. It is assumed that the Roman army was not going to be able to lift every blockade.

(The Navy, ch. 31–33)

31. Precepts of naval warfare.[1]

Now that by Your Majesty's command, Invincible Emperor, the accounts of land warfare have been cleared, the balance outstanding belongs in my opinion to naval warfare. Its arts require less to be said for the reason that the sea has long been pacified, and our struggle with barbarian races is played out on land.[2]

The Roman People for the pomp and advantage of their Empire used not to fit out the fleet on the spur of the moment in response to the needs of some crisis, but always kept it in readiness lest they should ever be in danger.[3] For no one dares to challenge to war or inflict injury upon a kingdom or people he knows is armed and ready to resist and avenge any attack.[4] So one legion was stationed with each fleet at Misenum and Ravenna, not too far away to protect the City and yet, when policy required, able to reach by navigation without delay or detour all parts of the world.[5] For the fleet at Misenum had nearest to it Gaul, the Spains, Mauretania, Africa, Egypt, Sardinia and Sicily. The fleet at Ravenna was used to reach by direct sailing Epiros, Macedonia, Achaia, the Propontis, Pontus, Oriens, Crete and Cyprus.[6] For in matters of war speed is often more useful than courage.

---

[1]Aen. Tact. 40.8 appended a treatment of naval warfare, lost; so too his successors in the Greek tactical tradition, Philo Byz. *Polior.* 104, cf. Ael. *Tact.* 2.1, Asclep. 1.1. See F. Lammert, "Die älteste erhaltene Schrift über Seetaktik und ihre Beziehung zum Anonymus Byzantinus des 6. Jahrhunderts, zu Vegetius und zu Aineias' *Strategika*", *Klio* xxxiii (1940) 280–282. It is included here not because V. wanted to write a complete art of war (he did not), but because he wanted to correct neglect of the navy by the Government.

[2]Points to a date at least before the Vandal naval capability which was already considerable by AD 419; cf. J.R. Moss, "The effects of the policies of Aëtius on the history of western Europe", *Historia* xxii (1973) 723–728, *CTh* 9.40.24 (419): *His, qui conficiendi naves incognitam ante peritiam barbaris tradiderunt... capitale... supplicium proponi decernimus.* "For those who have handed over to the barbarians previously unknown knowledge of how to build ships... we decree the imposition of capital punishment."

[3]Cf. the principle of Roman military readiness enunciated also by Jos. *Bell. Iud.* 3.72.

[4]A restatement of the famous dictum *si vis pacem para bellum,* cf. III praef.

[5]Suet. *Aug.* 49.1: *classem Miseni et alteram Ravennae ad tutelam Superi et Inferi maris conlocavit...* "(Augustus) stationed one fleet at Misenum and the other at Ravenna, for the protection of the Upper (Adriatic) and Lower (Tyrrhenian) seas."

[6]The list is V.'s own composition; Egypt was part of Oriens until c. AD 367, cf. Jones, 141.

32. The titles of the officers commanding the fleet.

The prefect of the fleet at Misenum was in command of the warships[1] stationed in Campania, whilst those located on the Ionian Sea were controlled by the prefect of the fleet at Ravenna. Under each of them were ten tribunes appointed one for each cohort. Each warship had a single navarch,[2] that is, a kind of skipper,[3] who was exempted[4] from the other duties of sailors and put in a daily responsibility and unfailing efforts to training pilots,[5] oarsmen[6] and marines.[7]

33. How warships got their name.[8]

Different provinces at various times held considerable naval power and therefore the types of ships were diverse. But when Augustus was fighting at the battle of Actium[9] and Antony was beaten mainly by the auxiliaries provided by the Liburni, it became clear from the experience of that great encounter that the ships of the Liburni were better-designed than the rest. Therefore usurping the likeness and the name, the Emperors built the fleet according to their pattern. Liburnia is a part of Dalmatia lying next to the city of Iadera;[10] ships of war are built today

---

[1] *liburnae.*

[2] *navarchus.* The captain of the ship, he is probably seen by V. as ranking with the centurion in the land legion, cf. Grosse, 116.

[3] *navicularius,* technically a merchant shipowner.

[4] v.l. *excepti* (pro *exceptis*), cf. A. Eussner, "Zu Vegetius", *Philologus* xliv (1885) 87.

[5] *gubernatores.*

[6] *remiges.*

[7] *milites.* Note that there is no evidence that the *navarchus* was the commander of a Roman naval vessel; this was in fact the *trierarchus.* But the *navarchus* was at any rate senior to the *trierarchus* on the same ladder of promotion. V.'s equation with a *navicularius* is misleading since the latter did not necessarily go to sea. Cf. M. Reddé, *Mare Nostrum* (Rome 1986) 542. See generally G. Forni, *Esercito e Marina de Roma Antica, Mavors* V (Stuttgart 1992) 298–323, 419–450.

[8] M. Reddé, 105. "Liburnian" was used for all warships of whatever size (cf. IV.37) by the late Empire, not only the light biremes of the first century BC which gave the name.

[9] 2nd. Sept., 31 BC, off the west coast of Greece; Augustus as C. Julius Caesar (Octavianus) *divi filius* with his admiral M. Vipsanius Agrippa decisively defeated M. Antonius and Cleopatra and took sole control of the Roman world.

[10] Zadar.

on their model and are called *liburnae*.[1]

(Shipbuilding, ch. 34–37)

34. The care with which warships are built.

As when building houses the quality of the sand or stone of the foundations is important, so the more carefully should all materials be obtained when building ships, because it is more dangerous for a ship to be faulty than a house.[2] So the warship is constructed principally from cypress, domestic or wild pine, larch,[3] and fir.[4] It is better to fasten it with bronze nails than iron; for although the cost seems somewhat heavier, it is proved to be worthwhile because it lasts longer, since iron nails are quickly corroded by rust in warm, moist conditions, whereas bronze preserve their own substance even below the water-line.[5]

35. The astronomical observations according to which timber should be cut.

Take particular observations so that trees from which warships are to be built are felled between the 15th moon and the 22nd. On these eight days alone is cut timber which is preserved immune from decay; that cut on the other days turns to dust even within the same year, eaten

---

[1]Appian *Illyr.* 3.7: καὶ ναυτικοὶ μὲν ἐπὶ τοῖς 'Αρδιαίοις ἐγένοντο Λιβερνοί, γένος ἕτερον 'Ιλλυριῶν, οἳ τὸν 'Ιόνιον καὶ τὰς νήσους ἐλήστευον ναυσὶ ν ὠκείαις τε καὶ κούφαις, ὅθεν ἔτι νῦν 'Ρωμαῖοι τὰ κουφα καὶ ὀξέα δίκροτα Λιβυρνίδας προσαγορεύ ουσιν. "Also sailors in addition to the Ardiaeans were the Liburnians, another Illyrian tribe, who used to raid the Ionian sea and islands using swift, light ships; hence even today the Romans call light, quick biremes 'liburnians'." Cf. Lucian *Am.* 6. Only V. gives the detail about the high performance of Octavian's *liburnae* at the battle of Actium, 31 BC, but the testimony may to some extent be corroborated by that of Cass. Dio 50.18.4 ff. Cf. also Hor. *C.* 1.37.30, *Epod.* 1.1, Prop. 3.11.44, Plut. *Ant.* 67.2, Prud. *c. Symm.* 2.530–531. See W.M. Murray, P.M. Petsas, *Octavian's campsite memorial for the Actian War*, Trans. of the American Philosophical Society lxxix.4 (1989) 147 ff., who argue that the "heavy fleet vs. light fleet" tradition of the battle derives from the appearance in the 20s BC of Augustus' own Memoirs.
[2]Perhaps an inept allusion to Biblia Vulgata *Matt.* 7.24–27, from the Sermon on the Mount. For the parallel should look to the quality of what the houses are built of, not what they are built on.
[3]v.l. *larice*, transmitted in all MSS of ε group, omitted by π.
[4]See R. Meiggs, *Trees and Timber in the Ancient Mediterranean World* (Oxford 1982) 86, 118–120.
[5]Cf. Caes. *Bell. Gall.* 4.31.2: *quae gravissime adflictae erant naves, earum materia atque aere ad reliquas reficiendas utebantur,* "as for the ships that were most seriously damaged, they used their timber and bronze to repair the rest."

away by destruction of worms.[1] This has been the lesson of science herself and the everyday experience of all shipbuilders, and we recognize it too when we contemplate the very religious festival which it has been decided to celebrate for ever more on these days alone.[2]

36. The months in which timber should be cut.

Timbers are best cut after the summer solstice, that is, through the months of July and August,[3] and through the autumnal equinox until the 1st January. For in these months the moisture evaporates and the wood is drier and therefore stronger. Avoid sawing timbers immediately after felling, or putting them into the ship as soon as they have been sawn, because both trees that are still whole and those divided into "double" planks[4] deserve a truce for further drying. Those fitted when still green exude their natural moisture and contract, forming wide cracks; nothing is more dangerous for sailors than for the planking to split.[5]

37. The size of warships.

So far as size is concerned, the smallest warships have one rank of oars a side, those slightly bigger two ranks, those of appropriate dimensions three, four, sometimes five ranks for their oarage. This should not seem enormous to anyone, because at the battle of Actium far larger vessels

---

[1] So Servius ad Verg. *Georg.* 1.256: *Tempestivam oportunam, maturam; nam tempore inoportuno hae caesae arbores cito termites faciunt: ita enim ligni vermes vocantur. (Tempestivam) nam hac re etiam rustici lunae cursum observare dicuntur; melius enim arbores luna decrescente caeduntur.* "*Tempestivam*: opportune, early; for these trees if felled at an inopportune time soon make 'termites', as woodworms are called. (*Tempestivam*:) for in this matter even country folk are said to observe the moon's course; for trees are better felled while the moon is waning."

[2] The rules for calculating the date of Easter Sunday were adjusted under the auspices of Theodosius I *c.* AD 388 consistently with lunar dates here offered, cf. H. Leclerq, *Dict. d'Archéologie-chrétienne et de Liturgie* XIII.2 (1938) 1553–1554, with refs. Cato's original lunar observations for cutting timber recommended the moon's last quarter for choice, or failing that, the new moon and first quarter, cf. J. Heurgon, "*Octavo Ianam Lunam*: traces d'une semaine de sept jours chez Varron et Caton", *REL* xxv (1947) 236–249, on Cato *de Agric.* 37.3–4 = Pliny *Hist. Nat.* 16.75.194, interpreted 16.74.188 ff. V. will have Christianized and distorted the source, which was easily misconstrued owing to its archaism: *diebus VII proximis, quibus luna plena fuerit, optime eximetur,* meaning "*after* the seven days immediately following full moon, it is best cut", not "*on* the seven days", etc.

[3] The superfluous mention of the two months named after Julius Caesar and Augustus immediately after the Christian religion may possibly follow a pattern in which V. regularly mentions the Emperor after God; cf. I praef., II.5, II.18, III.5.

[4] *tabulae duplices.* It is not clear what exactly these were.

[5] Cf. Meiggs, 349; in an emergency there was no option but to build with green timber.

are reported to have clashed, so that these were of six and even more ranks.[1] But to the larger warships are attached scouting skiffs,[2] having about twenty oarsmen on each side; these the Britons call † picati.[3] They are used on occasion to perform descents[4] or to intercept convoys of enemy shipping or by studious surveillance to detect their approach or intentions.[5] Lest scouting vessels be betrayed by white, the sails and rigging are dyed Venetian blue, which resembles the ocean waves; the wax used to pay ships' sides is also dyed. The sailors and marines put on Venetian blue uniforms too, so as to lie hidden with greater ease when scouting by day as by night.[6]

(The art of navigation, ch. 38–43)

38. The names and number of the winds.[7]
He who sails with an army in an armed fleet ought first to forecast the signs of storms. For storms and waves have often done greater damage to warships than hostile attack. In this connexion all the wisdom of natural philosophy should be applied, for the nature of the winds and tempests is deduced by studying the skies. So far as the roughness of the sea is concerned, as caution protects the provident, so carelessness

---

[1]Flor. 2.21.5–6 reports that Octavian's ships had up to six ranks of oars, Antony's from six to nine. Cf. IV.33.

[2]*scaphae exploratoriae.*

[3]The word is garbled in the MSS. Since the ships were payed with blue wax (as well as pitch and resin, cf. IV.44) they were in effect painted blue, so some such word as *pictae*—"painted"—may be right. Stewechius conjectured **pincae* as a putative plural latinized form of the M.Du., MLG, LG and mod. German and English word "pinke, pink". On the *scapha* cf. Reddé, 130, Caes. *Bell. Civ.* 3.24, *Bell. Gall.* 4.26.4 *speculatoria navigia,* Livy 36.42.8.

[4]*superventûs.*

[5]The counterpart of the use of scouts on land, cf. III.6. Tactical intelligence is meant, not strategic, of which V. is largely innocent.

[6]The blue disguise is uniquely attested here. Britain was still notoriously the country of blue woad, cf. Claud. *de bello Get.* 417–418, *pan. de Hon. cons. III* 54, *de cons. Stil.* 2.248. But the province was also very exposed to sea-borne barbarian raiders and will have needed special naval surveillance vessels such as these. However, they were not unique to British waters.

[7]IV.38–42 derive from Varro's "*libri navales*" (cited at IV.41), whether *de Ora Maritima* (lost), so R. Reitzenstein, "Die geographischen Bücher Varros", *Hermes* xx (1885) 514 ff., and Nielsen (see below), or *Ephemeris Navalis* (lost), so *RE Suppl.* VI (1935) col. 1252–1253 (H. Dahlmann), and E. Courtney (ed.), *The Fragmentary Latin Poets* (Oxford 1993) 246, or *de Aestuariis* (lost), mentioned in *de ling. lat.* 9.26.

drowns the negligent. Thus the art of navigation ought first to look into the number and names of the winds.

The ancients thought that following the position of the cardinal points only four principal winds blew from each quarter of the sky, but the experience of later times recognizes twelve. Their names we have set out in Latin as well as Greek for the avoidance of doubt, so that having stated the principal winds we shall indicate those adjacent to them on the left and right.[1] So let us take our beginning from the vernal equinox,[2] that is, from the eastern cardinal point, whence arises a wind called *Apheliotes*, that is, *Subsolanus* (E. wind); adjacent to him on the right is *Caecias* or *Euroborus* (ENE wind), and on the left *Eurus* or *Vulturnus* (ESE wind). *Notus*, that is, *Auster* (S. wind), occupies the southern cardinal point; adjacent to him on the right is *Leuconotus*, that is, *Albus Notus* (SSE wind), and on the left *Libonotus*, that is, *Corus* (SSW wind). *Zephyrus*, that is, *Subvespertinus* (W. wind), holds the western cardinal point; adjacent to him on the right is *Lips* or *Africus* (WSW wind), and on the left *Iapyx* or *Favonius* (WNW wind). The northern cardinal point is allotted to *Aparctias* or *Septentrio* (N. wind); close to him on the right is *Thrascias* or *Circius* (NNW wind), and on the left *Boreas*, that is, *Aquilo* (NNE wind).

These winds are accustomed to blow separately, sometimes in pairs, but in great storms even three at once. Under their attack the seas, which are naturally tranquil and quiet, rage with boiling waves. By their breath according to the nature of the season and location fair weather is restored after storms and fine conditions are turned to stormy again. When there is a following wind the fleet reaches its desired port, but an adverse wind compels it to stand at anchor or go back or risk danger. And so he is rarely shipwrecked who makes a thorough study of the science of winds.

---

[1] The original source of this 12-point wind-scale was Timosthenes; Poseidonios took it over and Varro incorporated this version in his work, from whence V. appears to have derived it. Cf. K. Nielsen, "Remarques sur les noms grecs et latins des vents et des régions du ciel", *C&M* vii (1945) 105–108, L. Edelstein, I.G. Kidd, *Posidonius, fragments* (Cambridge 1972) fr. 137a, theory of winds (Strabo 1.2.21), comm. II p.519 (P. has in mind the 12-point compass-card of Timosthenes), fr. 138, theory of tides (cf. IV.42), frs. 214–219, tidal and coastal waters (cf. IV.43).

[2] v.l. The "vulgate" reads *solstitio*, "solstice", which if genuine is V.'s mistake.

39. In which months it is safe to sail.

The next question is to consider months and dates. For the violence and roughness of the sea do not permit navigation all the year round, but some months are very suitable, some are doubtful, and the rest are impossible for fleets by a law of nature. When Pachon[1] has run its course, that is, after the rising of the Pleiades, from six days before the Kalends of June (i.e. 27th May) until the rising of Arcturus, that is, eighteen days before the Kalends of October (i.e. 14th September), navigation is deemed safe, because thanks to the summer the roughness of the sea is lessened. After this date until three days before the Ides of November (i.e. 11th November) navigation is doubtful and more exposed to danger, as after the Ides of September (i.e. 13th September) rises Arcturus, a most violent star, and eight days before the Kalends of October (i.e. 24th September) occur fierce equinoctial storms, and around the Nones of October (i.e. 7th October) the rainy Haedi, and five days before the Ides of the same (i.e. 11th October) Taurus. But from the month of November the winter setting of the Vergiliae (Pleiades) interrupts shipping with frequent storms. So from three days before the Ides of November (i.e. 11th November) until six days before the Ides of March (i.e. 10th March) the seas are closed. The minimal daylight and long nights, dense cloud-cover, foggy air, and violence of winds doubled by rain and snow not only keep fleets from the sea but also traffic from making journeys by land. But after the birthday, so to speak, of navigation[2] which is celebrated with annual games and public spectacles in many cities, it is still perilous to venture upon the sea right up to the Ides of May (i.e. 15th May) by reason of very many stars and the season of the year itself—not that the activities of merchants cease, but greater caution should be shown when an army takes to the sea in

---

[1]The word is garbled in the MSS, *pachnitae, phagnitae, phaenitae*; T. Mommsen, "Zu Vegetius", *Hermes* i (1866) 131, restored *Pachone*, the Egyptian month corresponding to 26th April–25th May. Why V. should cite an Egyptian month is unclear, but it may have been linked in his source to Isis Pelagia, for example (see below). For Pachon, cf. A.E. Samuel, *Greek and Roman Chronology*, Handbuch der Altertumswissenschaft I.7 (Munich 1972) 177. The true resolution of the corruption may be *Pachone itaque*; cf. IV.38 *a verno itaque solstitio, id est...* with *Pachone itaque decurso, id est...*

[2]*Navigium Isidis* or *ploiaphesia*, a nautical festival held on 5th March in honour of Isis Pelagia, cf. J. Rougé, *Recherches sur l'organisation du commerce maritime en Méditerranée* (Paris 1966) 33, Apul. *Met.* 11.8–17, *RE* IX (1916) 2084–2132 (Roeder), M.R. Salzman, *On Roman Time: the codex-calendar of 354 and the rhythms of urban life in late antiquity* (Univ. of California 1990) 173. V. is coy about naming the pagan goddess, whose festival continued to be celebrated even in the sixth century AD, cf. Ioh. Lydus *de Mens.* 4.45.

warships than when the enterprising are in a hurry for their private profits.[1]

40. How the signs of storms should be astronomically observed.

Also the rising and setting of other stars provoke very violent storms. Although fixed dates are appointed for them by the testimony of writers, nevertheless, since some details change on various occasions and, as must be admitted, the human condition prevents full knowledge of heavenly causes, they divide the results of nautical astronomical observation in three ways. It has been established that storms occur either about the appointed day, or before or after it. Hence they say in Greek terms that those occurring beforehand "storm before",[2] those arising on the regular date "storm",[3] and those following after "storm after".[4] But to list them all by name would seem either unnecessary or tedious, since very many authors have expressed in full the catalogue of both months and days. The transitions, also, of the stars they call planets, when they enter or leave signs of the zodiac by the course prescribed by the will of God the Creator, often tend to disturb fine weather.[5] The days of new moons too are filled with storms and are very much to be feared by navigators, as is understood not only by scientific study but the experience of the common people.

41. On signs of the weather.[6]

There are many signs, too, whereby storms are indicated after fair weather and fair weather after storms, which the moon's orb shows as though in a mirror. A red hue announces winds, blue, rain, a mixture of both rain-storms and furious squalls. A smiling and bright orb gives

---

[1]The greed of merchants which makes them brave the high seas was a commonplace; cf. Juv. 14.288–302, Ambr. *de Off.* 1.243, *de Elia* 70–71. According to *CTh* 13.9.3 (AD 380) the seas were open to merchant shipping from the Kalends of April (i.e. 1st. April) until the Ides of October (i.e. 15th. October).

[2]προχειμά ζειν.

[3]χειμάζειν.

[4]μεταχειμάζειν. These terms will have been transmitted by Varro. Cf. Pliny *Hist. Nat.* 18.57.207, probably from Varro; Paul. Fest. 249.22 L. has the translation *praesiderare* for προχειμά ζειν: *Praesiderare dicitur cum maturius hiberna tempestas movetur, quasi ante sideris tempus.* "*Praesiderare* is said when a winter storm arises early, as if before the time of the star."

[5]V. alludes to the pagan belief that the planets were gods, showing his Christian allegiance again.

[6]*prognostica*. Based largely on Verg. *Georg.* 1.393–463.

promise of fair weather for shipping which it wears on its face, particularly if at the fourth rising it is not red with the horns blunted or darkened by a covering of vapour. The sun is also significant when it rises or closes the day—whether it rejoices in evenly distributed light or is variegated by cloud in the way, whether it is brilliant with its wonted brightness or fiery from being beset by winds, or whether it is not pale or blotched by impending rain. The air, too, the sea itself, and the size and shape of clouds instruct attentive sailors. Some information is indicated by birds, and some by fishes, which Vergil included in his Georgics with almost divine skill,[1] and Varro studiously developed in his naval books.[2] If pilots profess to know this they do so only insofar as they have learned it by trial and error; no deeper knowledge has informed them.

42. On tidal waters, that is, ebb and flow.
The element of the sea is the third part of the world, and in addition to the blast of the winds it is quickened by its own breath and motion. For at appointed times, both day and night, there is a surge, which they call a "flow",[3] which runs forward and back and like rivers in flood now overflows onto land, now flows back into its own depths. This two-way reciprocal motion helps ships on their course when it is behind them, and retards them when in front. For one intending to do battle it is a thing greatly to be avoided. The force of a tide is not overcome by the help of oars, for even the wind yields to it on occasion. And since in different regions it varies at appointed times according to a different state of the moon's waxing and waning, he who is going to fight a naval battle ought to find out the characteristics of the sea and locality before any encounter.

---

[1]Verg. *Georg.* 1.351 ff.
[2]On Varro's *"libri navales"*, cf. IV.38 note. The information indicated by fishes is not in Vergil, nor in Aratus' *"Diosemeia"* (the last 400 lines of his *Phaenomena*), on which Vergil drew, nor in surviving parts of Latin poetic adaptations of the same by Cicero, Varro Atacinus, Germanicus and Avien(i)us. But it is in Pliny *Hist. Nat.* 18.361, from Varro, probably; see ibid. 18.348–350 for a quotation from Varro on weather-signs from the moon and Isid. *de Nat.* 38 (p.303 Fontaine) for similar from the sun.
[3]*rheuma*, Greek for "tide".

43. On navigational knowledge and oarsmen.[1]

It is the responsibility of sailors and pilots to acquaint themselves with the places in which they are going to sail and the harbours, so as to avoid dangerous waters with projecting or hidden rocks, shallows and sandbanks. Safety is greater, the deeper the sea is. In navarchs[2] close attention is required, in pilots[3] skill, and in oarsmen[4] strength, because naval battles are staged in a calm sea, and the massive warships strike through the enemy with their "beaks"[5] and avoid their attack in turn not by means of the breath of winds but by the beat of their oars. In this operation the muscle of the oarsmen and the skill of the officer who guides the rudder win a victory.

(Naval warfare, ch. 44–46)

44. On naval weapons and torsion-engines.

Land warfare requires many types of arms; but naval warfare demands more kinds of arms, including machines and torsion-engines as if the fighting were on walls and towers. What could be crueller than a naval battle, where men perish by water and by fire? Therefore protective armour should be a particular concern, so that soldiers may be protected with cataphracts, cuirasses, helmets and also greaves. No one can complain about the weight of armour, who fights standing on board ships.[6] Stronger and larger shields are also taken up against the impact of stones. Besides drags[7] and grapnels[8] and other naval kinds of weapons, there are arrows, javelins, slings, "sling-staves", lead-weighted

---

[1]The subject makes it likely that this chapter is derived from Varro de Ora Maritima also, or at least the first part is.

[2]navarchi, i.e. captains, cf. IV.32.

[3]gubernatores.

[4]remiges.

[5]rostra, i.e. rams.

[6]Cf. I.20. V. is still anxious about the alleged unpopularity of heavy armour; quite likely he has simply transposed the situation on land to that at sea. But the point is well-taken that there is no rôle for light-armed troops on board ship, because of the static conditions of close-quarters combat at sea. Cf. Leo Tact. 19.13 for the continuing influence of this chapter on ninth-century Byzantine tactici.

[7]falces.

[8]harpagones. Cf. Front. Strat. 2.3.24, Polyb. 1.22–23 (κόρακες = corvi, "crows"), Flor. 1.18.8–9, Zonar. 8.11 for the introduction of the harpago or manus ferrea, "iron hand", under C. Duellius in 260 BC during the First Punic War, and the stopping of fluid naval battle-tactics to facilitate stationary boarding operations.

darts, mangonels, catapults, and hand-catapults,[1] shooting darts and stones at each side. More dangerously still, those confident of their courage move up their warships alongside, throw out bridges and cross over to the enemies' ships to fight it out there with swords hand-to-hand, or *comminus* as it is called. On larger warships they even erect fortifications and towers, so that they may more easily wound or kill their enemies from higher decks as if from a wall. Arrows wrapped in "burning-oil", tow, sulphur and bitumen are planted blazing by catapults[2] in the bellies of hostile ships, and soon set light to the planking payed with wax, pitch and resin—so much kindling for fires.[3] Some are slain by steel and stones, others are forced to burn to death in the water. Among so many forms of death the bitterest fate is that the bodies are left unburied to be eaten by fish.[4]

45. How ambushes are set in naval warfare.
Just as in land warfare, descents are made upon sailors who are unsuspecting, and ambushes are laid about suitable narrows between islands. This is done with the idea of destroying them more easily, being unprepared. If enemy sailors are weary from lengthy rowing, if pressed by head-winds, if the tide is flowing against the ships' "beaks", if the enemy are asleep suspecting nothing, if the anchorage that they hold has no (other) exit, if a desired opportunity for battle occurs, one should take Fortune's favour in one's hands and give battle at the opportunity.[5] But if thanks to his caution the enemy avoids ambush and gives battle in a general engagement, the lines of the warships should be drawn up not straight as in a land battle, but curved like the moon, so that the wings are brought forward and the middle of the line is bowed. Then, if the adversaries try to break through, they may be surrounded by the formation itself and sunk. The chief strength of both warships and marines is placed on the wings.[6]

---

[1] *scorpiones*, i.e. *manuballistae*, cf. IV.22.
[2] Cf. IV.18 for fire-darts.
[3] Cf. IV.37 for paying ships' sides.
[4] Cf. Claud. *pan. de Hon. cons. IV* 628–629, Ovid. *Tr.* 1.2.53–56.
[5] V. transfers to a naval context III.19 init.
[6] So Philo Byz. *Polior.* 104.

46. What to do when naval battle is joined in an open engagement.
Moreover it is advantageous for your fleet always to use the deep, open
water, while the enemy's is pushed inshore, because those who are
thrust towards land lose the speed to attack.[1] In this type of encounter
it has been established that three kinds of weapon contribute most
towards victory, beams, drags and battle-axes. The "beam"[2] is the name
for a thin, long shaft like a yard-arm, which hangs from the mast and
has an iron head at both ends. When ships attach themselves to the
adversaries' starboard or port sides, they violently drive this instead of
a battering-ram. It is a sure method of cutting down and killing enemy
marines and sailors, and often pierces the ship itself.[3] The "drag"[4] is the
term for a very sharp iron blade curved like a sickle and mounted on
long poles. It quickly cuts the rigging[5] from which the yard-arm is
suspended, and the sails collapse rendering the warship slow and useless.
The "battle-axe"[6] is an axe which has on both sides a very broad and
very sharp iron blade. By means of these, in the midst of the heat of the
battle very skilled sailors or marines in small skiffs[7] secretly cut the
cables binding the adversaries' steering-gear. Once this is done the ship
is captured immediately, being disarmed and disabled. For what escape
is left for him who has lost his rudder?

On the subject of river patrol-boats,[8] which guard outposts on the
Danube with daily watches,[9] I feel I should keep quiet, because their

---

[1] Cf. Polyb. 1.51.4 ff.; F. Lammert, *Klio* xxxiii (1940) 278.

[2] *asser.*

[3] V. alone describes the *asser* as a naval *aries*. Otherwise it is the pole on which a
harpago or grapnel is mounted, cf. Livy 30.10.16, Appian *Bell. Civ.* 5.118 (491)–119
(496), Q. Curt. 4.3.24–25, Caes. *Bell. Gall.* 3.14.5–7.

[4] *falx*, literally "sickle".

[5] *chalatorii.* Lang rightly brackets *sub. funes* after Keller as a scribal gloss, *subaudi
funes*—"understand ropes". On V.'s use of the Greek word *chalatorius*, cf. *chalo* at IV.23.

[6] *bipennis*, battle-axe, double axe.

[7] *scaphulae.* Presumably the same as at IV.37; so Reddé, 130.

[8] *lusoriae.*

[9] Cf. *CTh* 7.17 (AD 412).

increased use has discovered a more advanced science for them than ancient theory had to show.[1]

F I N I S.

---

[1]So too at III.26 V. refused to discuss cavalry, modern advances having made the book-doctrines obsolete. The *Epit.* was not intended to be a complete Art of War, but a critique of current failings and strategies. In view of V.'s fondness for prologues and epilogues, book IV ends abruptly; comparison with III.26 suggests the possibility that a final epilogue may have fallen out of the tradition here. However, as the naval section is presented in the ancient Synopsis as an appendix, and is given short shrift in the prologue at IV.31, it may well be that V. did not consider another epilogue needful after IV.30.

Abbreviations and Bibliography

[Standard abbreviations for journals used by *L'année philologique* lviii (1987) are copied or slightly adapted in the commentary.]

ANRW   H. Temporini et al. (edd.), *Aufstieg und Niedergang des römischer Welt* (Berlin 1972–).

BAR   British Archaeological Reports (Oxford).

BGU Berliner Griechischer Urkunden I–IV, Aegyptische Urkunde aus den koeniglichen Museen zu Berlin (Berlin 1895–1912).

CCSL Corpus Christianorum Series Latina (Turnhout, Belgium).

Chron. min.   T. Mommsen (ed.), *Chronica minora,*   Monumenta Germaniae Historiae Auctorum Antiquissimorum I–III (Berlin 1892–1898).

CIL   T. Mommsen et al. (edd.), *Corpus inscriptionum Latinarum* (Berlin 1863–).

CJ   P. Krueger (ed.), *Codex Justinianus,* (Berlin 1877).

CSEL Corpus scriptorum ecclesiasticorum Latinorum (Vienna).

CTh   T. Mommsen (ed.), *Codex Theodosianus* (Berlin 1905).

Dig.   T. Mommsen (ed.), *Digesta Iustiniani Augusti* (Berlin 1868–70).

edn.   edition.

Epit. Epitoma Rei Militaris.

FGH   F. Jacoby (ed.), *Die Fragmente der griechischen Historiker* (Berlin–Leiden 1923–57).

JRMES   Journal of Roman Military Equipment Studies

lit.   literally.

MAMA   W.M. Calder et al. (edd.), *Monumenta Asiae Minoris Antiqua* I– (London 1928–).

Mul. Digesta Artis Mulomedicinae.

NCO   Non-commissioned officer.

Nov. Th. II   P.M. Meyer (ed.), *Leges novellae Theodosii II Augusti* (Berlin 1905).

Nov. Val. III   P.M. Meyer (ed.), *Leges novellae Valentiniani III Augusti* (Berlin 1905).

OCD   Oxford Classical Dictionary (1970^2).

O. Douch   H. Cuvigny, G. Wagner (edd.), *Les Ostraca grecs de Douch,* Inst. français d'arch. orient. XXIV fasc. I.1–57 (Cairo 1986), fasc. II.58–183 (Cairo 1988).

OLD   Oxford Latin Dictionary (1968–82).

P. Lips.   L. Mitteis (ed.), *Griechische Urkunden der Papyrussammlung zu Leipzig* (Leipzig 1906).

P. Monac. A. Heisenberg, L. Wenger (edd.), *Veroeffentlichungen aus der Papuryssammlung der K. Hof- und Staatsbibliothek zu München: Byzantinische Papyri* (Leipzig–Berlin 1914).

P. Oxy. B.P. Grenfell, A.S. Hunt et al. (edd.), *The Oxyrhynchus Papyri* (London 1898–).

PLRE A.H.M. Jones, J.R. Martindale, J. Morris (edd.), *Prosopography of the Later Roman Empire* I (Cambridge 1971), J.R. Martindale (ed.), vol. II (1980).

RE Pauly–Wissowa (edd.), *Real-Encyclopädie der classischen Altertumswissenschaft* (Stuttgart 1894–).

ref. reference.

S. O. Seeck, *Regesten der Kaiser und Päpste* (Stuttgart 1919).

SB F. Preisigke et al. (edd.), *Sammelbuch griechischer Urkunden aus Ägypten* I– (Strasbourg 1915–).

SEG J.J.E. Hondius et al. (edd.), *Supplementum epigraphicum Graecum* I– (Leiden 1923–).

SHA *Scriptores Historiae Augustae.*

Suda A. Adler (ed.), *Suidae lexicon* (Teubner edn., 1928–38).

TLL *Thesaurus Linguae Latinae.*

V. Vegetius.

v.l. *varia lectio.*

Select Bibliography

[A full Vegetius bibliography was published by R. Sablayrolles in 1984, and the general bibliography of the Roman army is truly vast. Accordingly only a representative selection of the chief works cited in the introduction and commentary are listed, together with a few other recent books and articles which seemed relevant.]

Alföldy, G., *Römische Heeresgeschichte: Beiträge* 1962–1985, Mavors Roman Army Researches III (Amsterdam 1987).

Anderson, A.S., "The imperial army", in J. Wacher (ed.), *The Roman World* I (London–New York 1987) Pt. 3.

Andersson, A., *Studia Vegetiana: commentatio academica* (Uppsala 1938).

Baatz, D., *Bauten und Katapulte des römischen Heeres*, Mavors Roman Army Researches XI (Stuttgart 1994).

Birley, E., *The Roman Army, Papers* 1929–1986, Mavors Roman

Army Researches IV (Amsterdam 1988).

Bishop, M.C., Coulston, J.C.N., *Roman Military Equipment from the Punic Wars to the Fall of Rome* (London 1993).

Blockley, R.C. (ed.), *The Fragmentary Classicising Historians of the Later Roman Empire: Eunapius, Olympiodorus, Priscus and Malchus* I–II, ARCA classical and mediaeval texts, papers and monographs, 6, 10 (Liverpool 1981–83).

Breeze, D.J., Dobson, B., *Roman Officers and Frontiers*, Mavors Roman Army Researches X (Stuttgart 1993).

Campbell, B., "Teach Yourself how to be a General", *JRS* lxxvii (1987) 13–29.

Campbell, B., *The Roman Army, 31 BC–AD 337, A Sourcebook* (London 1994).

Campbell, J.B., *The Emperor and the Roman Army 31 BC–AD 235* (Oxford 1980).

Cichorius—references are to the re-edition of C. Cichorius' plates by F. Lepper, S. Frere, *Trajan's Column* (Gloucester 1988).

Clarke, Lt. J., *Military Institutions of Vegetius* (London 1767).

Clauss, M., "Ausgewählte Bibliographie zur lateinischen Epigraphik der römischen Kaiserzeit (1. 3. Jh.)", *ANRW* II.1 (1974) 840–847 on the Roman army.

Davies, R.W., *Service in the Roman Army* (Edinburgh 1989).

Ernout, A., Meillet, A., *Dictionnaire Étymologique de la langue latine*, augmented edn. by J. André (Paris 1979⁴).

Feugère, M., *Les armes des romains de la République à l'Antiquité tardive* (Paris 1993).

Fink, R.O. *Roman Military Records on Papyrus*, Philological monographs of the American Philological Association XXVI (Cleveland, Ohio 1971).

Forni, G., *Esercito e Marina de Roma Antica*, Mavors Roman Army Researches V (Stuttgart 1992).

Garlan, Y., "Le Livre 'V' de la Syntaxe mécanique de Philon de Byzance, Texte, Traduction et Commentaire", *Recherches de Poliorcétique grecque*, Bibliothèque des Écoles françaises d'Athènes et de Rome CCXXIII (Paris 1974) 279–404.

Gilliam, J.F., *Roman Army Papers*, Mavors Roman Army Researches II (Amsterdam 1986).

Goffart, W., "The Date and Purpose of Vegetius' *De Re Militari*", *Traditio* xxxiii (1977) 65–100 = id., *Rome's Fall and After* (London 1989) 45–80.

Goodburn, R., Bartholomew, P. (edd.), *Aspects of the Notitia Dignitatum*, BAR Supp. Ser. 15 (Oxford 1976).

Grosse, R., *Römische Militärgeschichte von Gallienus bis zum Beginn der byzantinischen Themenverfassung* (Berlin 1920).

Hassall, M.W.C., Ireland, R.I. (edd.), *De Rebus Bellicis: Papers presented to Prof. E.A. Thompson*, BAR Int. Ser. 63 (Oxford 1979).

Hoffmann, D., *Das spätrömische Bewegungsheer und die Notitia Dignitatum*, Epigraphische Studien, VII.1–2 (Dusseldorf 1969).

Jones, A.H.M., *The Later Roman Empire* (Oxford 1964).

Jordan, H., *M. Catonis praeter librum de re rustica Quae Extant* (Leipzig 1867).

Kempf, J.G., "Romanorum sermonis castrensis reliquiae collectae et illustratae", *Jahrbücher für klassische Philologie*, Suppl. XXVI (1901) 338–400.

Keppie, L.J.F., *The Making of the Roman Army: from republic to empire* (London 1984).

Kolias, T.G., *Byzantinische Waffen*, ein Beitrag zur byzantinischen Waffenkunde bis zur lateinischen Eroberung, Byzantina Vindobonensia bd. XVII, Österreichische Akadamie der Wissenschaften (Vienna 1988).

Lang, C. (ed.), *Vegetii Epitoma Rei Militaris* (Teubner edn., Leipzig 1885²).

Le Bohec, Y., *The Imperial Roman Army* (Paris 1989, tr. London 1994).

Lenoir, M., *Pseudo-Hygin, Des Fortifications du Camp* (Budé edn., 1979).

Lepper, F., Frere, S., *Trajan's Column* (Gloucester 1988).

Liebeschuetz, J.H.W.G., *Barbarians and Bishops: Army, Church, and State in the Age of Arcadius and Chrysostom* (Oxford 1990).

Lommatsch, E. (ed.), *Vegetii Digesta Artis Mulomedicinae* (Teubner edn., Leipzig 1903).

Luttwak, E.N., *The Grand Strategy of the Roman Empire* (Baltimore–London 1976).

MacMullen, R., "How big was the Roman Imperial Army?", *Klio* lxii (1980) 451–460.

Marquardt, J., *Römische Staatsverwaltung* II (Leipzig 1884²).

Marsden, E.W., *Greek and Roman Artillery: Historical Development* (Oxford 1969).

Marsden, E.W., *Greek and Roman Artillery: Technical Treatises* (Oxford 1971).

Milner, N.P., *Vegetius and the Anonymus De Rebus Bellicis*, D.Phil.

thesis, Oxford 1991.

Neumann, A.R., *RE* Suppl. X (1965), s.v. "Vegetius", col. 992–1020.

Önnerfors, A. (ed.), *P. Flavii Vegeti Renati Epitoma rei militaris* (Teubner edn., Stuttgart 1995).

Phillips, T.R. (ed.), *Flavius Vegetius Renatus, the Military Institutions of the Romans* (Harrisburg, Pa. 1944), repr. Westport 1985.

Reddé, M., *Mare Nostrum: les infrastructures, le dispositif, et l'histoire de la marine militaire sous l'empire Romain* (Rome 1986).

Ruggiero, E. de (ed.), *Dizionario Epigrafico de Antichità romane* I– (Rome 1886–).

Sabbah, G., "Pour la datation théodosienne du De Re Militari de Végèce", Centre Jean Palerne, *Mémoires* II (Univ. de Saint-Étienne 1980), 131–155.

Sablayrolles, R., "Bibliographie sur l'*epitoma rei militaris* de Végèce", *CGRAR* III (1984) 139–146.

Schenk, D., *Flavius Vegetius Renatus: Die Quellen der Epitoma rei militaris, Klio*, Beiträge zur alten Geschichte XXII (N.F. IX) (Leipzig 1930), repr. Nuremberg 1963.

Speidel, M.P., *Roman Army Studies* I (Amsterdam 1984), II (Stuttgart 1992), Mavors Roman Army Researches I and VIII.

Speidel, M.P., *Riding for Caesar, The Roman Emperors' Horse Guards* (London 1994).

Stelten, L.F., *Flavius Vegetius Renatus: Epitoma Rei Militaris*, edited with an English translation (New York, Bern, Frankfurt, Paris 1990).

Tomlin, R.S.O., "The army of the late Empire", in J. Wacher (ed.), *The Roman World* I (London–New York 1987) Pt. 3.

Walde, A., Hofmann, J.B., *Lateinisches Etymologisches Wörterbuch* (Heidelberg 1938–54[3]).

Watson, G.R., "The army of the Republic", in J. Wacher (ed.), *The Roman World* I (London–New York 1987) Pt. 3.

Watson, G.R., *The Roman Soldier* (London 1969).

Webster, G., *The Roman Imperial Army of the first and second centuries* AD (London 1985[3]).

Wheeler, E.L., *Stratagem and the vocabulary of military trickery, Mnemosyne* suppl. CVIII (Leiden 1988).

Whitehead, D., *Aineias the Tactician* (Oxford 1990).

Index of Gods, People and Places

TRANSLATED TEXTS FOR HISTORIANS
Published Titles

Gregory of Tours: Life of the Fathers
Translated with an introduction by EDWARD JAMES
Volume 1: 176pp., 2nd edition 1991, ISBN 0 85323 327 6

The Emperor Julian: Panegyric and Polemic
Claudius Mamertinus, John Chrysostom, Ephrem the Syrian
edited by SAMUEL N. C. LIEU
Volume 2: 153pp., 2nd edition 1989, ISBN 0 85323 376 4

Pacatus: Panegyric to the Emperor Theodosius
Translated with an introduction by C. E. V. NIXON
Volume 3: 122pp., 1987, ISBN 0 85323 076 5

Gregory of Tours: Glory of the Martyrs
Translated with an introduction by RAYMOND VAN DAM
Volume 4: 150pp., 1988, ISBN 0 85323 236 9

Gregory of Tours: Glory of the Confessors
Translated with an introduction by RAYMOND VAN DAM
Volume 5: 127pp., 1988, ISBN 0 85323 226 1

The Book of Pontiffs (*Liber Pontificalis* to AD 715)
Translated with an introduction by RAYMOND DAVIS
Volume 6: 175pp., 1989, ISBN 0 85323 216 4

Chronicon Paschale 284–628 AD
Translated with notes and introduction by
MICHAEL WHITBY AND MARY WHITBY
Volume 7: 280pp., 1989, ISBN 0 85323 096 X

Iamblichus: On the Pythagorean Life
Translated with notes and introduction by GILLIAN CLARK
Volume 8: 144pp., 1989, ISBN 0 85323 326 8

Conquerors and Chroniclers of Early-Medieval Spain
Translated with notes and introduction by KENNETH BAXTER WOLF
Volume 9: 176pp., 1991, ISBN 0 85323 047 1

Victor of Vita: History of the Vandal Persecution
Translated with notes and introduction by JOHN MOORHEAD
Volume 10: 112pp., 1992, ISBN 0 85323 426 4

The Goths in the Fourth Century
by PETER HEATHER AND JOHN MATTHEWS
Volume 11: 224pp., 1992, ISBN 0 85323 426 4

Cassiodorus: *Variae*
Translated with notes and introduction by S. J. B. BARNISH
Volume 12: 260pp., 1992, ISBN 0 85323 436 1

The Lives of the Eighth-Century Popes (*Liber Pontificalis*)
Translated with an introduction and commentary by RAYMOND DAVIS
Volume 13: 288pp., 1992, ISBN 0 85323 018 8

Eutropius: Breviarium
Translated with an introduction and commentary by H. W. BIRD
Volume 14: 248pp., 1993, ISBN 0 85323 208 3

The Seventh Century in the West-Syrian Chronicles
Introduced, translated and annotated by ANDREW PALMER
including two Seventh-century Syriac apocalyptic texts
Introduced, translated and annotated by SEBASTIAN BROCK
with added annotation and an historical introduction by ROBERT HOYLAND
Volume 15: 368pp., 1993, ISBN 0 85323 238 5

Vegetius: Epitome of Military Science
Translated with notes and introduction by N. P. MILNER
Volume 16: 208pp., 2nd edition 1996, ISBN 0 85323 910 X

Aurelius Victor: De Caesaribus
Translated with an introduction and commentary by H. W. BIRD
Volume 17: 264pp., 1994, ISBN 0-85323-218-0

Bede: On the Tabernacle
Translated with notes and introduction by ARTHUR G. HOLDER
Volume 19: 176pp., 1994, ISBN 0-85323-368-3

The Lives of the Ninth-Century Popes (*Liber Pontificalis*)
Translated with an introduction and commentary by RAYMOND DAVIS
Volume 20: 360pp., 1995, ISBN 0-85323-479-5

Bede: On the Temple
Translated with notes by SEÁN CONNOLLY,
introduction by JENNIFER O'REILLY
Volume 21: 192pp., 1995, ISBN 0-85323-049-8

Pseudo-Dionysius of Tel-Mahre: *Chronicle*, **Part III**
Translated with notes and introduction by WITOLD WITAKOWSKI
Volume 22: 192pp., 1995, ISBN 0-85323-760-3

Venantius Fortunatus: Personal and Political Poems
Translated with notes and introduction by JUDITH GEORGE
Volume 23: 192pp., 1995, ISBN 0-85323-179-6

Donatist Martyr Stories: The Church in Conflict in Roman North Africa
Translated with notes and introduction by MAUREEN A. TILLEY
Volume 24: 144pp., 1996, ISBN 0 85323 931 2

For full details of Translated Texts for Historians, including prices and ordering information, please write to the following:
All countries, except the USA and Canada: Liverpool University Press, Senate House, Abercromby Square, Liverpool, L69 3BX, UK (*Tel* 0151-794 2233, *Fax* 0151-794 2235).
USA and Canada: University of Pennsylvania Press, Blockley Hall, 418 Service Drive, Philadelphia, PA 19104-6097, USA (*Tel* (215) 898-6264, *Fax* (215) 898-0404).